William Penn

John A. Moretta
Central College, HCCS

William Penn
and the Quaker Legacy

THE LIBRARY OF AMERICAN BIOGRAPHY

Edited by Mark C. Carnes

PEARSON
Longman

New York   Boston   San Francisco
London   Toronto   Sydney   Tokyo   Singapore   Madrid
Mexico City   Munich   Paris   Cape Town   Hong Kong   Montreal

Executive Editor: Michael Boezi
Executive Marketing Manager: Sue Westmoreland
Production Manager: Donna DeBenedictis
Project Coordination, Text Design, and Electronic Page Makeup:
   GGS Book Services
Cover Designer/Manager: John Callahan
Cover Image: © Lee Snider/Photo Images/CORBIS
Frontispiece Image: Bettmann/Corbis
Photo Researcher: Rona Tuccillo
Manufacturing Buyer: Roy L. Pickering Jr.
Printer and Binder: R.R. Donnelley & Sons Company/Harrisonburg
Cover Printer: Phoenix Color Corporation
Interior Photo Credits: p. 9, Bettmann/Corbis; p. 28, Library of Congress;
   p. 103, Corbis; p. 134, Bettmann/Corbis; p. 150 Bettmann/Corbis

Library of Congress Cataloging-in-Publication Data

Moretta, John.
   William Penn and the Quaker legacy / John A. Moretta.
      p. cm. — (The library of American biography)
   Includes bibliographical references and index.
   ISBN-13: 978-0-321-16392-9 (pbk.)
   ISBN-10: 0-321-16392-3 (pbk.)
   1. Penn, William, 1644–1718. 2. Penn, William, 1644–1718—
Influence. 3. Pioneers—Pennsylvania—Biography. 4. Quakers—
Pennsylvania—Biography. 5. Pennsylvania—History—Colonial
period, ca. 1600–1775. I. Title.

F152.2.M67 2007
974.8'02092—dc22
[B]   2006035528

Please visit us at www.ablongman.com

ISBN 0-321-16392-3

      6 7 8 9 10—DOH—12 11 10

For Ira Gruber and Chris Moretta, whose unswerving support made this book possible

Contents

Editor's Preface

William Penn (1644–1718), a Quaker who founded Pennsylvania colony, was arguably one of the most important figures in early American history, contends John Moretta, author of this biography. "It was the Quakers and their colony," Moretta explains, "that provided the foundation for many of the principles, beliefs, and liberties, which to this day Americans cherish."

This assertion may strike some as being excessively adulatory. Most Americans, many historians among them, believe that the American experiment began with Puritan leaders such as John Winthrop of Massachusetts Bay Colony or William Bradford of Plymouth. Puritanism, by emphasizing the importance of the individual and advancing the notion that individuals should have a say in their governance, established the foundations of a participatory political and social order.

Moretta makes a strong case that Penn's experiment has had longer-lasting and more profound resonances in American life. The Puritans did not believe in free speech, as evidenced by their expulsion of Roger Williams and Anne Hutchinson, and their execution of Quakers. The Puritans, too, were famously fractious; the Salem witch trials were simply the most lurid instances of this confrontational culture. By contrast, the Quakers under Penn's leadership endorsed freedom of speech, press, and religion and promoted a culture of conciliation. "What we find most appealing about the Quakers of Penn's day was their humanity," Moretta adds, "their embracing of all cultures and people, for Friends considered all human beings equal in God's eyes and thus entitled to just and fair treatment."

Quite apart from its historical significance, this biography recounts the story of an intensely interesting person. As an adolescent, Penn defied his father and his king in adherence to his religious beliefs. When he was 18, Oxford expelled him for his nonconformist convictions. When in his mid-twenties, Penn was imprisoned for writing Quaker tracts.

Penn's friends and family prudently arranged to get Penn out of harm's way—and thus to the Americas. This story of principled rebellion, too, foreshadows the emergence of the American nation a century later, as does the account of Penn's forging of a people and polity in Pennsylvania.

Moretta, who received his Ph.D. from Rice University, has written on various aspects of American history. Yet his career path had its own twists and turns. He was drafted as an outfielder by the Kansas City Royals; for two years he played in the minor leagues. When I asked why he left baseball to become a professor, he responded matter of factly: "The Kansas City Royals had George Brett, Hal McRae, Amos Otis, and a host of other superstars," Moretta explained. "I was not going to take their jobs."

Moretta's departure from baseball was perhaps no great loss to the national pastime; but as this engaging and wise biography suggests, readers can be grateful for his career choice. Moretta lives in Houston and teaches American history at Central College of the Houston Community College System, and for the University of Houston, Main Campus. He is also Chair of the Social Sciences Department at Central College.

Mark C. Carnes

Author's Preface

When I ask my students in the first half of the United States survey, "Who was William Penn and who were the Quakers?" responses range from completely blank faces to the inevitable "he's the guy on the front of the Quaker Oats box." Sadly, in twenty-four years of college teaching, I have watched William Penn and the Quakers slip ever deeper into the recesses of historical memory and importance. It was with my students in mind that I set out to resurrect from possible historical oblivion an individual who had contributed so much to the shaping of the American creed and ideal. I have great hope that this comparatively brief but encompassing biography of William Penn succeeds in reacquainting students and fellow citizens with this most extraordinary individual, and the dynamic faith with its great humanitarian tenets that he and his fellow Quakers brought to North America in the seventeenth century.

Of all the utopian dreams imposed on the North American landscape in the seventeenth century, the most remarkable was that of the Quakers. During the English civil war, the Society of Friends (the Quakers' official name) emerged as one of many radical sects searching for a more just society and a purer religion. Their visionary ideas and defiance of civil authority cost them dearly in fines, brutal punishment, and imprisonment. Quaker persecution intensified during the Restoration, and as a result, Quakers began emigrating to the New World, ultimately by the thousands to their "promised land," the "holy experiment" of Pennsylvania. More than any other colony, the society they founded in Pennsylvania foreshadowed the religious and ethnic pluralism of the future United States. The individual most responsible for bringing such enlightenment to the wilderness was William Penn, a convert to the faith and the son of a warrior aristocrat.

A genial Founding Father image has influenced many interpretations of Penn's life. In such renditions, an aura of saintliness surrounds

Penn, out of which emerges an individual possessing godlike wisdom, purity, and sanctity—an almost mythic, superior being much too good to be true. The overarching theme in many Penn biographies has been religious—that motivating Penn to accomplish all he did was a desire above all else to promote and protect his faith and fellow saints and to bring about God's kingdom on earth. Although Penn was most definitely a deeply spiritual man, a devout Quaker, in many areas of his personal and professional life, other, more profane factors, frequently propelled him to action.

What the Founding Father image as well as the religious portrayals fail to project was that Penn was a man of intense action, of incredible tenacity, of boundless intellectual curiosity, imagination, and creativity, and as the son of one of England's greatest naval war heroes, a man possessed of wealth and status, which gave him almost immediate access to the halls of power in Restoration England, even after he became "convinced" in the Quaker faith. Indeed, rarely do textbooks mention this most important aspect of Penn's life and career to which he owed much of his success both as a leading dissenter for toleration and as the proprietor of England's largest North American colony.

Over time, Penn developed a political savvy and influence at the Stuart court that exceeded his father's and rivaled as well the wiles of even the most experienced and seasoned courtiers and placemen. Throughout his adult life Penn shrewdly cultivated close relationships with some of the most powerful men in England to whom he could turn for help and redemption, whether it involved his personal well-being, that of his fellow Quakers, or that of his colony.

Although we (Americans) like to claim Penn as one of our own, Penn would flat out reject such an "absurd" connection. Penn saw himself first and foremost, and with great pride, an Englishman, as head and heir of a proud and well-connected family, and loyal supporter of the Stuart monarchy, to whom he believed he had a dynastic responsibility to serve. Even when his life was in danger in England, Penn never seriously contemplated seeking refuge in his colony, making Pennsylvania his permanent home. He simply could not bring himself to leave his beloved England. It would thus be a historical mistake to assume that Penn's actions relative to his colony were separate from his activities in England. They were at all times inextricably linked, and if we view Penn in that context his life becomes even more complete and extraordinary. To understand Penn better, it is vital to examine the imperial context in which he operated, for to neglect one side of the Atlantic does neither Penn nor the Quakers justice as significant contributors to the histories of Great Britain and the eventual United States.

Not all Englishmen who came to North America stayed permanently; many, like Penn, saw the New World as a place for personal salvation or opportunity; or as a place of service to their countrymen, which also implied the potential for greater glory and wealth for king and country. They believed such objectives could be attained without having to take up permanent residence, which meant becoming a "colonial"—a status completely unacceptable to a hardcore, aristocratic Englishman like Penn.

Rather, Penn's significance was found in his ability to visualize both in his mind and heart, and translate into reality in the New World, an asylum for the persecuted and a refuge from arbitrary state power. Puritans had strived for social homogeneity and religious uniformity, excluding all not of like mind. In the Chesapeake and Carolina colonies, aggressive, self-serving men had sought to exploit their lands and bondspeople. Penn, however, dreamed of inviting to his colony folk of all religions and national backgrounds, promising them liberty of conscience and peaceful coexistence. Penn foresaw his colony as the centerpiece of England's New World empire, for the wealth it would bring to his nation as well as testimony to England's self-proclaimed status as the most enlightened nation in the world.

Despite commercial success and prolonged peace with Native Americans, much to Penn's dismay and eventual heartbreak, early on his colonists proved to be a much less righteous, God-fearing people than he initially reckoned. They rarely, if ever behaved as if they were participating in a holy experiment. Despite granting his brethren greater political autonomy than existed anywhere in the empire, Pennsylvania politics became especially contentious, bitter, and ultimately filled with animosity toward Penn. Although at the beginning of his holy experiment he was a much-loved proprietor, Penn contributed to his vision's demise, as well as to the incessant rancor and turbulence that affected his colony, by not remaining long in Pennsylvania. He returned to England in 1684, two years after acquiring his charter, and did not revisit his colony again until 1699, and staying then for only twenty-three months. Penn's prolonged absence from Pennsylvania caused him to lose touch with his province, and when he returned in 1699, it was too late; he faced a hardened and hostile antiproprietary combination of both Quakers and non-Quakers determined to wrest from him what little authority he had left after a fifteen-year withdrawal. In effect, while in England attending to his other affairs, Penn neglected his colony, causing its inhabitants to feel abandoned, and many to take opportunities politically and economically at his expense.

Perhaps a more important cause of disunity resided in the Quaker attitude toward authority. In England, resistance to authority had become a daily part of Quaker life. However, in Pennsylvania, the absence of persecution eliminated a crucial unifying element from Quaker society. The factionalism that developed among the Friends demonstrated that people never unify better than when under attack. Rather than looking inward and banding together, they looked outward to an environment filled with opportunity. Their squabbling filled Penn with dismay. Why, he asked, were his settlers so "governmentish, so brutish, so susceptible to scurvy quarrels that break out to the disgrace of the Province?" Much to Penn's disheartening realization was the reality that his Quaker brethren could not resist the vast opportunities for individual accrual his colony provided. Continued adherence to Old World creeds would gain only a modest existence in a land of plenty, while the development of more profane standards was better suited for conquering the wilderness. Penn had assiduously planned a godly utopia, delicately balanced between democracy and deference, deeply religious yet utterly tolerant. Sadly, he lived to see his holy experiment vanish in a quarrelsome, commercial metropolis controlled by a self-serving, acquisitive group of former saints.

William Penn was an inveterate pamphleteer and prolific writer, producing 150 books and essays during his lifetime. Penn did not limit his writing to exclusively religious treatises or Quaker apologias. He wrote on a variety of topics, ranging from the law, politics, and international relations to business, education, science, and on to philosophy and theology. Penn usually wrote for an immediate, specific purpose or objective, typically in response to an important religious issue, but just as frequently a secular matter such as the right to a trial by jury, prompted him to take pen in hand in defense of such liberties. Penn also wrote to agitate, to provoke readers, particularly non-Quakers, to reconsider their current beliefs, attitudes, and behaviors, especially when it came to profound questions such as liberty of conscience. For Penn, writing became an inextricable part of his Quaker wholeness; he believed it was his duty both as a Quaker and as an Englishman to put on paper not only cogent defenses of his faith but to address other issues as well that affected his fellow countrymen. In the process, he framed perhaps the most enlightened and liberal plan of government prior to the eighteenth century.

On a personal level, William Penn definitely was not the beaming, jovial, and amicable fellow depicted on the Quaker Oats box. Much to his adorers' chagrin, Penn often was temperamental, petty, tactless, vindictive (especially toward those who personally reviled him or his faith) and given to self-pitying. All too frequently he treated his Quaker brethren, especially those not his social equal (which was the majority), with the condescension of noblesse oblige. He had few close male friends within the Quaker community, largely because he was so patronizing. Yet, when attending the Stuart court or when needing the help of powerful courtiers, Penn could be most charming, gracious, and warm. He had to have been of such countenance, for had he been his more aloof and irascible self, it is unlikely he would have been able to keep his colony, even his life, in the capricious and vicious world of Restoration and post-Glorious Revolution England. Nor was Penn much of a family man, spending more time away from his wives (he married twice) and children than with them. In short, William Penn was not the most likeable of human beings.

Thus, the William Penn revealed in this book is not the "warm and fuzzy" character of hagiography or the American stereotype of the humble, benign, and saintly founder of one of the original thirteen colonies. History is replete with individuals who have attained the status of historical significance with personalities even more crusty than Penn's. History does not ascribe greatness based on whether someone was personable. Rather, history awards distinction by assessing what that individual accomplished not only during his or her own time, but for posterity as well. Whether William Penn was liked by either his contemporaries or by us is moot; we must look beyond such facile criteria, accept him as he was, "warts and all." We must lay aside his cantankerousness and see a man of singular vision, uncompromisingly devoted to making real in his colony his faith's belief in human equality, racial and ethnic pluralism, liberty of conscience, and a world without war.

As a result of his admirers' failure to make him human, even in his own city of Philadelphia, Benjamin Franklin is not only better known, but sadly, the object of more heartfelt admiration as well. Even among Americans who have some knowledge of who Penn was, they nonetheless see him only as a well-fed, beaming man in a broad-brimmed hat with no human foibles. Franklin is affectionately called "Ben"; how many Americans ever refer to Penn with equal familiarity and sentiment as "Bill"?

William Penn and his fellow Quakers offered a new concept of community, in which differences of birth, background, and belief were ignored or downplayed, allowing everyone equal opportunity to succeed. Even if Pennsylvania fell short of what Penn envisioned as a holy experiment in righteous living, it nonetheless was a place where men and women lived together peacefully, regardless of differences in faith, skin shade, and place of origin. If there is anything permanently abiding in the nation's history, it is the respect for human dignity and human rights. These ideals have come to inform the American creed, and thus the Quaker legacy and that of the man who brought it to North America, William Penn, endures.

John A. Moretta

Acknowledgments

Rarely does one earn the distinction of having written a book without the key support of friends, relatives, colleagues, and mentors. Thus, it is a pleasure to thank the many people who helped and encouraged me with this biography. My first, most sincere thank you goes to Ira Gruber, Harris Masterson Jr. Professor of History at Rice University, who, since my days as a graduate student at Rice, has been one of my strongest supporters in all of my scholarly endeavors. Ira took the time from his own scholarship to meticulously read every chapter of Penn and discussed with me for several hours how I could improve the manuscript's focus and intent. Also invaluable and incorporated into the final draft, was Ira's vast knowledge of the time period in which Penn lived. Ira continues to inspire me, for he is a great model for what it means to be totally dedicated to the life of the mind.

A number of friends and colleagues have always been there for me, never wavering in their support and confidence in my abilities as a scholar. In this most crucial area, I am especially indebted to Joe Glatthaar, Jim Martin, and David Wilcox. Joe Glatthaar, currently Stephenson Distinguished Professor of History at the University of North Carolina at Chapel Hill, was in many ways, the impetus for this book. Joe is one of the most disciplined, prolific, and wonderfully gifted scholars in the profession. Joe and I have been friends for almost three decades, and in that time, usually during one of our daily three-mile jaunts, when we were not talking about sports, usually baseball, we talked about history. On one particular day, I bemoaned to him that I wish there was a short biography, similar to Edmund Morgan's work on John Winthrop, of William Penn. We had both used Morgan's book for several years in the first half of the United States survey, but it seemed students were growing weary of the Puritans and that perhaps it was time to look at another group of early American dissidents, the Quakers, who were just as important as the Puritans, in leaving an imprint on the American character. Joe said "then stop complaining and write a biography of William Penn for that series. You can do it. You have the credentials." With such a vote of confidence, I proceeded to contact Ashley Dodge, acquisitions editor at Longman at the time, sent her a prospectus, and she agreed that William Penn indeed would be a valuable contribution to the Library of American Biography Series.

After writing the first six chapters, I wanted to make sure I was headed in the right thematic and stylistic direction. I thus turned to Jim Martin, Moores Distinguished Professor of History, at the University of Houston, who is one of the finest historians and writers in the profession, and whom I have had the pleasure and honor of having as a friend for several years. Jim also took time out from his own work to read not only the first six chapters, but the "Preface" and "Epilogue and Legacy" as well. Jim did not hesitate to offer insights and criticisms that forced me to go beyond where I was in my own thinking about Penn's time and place in history. I thank him profusely for his ideas and guidance.

Within my home department at Central College of the Houston Community College System, I received the kind of support that represents the college at its best. I am especially grateful to David Wilcox, one of my closest colleagues, who also happens to be a Friend (a Quaker). From the beginning to the end of this project, but especially during some of my lowest ebbs, which usually occurred after I received some of the readers' reports, David's friendship and support knew no boundaries, as he encouraged me to keep going, telling me that in the end he knew that I had it in me to produce a work of admirable quality. I hope I have not disappointed him.

I would also like to thank Cheryl Peters, Academic Dean at Central College, who has been over the years, one of my strongest supporters in my efforts to continue to research and write. Whether it was giving me time off from my position as department chair to take research trips, to reading everything I have written and telling me candidly whether she liked it or not, Cheryl has never wavered in doing all she can to promote my scholarly endeavors. I thank her most sincerely. I am also grateful to another Central colleague and good friend, Alan Ainsworth, chair of Central's English department and a gifted writer and scholar in his own right. Alan has also read and appreciated most of everything I have written, and graciously volunteered to edit several chapters as well as offer some insightful observations along the way about Penn's "ideological dilemmas and contradictions." Another colleague, who also provided invaluable editorial suggestions, was Ms. Audrey Crawford. Audrey is a talented writer and editor in her own right, as she currently serves on the editorial board of *The Houston Review,* a Gulf Coast/Texas historical magazine published by the University of Houston under the general editorship of Joe Pratt, Cullen Professor of History and Business at the university. Last but not least, my thanks to a most wonderful, patient, and understanding human being, who graciously listened to me talking to myself about Penn, sometimes swearing when I could not get a thought or sentence right, whom I know probably thinks I am crazy, Ms. Julann Sam. Thank you Julann for a thousand kindnesses.

At Pearson Longman, I would first like to thank series editor Mark Carnes for all his encouragement and help in getting this manuscript "polished" and ready for publication. His candor, insight, years of experience, and endorsement for what I have produced, has been most welcomed and sincerely appreciated. Michael Boezi, Executive Editor for the series, has been a pleasure to work with. From the start he recognized Penn's significance in history, and encouraged me to write a book that would illustrate Penn's signal contributions to the histories of both early America and England. Perhaps most important, Michael never wavered in his faith in my abilities as a historian to produce a quality book that he believes will be read by students for years to come. I hope he is right. I would also like to thank Ashley Dodge, who honored me with the invitation to contribute to the esteemed Library of American Biography series; Priscilla McGeehon, who approved the Penn project, Vanessa Gennarelli, who guided it through the editing process; and Ginger Logan, our Central College Pearson Longman "book rep," who several years ago encouraged me to write a biography for the series.

In addition, I would like to acknowledge the following manuscript reviewers: Alan Abbott, Indiana University Southeast; Archie MacDonald, Stephen F. Austin State University; Brian Ethridge, Louisiana Tech; Bruce Bendler, Wesley College; Carol Keller, San Antonio College; Cynthia Carter, Florida Community College at Jacksonville; David Hudson, California State University—Fresno; Hal Friedman, Henry Ford Community College; Jennifer Fry, King's College; Patricia Gower, University of the Incarnate Word; Richard Filipink, SUNY Fredonia; Robert Cray, Montclair State University; Robert Glen Findley, Odessa College; Sean Busick, Kentucky Wesleyan College; Stephen M. Leahy, University of Wisconsin-Fox

Valley; Stephen Tootle, University of Northern Colorado; Steven Prewitt, Tomball College; Virginia Jelatis, Western Illinois University; William Kerrigan, Muskingum College.

Family members provided unfailing support. I am especially indebted to my mother-in-law, Ms. Gail Tycer, whose years of experience as a professional writer, and whose willingness to put her marvelous editing skills to work on my behalf, proved indispensable to the completion of this manuscript. Of all the encouragement I received to complete this undertaking, no one was more reassuring and confident in my ability to do so than my wife Chris. From her understanding of this project's importance to her reading of every paragraph, she was always there, never hesitating to help in whatever way she could. She was my sharpest critic, most determined advocate, best editor, and closest friend and confidante. No written tribute could ever express my deep appreciation for the faith, patience, and love she has demonstrated throughout the thirty years of marriage.

J. A. M.

CHAPTER

1

"Gold to Me Is Dirt"

As Captain William Penn walked the deck of his new ship, he could not help but think about the birth of his firstborn, a son, on October 14, 1644, who would be his namesake and whom he had seen only a few times before getting his orders to put to sea. He wondered, like all parents in seventeenth-century England, whether his son would survive infancy, let alone adolescence, at a time when even among the upper classes, one child in three died before the age of five. Captain Penn, however, had little to fear, for not only would his son survive smallpox as well as England's last outbreak of the plague during his early youth, but he would die peacefully in his bed at the remarkable age of 73.

Though devoted to his family, Captain Penn's was a seaman's kind of devotion, and for many years the sea had more command of his time than his family did. The pattern of long absences and hasty farewells had already been established as he set sail once more. His new vessel, the *Fellowship*, was his first important command. He was only 24, but years of going to sea with his father, Giles Penn, had prepared him well.

Giles Penn, the future Proprietor's paternal grandfather, was one of early Stuart England's most legendary and wealthy merchant sea captains. By the 1630s Giles owned a fleet of six ships, which sailed out of Bristol and into the Mediterranean, where he traded with Spaniards, Moors, and even Algerian pirates. Although bartering with people most Englishmen considered to be inferior rogues and enemies, King Charles I did not mind Penn's "business relations," for the mariner provided the Stuart court with all manner of exotic finery, including Arab horses and hunting falcons. So pleased was Charles by Penn's gifts that he appointed the captain the official agent for ransoming English captives taken by the Moors and other North African corsairs.

For several years Giles's two sons, George and William, participated in their father's lucrative Spanish and North African trade. George was resident merchant at Seville, while William captained a vessel taking goods to Bristol, where the influential merchant Thomas Callowhill (William Penn, Jr.'s future father-in-law) sold the cargo and supplied a return consignment. Such an arrangement allowed the Penns to control, if not monopolize, for many years the commerce of North Africa and Spain. However, sometime in the late 1630s everything went wrong. For reasons still unclear, Spanish authorities arrested George in Seville, confiscated his property "down to the nail on the wall," threw him in prison and for weeks fed him nothing but bread and water while beating him regularly with a knotted whipcord.

Soon after hearing of his brother's arrest, William decided that such a fate awaited him as well if at any time on one of his sojourns his father's trading partners decided they were being cheated or war erupted, which was always an imminent possibility, especially between Spain and England. In 1640 William left the trading company and joined the Royal Navy. When Giles pointed out that merchant shipping provided larger and quicker returns, William answered in words that his son, the founder of Pennsylvania, might well have spoken: "Gold to me is dirt; 'tis the goodness of the cause that hath only to put me on, and nothing shall take me off the service." Nothing did. William, the Sailor, remained a naval officer all his life.

Two years after joining the Royal Navy, William found himself, like many Englishmen, having to choose between remaining loyal to a king who had favored his family, but who had become a tyrant in the eyes of many of his countrymen, and allegiance to Parliament, which proclaimed itself to be the champion and guardian of the people's rights and liberties against Charles's arbitrary rule. Although still wondering how relations between the king and Parliament had become so strained, Penn nonetheless momentarily absolved himself of his sentimental attachment to the tradition of monarchy. Like the majority of his compatriots, he realized that his king was unwilling to accept even the slightest check on his power, and thus had no intention of ruling England even occasionally with Parliament—a concept no true Englishmen could ever accept, for Parliament was as sacrosanct an institution as the monarchy. Largely as a result of this issue as well as Charles's determination to impose religious conformity within England and Scotland—that of high-church Anglicanism, which many Englishmen, especially the Puritans, believed was code for the ultimate return to Catholicism—Parliament rebelled in June 1642. For the next four years (1642–1646), civil war engulfed England.

Although initially reluctant to side with Parliament against the king, and remaining throughout the war a "closet" royalist, Captain Penn nonetheless took up arms against Charles. By the time Penn took command of the *Fellowship*—300 tons, 110 men, and 28 guns—Parliament had won its first major victory of the war, the Battle of Marston Moor, near York in northern England. Until then, the king's armies had prevailed. Most important for Penn was Parliament's appointment of the Earl of Warwick as Lord High Admiral and Captain William Batten as Vice Admiral, both of whom believed Penn to be one of the navy's finest young commanders. They showed their confidence in Penn by assigning him to patrol the Irish Sea, an important command because Ireland was Catholic, royalist, and still waging war against the English Protestant "invaders."

Penn was relieved by his orders to proceed to the Irish Sea because it meant he would not have to fight directly against his king. The captain, like many of his cohorts, shared the sentiments of the Earl of Manchester, who declared early in the conflict that "if we [Parliament] beat the king ninety-nine times yet he is still king, . . . but if the king beats us we shall be hanged and our posterity made slaves." Penn became a rebel when he sided with Parliament, and rebels carried the stigma of treason. The habit of loyalty to God (an Anglican or Protestant God, not a Catholic one) and king remained strong and Parliament had the difficult task of building the machinery of war upon unconstitutional foundations and of convincing a doubtful nation that God and justice were on its side.

From October 1644 to August 1645, Penn helped suppress the Irish rebellion. From bombarding Irish fortresses to the razing of Irish villages to the transporting of troops to the executing of scores of Irish rebels, Penn's activities proved pivotal in quelling the uprising. After ten months patrolling the Irish sea, in the middle of August 1645, Penn received orders "to repair to England, so for London."

Penn's exploits got the attention of the Puritan Oliver Cromwell, who was fast becoming the most powerful man in England as the result of helping to create Parliament's New Model Army and then lead it to pivotal victories over the king's forces. Under Cromwell's auspices, Parliament forged a weapon of righteousness and discipline, dedicated to victory. Boding well for officers like Penn was Parliament's policy of promoting individuals based on their accomplishments or merit, not blood; thus, both the army and navy became staffed with men who "made some conscience of what they did." Cromwell realized that though the New Model Army had been the key to victory over the king's forces, he needed the navy to be as well led and proficient as the army. Cromwell was quick to notice gifted officers, and as a result of his influence and power he was able to persuade Parliament to promote Penn to the rank of Rear Admiral of the Irish Seas.

Penn returned home to visit his wife and two-year-old son. For the moment, Penn forgot his country's turmoil, worrying more about his family's future well-being. When he stepped into his London home, he found a frightened wife who had endured over a year of civil war without her husband and had nursed her son through smallpox. There was grim comfort in the fact that once the dreaded disease struck it would not visit a second time, and thus young William Penn survived one of the deadliest contagions of his time. However, he did not escape unscathed: the high fever that accompanied the affliction had burned every remnant of hair from his head, and soon he would have to be fitted for a wig, *de rigueur* among the English upper classes to hide the fact that even they were susceptible to the most common of epidemics. Plague also haunted civil war London, as garbage-strewn streets and flea-ridden houses increased in number. However, the Admiral did not have to despair about his family being exposed to the plague. His promotion and profits made from captured ships gave him enough money to buy a country house in Wanstead near the village of Chigwell in Essex County, only ten miles northeast of London.

Penn's move to the country pleased him, for not only did he have a fine estate complete with forest, wild game, sheep, and grain fields and a staff of ten servants, but more important, it was a far healthier and safer environment than disease-ridden, raucous, and conspiring London. At Wanstead, secure from the vagaries of civil conflict, Margaret Penn could oversee her son's early education. Penn's mother had been born in Rotterdam to Anglo-Irish parents. Her father, John Jasper, came to Ireland in the early seventeenth century from England, married an Irish woman, and prospered as a merchant in the Dutch-English colony of Kilrush, County Clare, on the River Shannon, near the Atlantic coast in southwest Ireland. While still in her teens, Margaret married a Dutch merchant, Nicasius Vanderschuren, who died in 1640, one year before the occurrence of a massive Irish-Catholic uprising against Protestants. The insurrection quickly spread throughout southern and central Ireland, forcing Protestants like the widow Vanderschuren and her parents to flee for their lives to London, where Margaret met and eventually married Captain William Penn in June 1643.

Although very little has been written about Penn's mother, from what can be pieced together she apparently was a hearty, zestful woman. However, according to some contemporaries, she was a little too raucous and bawdy for proper English society. Not wanting to embarrass or jeopardize her husband's status, Margaret accepted the tutelage of the aristocratic wives with whom she associated, and they, in short time, "cured" Margaret of her alleged "slatternly ways." By the time of her son's birth she had calmed considerably, becoming the perfectly mannered wife of a respected naval officer.

While Margaret Penn learned protocol, the civil war entered its final phase. After surrendering to a Scot army that had invaded England after the Battle of Naseby in the summer of 1645, Charles formed an alliance with the Scots, who suddenly remembered that, after all, Charles was a Stuart and a Scotsman. Joining Charles's makeshift army were conservative Parliamentarians, mostly Presbyterians, who had been driven out of Parliament by the extremists and the military, which had taken control of the government by coup d'etat in 1647. In August 1648, at the Battle of Preston Pans, Parliament's soldiers of righteousness routed Charles's forces. In December, Cromwell and his victorious army marched to London, surrounded Westminster, and purified Parliament of the fearful of heart, the sinful of soul, and the uncertain of politics. In the year 1648–1649 the tempo of constitutional change attained revolutionary proportions. In January 1649 the House of Commons declared itself to "have the supreme power in this nation," and whatsoever it enacted "hath the force of law, . . . although the consent of the king or the House of Peers [Lords] be not had thereunto." The newly sovereign House of Commons then declared kingship to be "unnecessary, burdensome, and dangerous," and thus ordered the execution of Charles I, which was carried out on Sunday, January 30, 1649. A week later, the House of Lords disappeared from England's body politic, joining the episcopacy of the Church of England, which had been abolished three years earlier.

Charles's execution and Oliver Cromwell's rise in political power also meant the ascendancy of Puritanism, a religious movement that emerged during the reign of Elizabeth I. Although of the more radical, rabidly anti-Catholic congregational ilk of the Puritan movement, Cromwell nonetheless granted a limited religious toleration to all Protestants but not "papists" (Catholics). Although wisely allowing religious toleration for Protestants, Cromwell nonetheless imposed on England a moralistic military dictatorship. From 1649 to 1660, England officially became a Puritan republic, although for much of that time Cromwell dictated national policy. During this period, Cromwell's army conquered Ireland and Scotland, creating the single political entity of Great Britain. Particularly brutal was Cromwell's subjugation of Ireland, where the fire of the 1641 uprising continued to smolder. Ireland was Catholic, royalist, and seditious—three good reasons to warrant God's vengeance—and in the summer of 1649 His instrument, in the shape of Oliver Cromwell, arrived to punish the ungodly and disloyal Celts. By outright ruthless slaughter and pillage and the selling of Irish Catholics into slavery in the West Indies, he won a terrible kind of submission. Within a year Ireland was prostrate and bleeding, and by the 1652 Act of Settlement, two-thirds of the land was expropriated, the bulk of the Irish population forcibly removed and confined to County Connaught, and the island populated by London land speculators and Cromwell's soldiers. The terms of the settlement were never carried out in full, but enough was accomplished to embitter English–Irish relations for over 300 years.

With Ireland and Scotland subjugated, Cromwell then pushed for war against the Netherlands, a conflict that had been brewing since England had made peace with Spain in 1604. War finally erupted between the two nations, the result of decades of escalating maritime rivalry and tensions. The First Dutch War (1652–1654) was disastrous for the Netherlands: her navies were defeated, her commerce disrupted, and her ports blockaded. Admiral Penn commanded one of the three great squadrons that brought England victory at sea. Penn came home from the war "noble and renowned," with a long list of sunken men-of-war, prisoners, prizes, wounded, and dead to his credit. Though still suspicious of Penn's royalist sympathies, Cromwell nonetheless rewarded the Admiral for his exploits by commissioning him General at Sea, a rank that had heretofore always gone to an army field officer.

The Commonwealth lasted for eleven years, throughout most of young William Penn's boyhood and teens. Its impact on his thinking, however, did not manifest itself until he reached college. Until that time, all he understood was that his father continued to rise in rank and importance under Cromwell's Protectorate and achieved the proportions of a national hero with his successes at sea. To young Penn, his father was his hero and standard, yet, at the same time, he remained a remote, not-quite-real, romantic figure, who descended upon his family—which now included daughter Margaret—for short exciting visits and then disappeared again.

While his father was off achieving more fame and fortune, young Penn learned how to read and write under his mother's tutelage, for the grammar schools of Penn's time did not want to teach the basics. Penn's formal education did not begin until he was ten, when he was admitted to the Chigwell School, established in 1629 by Samuel Harsnett, Archbishop of York. The academy comprised two schools within the same building. The lower school focused its curriculum on developing or enhancing an individual's more practical education and skills—reading, writing, and mathematics. The upper school was more classically oriented, teaching Latin and Greek as well as sharpening the fundamentals.

Young Penn spent time in both tiers; thus, while attending Chigwell he received a classical as well as a practical education—a rigorous curriculum of Greek, Latin, English grammar, spelling, mathematics, history, and geography. Since the Cromwellian Protectorate had been established by the time of young Penn's attendance, students were no longer required to take Anglican catechism and prayers or attend chapel. Young Penn was a good student, at the top of his class in all of his subjects. Penn liked Chigwell—his teachers, his friends, and his Latin and Greek classes.

The year 1653–1654 marked the longest time Admiral Penn spent at home since young William's birth. During his first impressionable seven years, young William saw almost nothing of his father. Sadly, even though he was now at home, the Admiral apparently paid little attention to his son, spending most of his time either eating copious amounts of mutton and drinking tankards of English beer and socializing with his naval comrades or tending to the business of his estate. The Admiral was an energetic warrior; to his ingenuous son, the epitome of the swashbuckling, larger-than-life Elizabethan "sea dog," who plundered enemy ships with the same savoir faire as Francis Drake and Walter Raleigh. He was the stuff of legends. He was also an ambitious man, who had dreams of worldly glory, of social and political success for both himself and his son. Although the Admiral may have longed for the comforts of home and family, his naval career was paramount, for without it he could not ensure his family's present and future status and security.

Like most seventeenth-century fathers, especially those of the Admiral's status and occupation, William, Sr., believed his most important role as father and husband was to provide for his family's financial stability and security—to ensure that his wife and children had all the appropriate requisites (country home, servants, and education) as befitted his status as an Admiral in the vaunted English navy. Thus, when at home, even if it was for several months, William, Sr., did not believe it was his role to help raise his son, to observe and influence the boy as he learned to negotiate his way in the larger world. Rather, that was his mother's and his school's domain. Thus, young William did not "bond" with his father in a modern-day sense, nor did he ever absorb his father's standards of manliness and success.

Because young William interacted with his father on only a most fleeting, superficial basis, he turned to his mother for closeness and attention, which she gave most affectionately and readily. Consequently, young Penn developed a quieter, more introspective personality compared to his lusty, robust father. Indeed, young Penn bonded with his mother so strongly that he may have viewed his father as an interloper, who deprived him of his usual measure of his mother's solicitude. The occasional presence of various male relatives, such as Uncle George, freed from captivity in Spain, or Grandfather Jasper, or of some others vaguely described as cousins, afforded some masculine influence. However, the men were either sickly or ineffective and were, to William's childish mind, ancients from another world.

Young Penn's only other male role models were his teachers at Chigwell, and they certainly were not even remotely the same kind of men as his father. They were as circumscribed as his mother into specific roles, none of which came close to approximating the sheer manliness and courage of his father. His teachers were pedantic, stuffy, and somewhat effeminate personalities, who were charged with his education, not in the ways of the world but in a purely academic, nontemporal way. In this rigidly controlled environment young Penn grew into a somber lad much given to reading. The child being father to the man, he matured into a sober, introspective adult; a boy who in later life declared he had never wasted time in play. In the long record of his fully documented life there are only two instances when anyone saw him laugh.

Although we know on the surface that William, Jr., respected his father for the Admiral's exploits, perhaps on a deeper level, young Penn knew he could never become like his father, for how could he, without the Admiral's presence and tutelage? It would be only natural for a young boy, surrounded by a constant yet almost illusory image of a larger-than-life father, to want to emulate him. The Admiral, however, shut his son off from his world.

Thus, as Penn grew older he came to resent his father for having failed to help him evolve into the man his father expected him to

Admiral Penn on deck
of ship gazing at sea.

become. Such feelings produced in Penn not only complete rejection
of his father's world but a constant rebellion against all forms of
parental as well as established authority and expectations. Perhaps
it was Penn's own inherent antiauthoritarian personality, developed
during adolescence as a way to cope with his father's neglect that
made Quakerism so appealing to him in later years. As will be seen,
Quakers became notorious for their refusal to accept any human or
institutional restraints—civil, political, or religious—on what they
perceived to be their God-ordained freedoms. To Penn, Quakerism
provided the perfect and safe circle of kindred rebels with whom he
could identify and embrace as codissenters from the established
political-religious order.

It was perhaps this estrangement from his father's world and the
overwhelming influence of his mother, and the feeling of being
alone, that led to young Penn's mystical streak and ultimately to his
becoming a Quaker. Young Penn was eleven and still attending
Chigwell when he had his first recorded mystical experiences. In a
moment of solitude, in prayer, he felt a sudden inward peace, an

enlightening of himself and a brightening of the room around him. It was his "Discovery of God." There was no pattern for such "Revelation" in his family; he said, pathetically, "I had no Relations that inclined to so solitary & Spirituall a Way; I was as a Child alone." Thus, Penn's mysticism may have been an early attempt to escape from his father's world, a world he believed himself unprepared for because of his father's prolonged absences and inability or unwillingness to instruct him in such ways. Not until William, Sr., exiled himself temporarily to Ireland in 1656 would father and son try to begin any sort of meaningful relationship.

Young Penn was a few days from his eleventh birthday when he was abruptly called out of class at Chigwell by the headmaster, who told him that servants were waiting to take him, his mother, and baby sister Margaret to London. They would be staying in rooms on Tower Hill. William had no idea what all this meant or what had happened to cause such a sudden upheaval in his world. He was told first by the headmaster, then by his mother that his father had returned from the West Indies but was not coming home to Wanstead. Instead, he was being sent to London in custody, to await his fate in the infamous Tower. Young Penn did not know that historically, confinement there was for those accused of treason, their final residence before their execution.

Up to this point in his life, thanks to his father, young William had been insulated and protected from the insecurities and uncertainties caused by civil war, the end of the monarchy, and the transformation from monarchy to Commonwealth or republic. This was why the Admiral moved his family to the country, to Wanstead, so hopefully they would indeed be in a safer, less exposed environment. The Admiral, like many Englishmen, sensed that civil war, once unleashed, would deliver unforeseen, revolutionary changes, that his nation would be in turmoil for years to come, especially once the monarchy was declared "unnecessary and dangerous." What had the Admiral done to warrant such dire consequences?

Soon after Cromwell initiated war with Spain in 1655, Penn sailed for the West Indies under sealed orders. Accompanying the Admiral was army General Robert Venables, who had under his command more than 7,000 troops. When his ships were well at sea, Penn opened his orders and found that he was to transport Venables and his soldiers to the island of Hispaniola (present-day Haiti and the Dominican Republic), which the general was to take for England. No sooner did Venables land than the scheme unraveled, becoming a most embarrassing defeat for Cromwell's once-invincible New Model

Army. The troops suffered horribly from heat, insects, diseases, and lack of drinking water. Cromwell had believed that 7,000 troops would be enough to take Hispaniola because he was certain that the island's thousands of African slaves would rise up against their Spanish masters and join this army of liberation. They did not, and once that fear was put aside, the Spanish attacked the weakened English forces and easily routed them, driving them off the island and back into the Admiral's ships.

Neither Penn nor Venables wanted to return to England in such disgrace and so they set sail for Jamaica, another Spanish possession, and with depleted forces, captured the island in a relatively short time, "sacking their towns and returning with very rich booty." Apparently Jamaica was not as well garrisoned or protected as Hispaniola and fell rather easily to a token English force. At the time, neither Penn nor Venables realized the significance of their triumph. To both men, the decision to attack Jamaica was simple: neither warrior wanted to return to England as an empty-handed failure. Whether they knew the island was so poorly defended and that they would take it with relative ease is uncertain. What is certain is that they captured a prize of greater importance than either man realized at the time.

For one, Jamaica was the first of Spain's Greater Antilles possessions to be lost, and its seizure by England inaugurated a new epoch in that nation's commercial policy. Not only did Penn and Venables capture one of the Caribbean's richest sugar islands but also one that would soon become a most valuable entrepot for slaves for England's expanding New World empire. Especially benefiting from Jamaica as a source for slaves was England's North American southern colonies. Because of the region's burgeoning tobacco, rice, and indigo production, its planters' demand for slaves increased commensurately, making Jamaica the perfect place to purchase already "seasoned" slaves.

Despite bringing home to England such a boon to its commercial expansion, both Penn and Venables were arrested and taken to the Tower as soon as they arrived at port. Reasons (or conjecture) for their arrest vary in the extreme. Some scholars believe Cromwell was simply so embarrassed that his grand plan had failed that he needed scapegoats for the Hispaniola debacle. Penn and Venables became the perfect foils for his humiliation and subsequent rage. He accused them of incompetence and then disgraced them publicly, as they allegedly had done to Cromwell by their ineptitude, by throwing them in the Tower. Other historians proffer that Penn's and Venables's failure to take Hispaniola was deliberate; that is, they purposely muffed the whole operation, hoping to so discredit Cromwell that he would be overthrown and the Stuart monarchy returned to power. Some even believe that Penn and Venables may have offered the fleet and army to Charles II in exile, to be used by him as an invasion force to reclaim the throne.

The notion that Penn might have been involved in some sort of conspiracy to help Charles II come to power is probably far-fetched. He was too able a commander, too deeply entrenched in naval traditions, and too proud of his previous victories and the acclaim and wealth it had brought him, to deliberately sabotage an armed engagement.

In the end, all Cromwell could rightly claim was that Penn had no orders to attack Jamaica, nor did he have permission to return home. Whatever Cromwell may have suspected, he wasn't able to make his mistrust or vendetta stick. After five weeks in the Tower, punctuated with questionings before the Council of State, Penn was released and all charges against him dropped with full apology from both Cromwell and the Council of State. Although Cromwell atoned for his charges, the Admiral never forgave his humiliation. He became involved actively, although secretly, in the scheme to restore the monarchy.

The Admiral was so disquieted by his arrest that he decided on a hiatus from the navy. In many ways it was self-exile; he wanted to remove himself and his family as far as possible from any future events or accusations that could ruin him personally, destroying all he had accomplished. His brief but humiliating imprisonment in the Tower was a painful reminder that the reputation and status of even the greatest of heroes could be obliterated by the jealousy and suspicion of one man. For a few months after his release, Penn and his family stayed in Wanstead, but by the summer of 1656, the Admiral thought it wise to leave England altogether, taking his wife and children—young William, Margaret, and his new son, Richard, as well as a tutor for young William—to his recently acquired lands in Ireland, to his manor and castle at Macroom, about twenty miles west of Cork in southern Ireland.

Three years earlier Penn had taken advantage of his favor, petitioning the Lord Protector and his Council for restitution for damages done to his wife's Irish estates during the 1641 rebellion. Not only would the land lost be returned to Penn but more added to it, about 300 acres, worth hundreds of pounds in annual revenue. In addition to his manor house, Penn was given a castle garrison to use at his discretion to keep the peace. Penn was just one of scores of military commanders benefiting from Cromwell's 1652 Act of Settlement. The measure served a twofold purpose: to reward men like Penn for services to the Commonwealth without disturbing the aching national treasury, and to initiate the colonization of Catholic Ireland with English Protestants. Hopefully the majority of the expatriates would be rabid Puritans, who would welcome the opportunity to further subjugate the Irish by acquiring their land and using whatever force necessary to keep them from rebelling again. Such was incumbent on Penn when he received his new grant. Moreover, in a land where the law of primogeniture guaranteed him his father's shoes, young Penn's future appeared financially secure.

Young Penn's Irish experience proved to be one of the most influential of his early years. He was venturing into a land and encountering a people, the likes of which he could not have previously imagined in his insulated worlds at Wanstead and Chigwell. He was in an unknown country of mountains and forests and bogs; of mists and mysticism; of sullen and vengeful Celtic Catholics, who looked upon him and his family with perpetual suspicion and hostility, regardless of how "well" his father provided for them. He had been uprooted from public school to private tutor, from England to an un-English soil. His previous life patterns of school, prayers, and his mother's constant companionship and solicitude were shattered by the move to Ireland. He understood why his father left England and yet, despite the repression and isolation of his life there, young Penn initially longed for England's familiarity and constancy. Despite all that the exile represented to young Penn, within months of coming to Ireland he found that expatriation gave him an opportunity to mend years of estrangement with his father and try to create a more meaningful relationship as he entered early manhood.

To young Penn's surprise, his father, the seafaring-warrior–cum–land-dweller, was eager to help his son prepare for the ways of the world. The Admiral became a constant companion, teaching his son how to manage an estate, delegate work graciously to those of lower caste, and become skilled with a sword so he could defend himself in a quarrel or against highwaymen when he traveled abroad; in short, the elder Penn helped young William attain the manner, mien, and finesse of a courtier and gentleman, so that when the exile ended he would be ready to assume his proper place, alongside his father in the courts and salons of London. Although father and son spent much time together, it unfortunately was too late for William, Jr., to embrace his father as friend and confidant and certainly not as a behavioral model. Superficially they interacted with great civility toward each other, the younger Penn showing appropriate deference to his father's worldly instruction. The two rarely quarreled; they simply coexisted.

More important than his father's tutelage in the ways of the world was young Penn's intensifying interest in religion. His tutor as well as the two headmasters—men "of grave behavior"—of the grammar school he eventually attended, were dissenters, who helped young Penn better understand the Puritan critique of Anglican ritual. They also further encouraged his already passionate reading of the Bible, which he had been doing on his own since his days at Chigwell. Young Penn read the Bible with such fervency that, as he later recalled, he frequently "was ravished by joy and dissolved into tears." Revelations followed, although Penn, even in later recollections, never fully revealed how affected he was by their clarity and force. Nonetheless, their impact was sufficient enough to convince him at 13 that he was destined to lead a holy life. Such feelings, however, he carefully concealed, especially from his father, who would have been beyond consolation if he knew his son had chosen such a path. The elder Penn hoped that since he was spending so much time with his son, instructing him in the ways of an English gentleman, that young William was beginning to accept the idea that he was to follow in his father's footsteps; not necessarily precisely a career in the navy but certainly to at least maintain if not enhance the family status by distinguishing himself in politics or the law.

Young Penn's Irish years also marked his first exposure to the Quaker faith. The sect was less than ten years old when one of its itinerant preachers, Thomas Loe, came to Ireland in 1657 to spread the Quaker message and hopefully win converts among expatriate Englishmen, especially those who were dissenters (non-Anglicans). Even the Catholic Irish could not escape the proselytizing zeal of the Quaker evangelist. Founded in the 1640s by George Fox, The Society of Friends (derisively named Quakers because they allegedly shook or trembled when experiencing a union with the Lord), was just one of the many sects that emerged out of the cauldron of religious experiments that boiled over after the dismantling of the established Church of England soon after Charles I's execution. The son of a humble weaver with only the bare rudiments of formal schooling, Fox nonetheless became one of England's most legendary religious voices and leaders. Fox possessed a magnetic, almost hypnotic personality that attracted a host of individual seekers as well as groups of searchers dissatisfied with, if not alienated completely by, the "popery" of the Church of England, or the sterile, doctrinaire, and emotionally stifling rigidity of Calvinism. Fox appealed to so many of the religious and spiritually disillusioned because he rediscovered in the Christian faith what the Protestant reformation had lost—its inner core of mysticism.

An itinerant preacher who traveled for years in search of a true church, Fox ultimately came to reject nearly all outward forms of worship. The essence of his belief was that people's souls communed directly with God, who revealed Himself to the faithful through an "Inner Light," which was the Holy Spirit, Jesus Christ, who potentially dwelled within every person. How was one to discover their Inner Light and thus find and know God? Fox asserted that the awakening of this Spirit could come about only by a mystical experience, by an emotional and spiritual exchange and ultimate union between believer and God. Anyone truly awakened by that Spirit could thereafter live in sanctity, for he or she was filled with God's living grace and constant love. They could go out into the world knowing they had God's blessing and guidance to do good by helping ("convincing") others to discover their Inner Light.

The Quakers, took to an extreme the Puritan condemnation of elaborate ritual and church hierarchy, rejecting all sacraments, liturgies, and paid intermediaries—ministers as well as bishops—for all interfered with the direct communion between the human soul and God. Renouncing formalized worship of any sort, including prayers and sermons, Quakers met together as spiritual equals and sat silently until the divine spirit inspired someone, anyone, to speak. A Quaker service thus consisted of potentially long periods of silence interspersed with brief fits—the "quaking"—of testimony or revelation as a member or several members simultaneously experienced that mystical awakening of their Inner Light. Meetings often lasted for several hours and ended when no one felt further compelled to speak. When that occurred, the meeting simply broke up.

The close relationship between the human soul and the divine being in the Quaker creed diminished the role of not only the clergy but of Christ himself. Although professing to be Christians, the Quakers attenuated the concepts of original sin and salvation through Christ. More than a remote deity or ancient person, their Jesus Christ was omnipresent and eternal, a living symbol of salvation but not a necessary agent, and he certainly did not rank on a Trinitarian par with God. This notion led more orthodox Christians to accuse, condemn, and promote the persecution of Quakers for being Unitarians—those who believed in the humanity of Jesus rather than in His divinity, and thus denying that God the Father, Jesus the Son, and the Holy Spirit were one sacred personage. Although the charge was not completely true, the Quakers' Christ was nonetheless not part of the same holy trinity of both Catholic and Protestant orthodoxy. Moreover, the Quakers' God was not the wrathful, vengeful, omnipotent Jehovah of the Old Testament, which the Puritans claimed He was because of mankind's inherent depravity and sinfulness. To the Quakers, since man was inherently good or at least predisposed to do good rather than evil, especially after accepting God's grace—the revelation of one's Inner Light—then God must be a forgiving and loving deity who expected the best, not the worst, from mankind, His most perfect creation.

Equally disturbing to Puritans was Quakerism's anti-intellectualism, which offended their premise that religion must be rational and at all times under the stewardship and scrutiny of an educated ministry. From the point of view of both Puritans and Anglicans, without a learned clergy, religion would degenerate into ignorance and mysticism; the church itself would collapse as each saint went off on a theological tangent. George Fox, of course, did not care. An institution that required conformity was precisely what he and his followers were trying to avoid.

Fox also believed that Friends were to be practicing, activist witnesses and examples to their faith in their daily lives. Humble sobriety was not for Sunday alone; it ought to be part of the daily regimen, along with plain dress and the use of plain, familiar if archaic language—the use of "thee" and "thou"—with all people, regardless of their social status, including the king! Deference was not a part of Quaker vocabulary, even when it came to something as customary as doffing one's hat in the presence of a supposed social superior. In the Quaker faith, only God warranted such submission. Such behavior only reinforced suspicion that the Quakers were dangerous radicals, intent upon subverting the social order. Christ had preached the brotherhood of man, so Quakers refused to carry arms or make war. God had warned against false swearing, so Quakers refused to take oaths of allegiance or for testimony. An honest man's word, they insisted, was as good as his oath anyway. In a society that perceived all Europe to be a potential military threat and which regarded all dissidents as subversives, a group that refused military service and rejected loyalty oaths was naturally suspect. Finally, Friends accepted and promoted the democratic implications of their faith. The concept of the inner light meant that all men *and women* were equal before

God, and thus all should have the same rights and privileges not only within the Quaker community but in the larger society as well.

Had the Quakers been content to practice their faith quietly, behind closed doors, they might have been tolerated, although their refusal to swear oaths automatically excluded them from government service, politics, and the universities. Unfortunately for their well-being, they could not remain quiet or passive. True evangelists, they believed God called upon them to spread His word. Even so, they might have become lost among the host of religious seekers and exhorters that emerged and roamed the English countryside and cities during the 1650s. Their peculiar mannerisms, however, drew attention and aroused suspicion, resulting in physical assaults on many a Friend. So hostile did many Englishmen become toward the Quakers, that hundreds of the faith's itinerants were placed in stocks, whipped, or locked in jail, depending on the facilities available. Even Quaker meetings were frequently violently disrupted by angry mobs and those at the gathering hauled off to jail en masse.

Despite Cromwell's granting of religious toleration to all Protestant sects, the harassment and intimidation of Quakers was meted out with impunity. Such was the fate of James Naylor, who symbolically rode into Bristol in 1656, with women strewing palms before him as if he were reenacting Jesus's entry into Jerusalem. For his audacity, Naylor was arrested, flogged, branded, and bored through the tongue. Although only a handful of the sect's more zealous leaders exhibited the "peculiar" behavior associated with the movement's creed, the majority of Englishmen nonetheless regarded the Quakers as threats to the established political, social, and religious order.

The previously persecuted Puritans, both in England and in the New World were the most brutal in their treatment of Quakers. The colony of Massachusetts in particular treated Quakers most atrociously. There, in towns such as Salem, Friends' ears were lopped off, bodies whipped, tongues bored, fines levied, and people imprisoned. Boston's hostility was almost psychopathic with its cored whips and starvation of prisoners. One Quaker was encased in irons and whipped; when he refused to recant he was taken out and beaten until the flesh of his back and arms became jelly. Others were stripped to the waist, lashed to the back of a cart, and whipped out of town. In 1658 Boston passed an act against the "pernicious sect," making it possible to arrest them without warrant, imprison them without bail until tried, and if found guilty, banish them, and if they dared to return they would be put to death.

When the Quakers carried their gospel to Ireland, they quickly found that there, too, they were *persona non grata*, not among Irish Catholics, but among their fellow Protestants. Despite arrests, beatings, loss of goods, imprisonment, and banishment, their preachers, like Thomas Loe, persevered, determined to "convince" ("convincement" was the term used by Quakers to describe a convert to their faith) anyone willing to open up their hearts and souls, and embrace the Inner Light. They rode throughout Ireland, preaching in the open air, often from the backs of their horses, telling gatherings that everyone assembled could know God; that all they had to do was let Him in and their Inner Light would emerge, and from that moment on, they would know what God wanted them to do with their lives.

Such was to be William Penn's first encounter with the Quaker faith when the Admiral invited Thomas Loe to hold a meeting in his home. William Penn, Sr., the epitome of the English gentleman, and apparently not at all threatened by the Quaker movement, believed it was incumbent upon him as a "noble Berean [sic]" to at least hear Loe before judging him. Loe came eagerly and joyfully to Macroom, gathering the Penn family and their servants around him. Apparently Loe's "sermon" was so moving that not only was the future Quaker convert, William Penn, Jr., "caught up in the emotional appeal," but much to the son's surprise, so was his father, who had "tears running down his cheeks." Thomas Loe traveled on and the glow of his visit to Macroom faded, but it never fully disappeared in the heart and mind of young William Penn.

While the Admiral idled away his days on his estate, momentous events occurred in England that hastened the end of the family's exile. While in Ireland, the Penns heard that England had become a "republic"; that Parliament had sponsored the nation's first written constitution, the Instrument of Government; what they did not know was that the document inaugurated the drift that would end in the monarchy's restoration and when that happened, they would be able to return to England. Promulgated in 1653, the Instrument of Government lasted less than two years. In 1655 Cromwell dissolved his parliament, choosing to rule alone, thus beginning twenty-two months of dictatorship. As Cromwell's regime became more arbitrary and oppressive, increasing numbers of Englishmen longed for the restoration of the ancient constitution—king and Parliament—which they believed would safeguard property and assure to "the natural rulers" of society—the aristocracy and gentry—their control of local and national government.

To royalists everywhere, including Admiral Penn, the news of Cromwell's death in September 1658, meant not only the end of exile and a return to England, but more important, the restoring of the way things political should be—a king and a Parliament, who together would rule England and bring back peace and prosperity for all Englishmen. Within eighteen months of Cromwell's death, Charles II reclaimed his throne, ironically, at the behest of the army that had rebelled against him.

With Cromwell dead, the Commonwealth would soon follow the Protector to the graveyard of history. How much longer could such a political state last that had so much invested in a single personality? If indeed the Commonwealth collapsed soon, and the monarchy was restored, Admiral Penn was confident he could go home to England, for the man and the regime that had forced him into exile was no more. To young William, returning to England meant his father would once again be involved in national affairs, once again a man of influence and affluence. Once back in England, young Penn would be able to resume his formal education, something he had missed dreadfully while exiled in Ireland.

Young Penn was old enough to understand what was happening, for his father confided in him that he was helping to pave the way for the restoration of the Stuart monarchy. In the first week of April 1660, his father, accompanied by other Royalists, boarded the *Naseby*, one of the thirty-one ships sailing for Scheveningen, Holland, to bring home their king. Admiral Penn had no command on this voyage; he went as a Stuart loyalist. Whatever secret role Penn played in the service of his king was fully appreciated and rewarded. When Charles boarded the *Naseby*, one of his first acts was to lay the flat of his sword on the back of the kneeling figure, his devoted subject, William Penn, and pronounce him a knight. En route home, the *Naseby* was renamed the *Royal Charles*, and its most prestigious passenger went ashore at Dover to the cheers of waiting throngs.

On Friday, May 25, 1660, Charles II's exile came to an end. Four days later, on his thirtieth birthday, the Merry Monarch made his triumphal entry into London. "The shouting and joy" were "past imagination." His way was strewn with flowers, bells rang out a noisy welcome, the streets were hung with tapestries, fountains ran with wine, balconies were crowded with gaily decked ladies, and the procession took seven hours to reach the royal palace at Whitehall. There, in the same room where his father had waited eleven years before to walk out upon the scaffold, Charles II was acclaimed as monarch by Parliament. King, Lords, and Commons were united in their determination to turn back the clock to 1641. The skeletons of war, rebellion, and regicide were firmly and securely shut into the closet of forgetfulness. All in attendance at the coronation pretended that twenty years of treason never existed. Two decades of civil war and Cromwellian dictatorship became an Interregnum, a limbo between periods of legality.

Naturally, *Sir* William Penn relished the festivities and breathed a great sigh of relief watching the coronation ceremonies, for his beloved England had found its way back to the security and stability of its ancient constitution. Young William accompanied his father to the coronation, for the Admiral intended to bring the promising young man to the royal attention at the earliest possible moment. Indeed, as the king's procession passed the Penns, both Charles and his brother, James, Duke of York, nodded their acknowledgment of Sir William and his son. No doubt young Penn was impressed by the king's gesture. At that moment, he believed it was recognition of only his father, who obviously deserved such observance. However, in many ways, it was also an acceptance of the Admiral's plan to have his son as prominent in the royal eye and patronage as he had been. As will be seen, young Penn far exceeded his father's visibility and connections when it came not only to royal favor but friendship as well.

A month after the king's coronation, the navy's top administration was completed, with the Duke of York, Charles's brother James, as Lord High Admiral. Sir George Carteret was appointed Treasurer, Sir Robert Slingsby, Comptroller, Sir William Batten, Surveyor; and Lord Berkeley, Sir William Penn, and Peter Petts, Esquire, as Commissioners. Within weeks of their respective appointments, Sir William Penn and Sir William Batten emerged as the Duke of York's two closest advisers and confidants. Penn's relationship with the future King James II augured well for both himself and his son. The younger Penn developed an even more intimate association with James, one that proved most beneficial to his role as the Great Colonizer.

The world of opportunity was opening up to Sir William Penn's son just as adult life was beginning. The Admiral could now give his son everything: contacts with the most influential men in the realm, a well-furnished home, the finest, appropriate apparel, and most important, the best and most fitting education for an English gentleman: Oxford University. Sir William had come home to London in March 1660; October 26 of the same year saw his son enrolled at Christ Church as a gentleman commoner and a knight's son.

"Hellish Darkness and Debauchery"

To a royalist such as Sir William Penn, Oxford University was the only logical place for his son to pursue the next phase of his education in becoming the complete English gentleman. The Admiral also believed it was politically imperative that both he and his son affirm their loyalty to the House of Stuart; having William, Jr., attend Oxford would go far toward accomplishing that objective. The university had avowed its loyalty to England's kings through the centuries. It was the financial darling of many monarchs as well as the host of royal families and their parliaments. Charles I was the school's most recent guest, with the king making the university his headquarters during the civil war. Oxford had loaned the king money and allowed its buildings to be used as barracks for troops, as arsenals for weapons, and as granaries and warehouses. Cavaliers drilled on its grounds, and when the Roundheads attacked, students showed their devotion to the university's royalist tradition by taking up arms for Charles.

Sixteen-year-old William Penn arrived at Christ Church just as Oxford was about to experience another trauma—the Restoration. No sooner was Charles II on the throne than both he and a royalist-dominated Parliament pursued a policy of purging from the university all vestiges of Puritanism. Oxford was once again to be the bastion of both Anglican orthodoxy and of monarchical support. To help return Oxford to such a fold, the hardcore Anglican, John Fell, was appointed Dean of Christ Church. Fell gave special attention to purifying his students' thinking, believing it his sacred duty to inculcate devotion to king and church.

Although determined to restore Oxford to its rightful place as both the nation's leading university and the center of orthodoxy and loyalty, Fell could not suppress the challenge to dogma, whether religious or secular, or the encouragement of inquiry and free thinking. These remained traditions too deeply rooted for even the most zealous of reformers to extirpate. Some of England's greatest dissenters, both political and religious, ranging from John Wycliffe to John Pym and Thomas Loe, were Oxford graduates. A voracious reader, young Penn absorbed these men's works as well as those of scores of other noted scholars from antiquity to the more contemporary writings of Descartes, Hobbes, and Hugo Grotius. Penn found the ideas and theories of the nonconformists particularly insightful, for they helped him to understand better his own emerging recusancy.

At the time of Penn's admission to Oxford, the university had 2,500 students in attendance, of which 100 were enrolled at Christ Church. Oxford was still a walled, medieval town in its design and in its lack of comfort and amenities. Its narrow streets were perpetually littered with garbage and other detritus, causing a pervasive stench that hung constantly in the air. Oxford's chronic housing shortage, with residences for students and townsfolk cramped and filthy, earned the city the reputation of being one of the most unsanitary places in all of England. Compounding the wretched and unhealthy living conditions was the ongoing tension and rivalry between the city's residents and the students, as well as between warring student factions. Oxford students also gained a reputation for consuming as much beer as the town could brew and in upholding the university's tradition for riotous feasts and celebrations as well as roaming the streets at night searching for "mischief."

Introspective, shy, and protected, young Penn initially had difficulty adjusting emotionally and socially to such a raucous environment. Indeed, he later referred to his university life as "hellish darkness and debauchery." William undoubtedly felt uncomfortable in such a setting, for he had never been exposed to such a world, living as he had until then in isolated, rural enclaves with minimal contact with other young men, especially with the rowdier types whom he encountered at Oxford. Much to his father's chagrin, young Penn refused to associate with the revelers, spending most of his time studying or simply reading in the library. Sir William wanted his son to step out of his insulated existence and his mother's coddling and mix with the "rowdies," hoping such camaraderie would help young Penn become more of a "man." Sir William expected the younger Penn to assume his role as heir apparent, fulfilling all the hopes and ambitions that the son would participate in his father's domain of politics and business. In Sir William's mind, Oxford was the perfect place for his son to attain the appropriate requisites of contacts, education, and savvy in order to someday play an essential role in England's destiny. While William Penn indeed became a significant personage in England's future—far greater than that of his father—at the moment the Admiral saw only a son who refused to accept what was incumbent upon him to do in order to sustain the family's status.

Penn felt more comfortable at Oxford by his second year. He was more willing to engage other students and ideas, and in fact, began to bond with the students labeled as dissenters for their refusal to wear the required surplice and attend chapel service. Instead, they held their own worship meetings and attended the lectures of the well-known Puritan theologian, Dr. John Owen, who had not yet been dismissed. This small group of nonconformist lads appealed to William, not only because of their devotion to Puritan traditions, but also because they were less obscene in language and conduct, less cruel, and less vain. Penn believed such temperate and serious individuals did not exist at Oxford, so when he discovered that there were indeed students of such character, he naturally gravitated to them, joining in their protests against forced conformity.

Needless to say, Sir William was not all pleased by his son's companions and their activities. Although a former dissenter himself (a Presbyterian), the Admiral, ever the pragmatic survivor, converted to Anglicanism, and thus saw no problem in obeying the new laws. He expected his son to do likewise. Sir William should have known that young William was not going to follow his lead, conforming for purely political or social reasons. Penn, Jr., was the Admiral's complete antithesis, especially when it came to sensitive issues such as religion. Although by no means a nonbeliever, Sir William, like so many of his Restoration comrades, saw conformity, not for religion's sake, but because it was one of the pillars of respectability and an essential prop to oligarchical rule.

Penn's increasing association with the dissenting students, visibly joining them in all their protests, inevitably led to reprimands. Initially Christ Church levied an ineffective fine on Penn for his participation, but his later writings suggest that physical punishment was also meted out during his "persecution at Oxford." "The Lord sustained" him, and he refused to recant. Christ Church endured the 17-year-old recalcitrant as long as its patience would allow. In March 1662, its tolerance ran out and Penn was expelled and sent home.

Penn came home to an embarrassed and enraged father. Sir William had been unaware of the developing problem, so when his son arrived home in disgrace for having been "sent down" (expelled), the Admiral, in Penn's own words, unleashed a tirade of "bitter usage" that included not just a verbal harangue but "whipping, beating, and turning out of Dores" (thrown out of the Admiral's home). Sir William's hot-headedness caused Lady Penn to intervene on her son's behalf. To Lady Penn, her husband's demand that their son leave their home was foolish. Where would he go? How could he live without their financial support? Most important, how could they protect him from further "infection"—becoming even more deeply involved with dissenters—if he were turned loose on the world and beyond their jurisdiction? After a few days' absence, Penn, Jr., returned home, withdrew to his room and into himself, to reflect, to consider how his life would turn out if he and his father could not agree—and they could not.

For Sir William the whole affair was simple: His son's behavior had humiliated and betrayed him. The "cure" for such youthful indiscretion, which the Admiral's Whitehall friends assured him was his son's problem, was typical for the time among the upper classes: One simply sent the wayward on a grand tour of the continent, which was an essential component to a gentleman's education. A prolonged stay in France was considered especially necessary because that was where a young man acquired fine manners, subtle ways, and a genteel air; and its Court, especially now that it was dominated by its most illustrious monarch, Louis XIV, could certainly divert an impressionable youth's thoughts from his soul.

In July 1662, 17-year-old William Penn crossed over to France in company with "some persons of quality," most notably Robert Spencer, the future Earl of Sunderland. Spencer was the complete opposite of Penn—carefree, secure in his status as an aristocrat, not troubled by inner conflicts, and in no danger of becoming a spiritual seeker. Spencer was exactly the type of person Sir William wanted his son to be around, hoping that Spencer's buoyant personality and gentlemanly bearing could help young Penn regain his "senses" and return to England as a different man—urbane, mature, cured of his spiritual wanderlust, and most important, ready to assume his filial responsibilities.

Young Penn and his traveling companions arrived in Paris in the summer of 1662, and according to some sources, thanks to a letter of introduction sent by the Duke of York, attended the French Court at Fontainebleau, since Versailles was still under construction.

There, nearly forty miles from Paris, the Bourbons were at the height of their glory. William Penn was not quite 18 when he stepped into what was fast becoming the most extravagant and envied royal court in all of Europe, one that would soon be copied by monarchs everywhere, including the Stuarts. Penn and his companions could not help but be affected. Although he had spent two years in Ireland, that country was hardly "foreign" to an Englishman. Indeed, thanks to Cromwell's policies, the Emerald Isle had become more English than Irish. Thus, Penn's French sojourn was his first real exotic experience, and while in Paris and at Court, he momentarily immersed himself in the sportive life, donning the latest French apparel and taking lessons in dancing and swordsmanship. Penn later confessed that he engaged in such activities mostly to please his father.

That young Penn was capable of becoming the man his father hoped is reflected in an interesting episode that occurred one evening on a Paris street. As Penn was walking to his lodging, he was "set upon by a person . . . with his naked sword in his hand," demanding "satisfaction"—a sword duel—because Penn had insulted the Frenchman by failing "to take notice of him, at a time when he civilly saluted me with his hat." The Frenchman rejected Penn's apology for the slight, drew his sword and "made several passes" at Penn. Penn fought back, ultimately disarming his opponent. At that moment, Penn was "legally" entitled to slay his attacker, but he did not. As he later revealed, he could not bring himself to "run the man through" because "adherence to such ceremony is never worth the life of a man, considering the dignity of the nature, and importance of life, both with respect to God his Creator, and himself." Penn, in a moment of complete clarity, saw the absurdity of man-made rank and complex custom. Even among all the French finery and influence, Penn could still hear the words of Thomas Loe and those of other Quakers, who proclaimed the sanctity of all human life and the profanity of taking it from an individual for the sake of attachment to antiquated custom or convention.

Even before his "affair of honor" with the Frenchman, Penn had grown weary of Paris and what was becoming, in his view, his life of a superficial fop. The duel simply confirmed such feelings. He thus decided to leave Paris and journey to western France to attend the famous Protestant Academy of Saumur on the River Loire. At the time of Penn's arrival (sometime in late 1662 or early 1663), the academy was under the directorship of Moise Amyraut, one of Europe's leading Calvinist theologians. Although Penn's relationship with Amyraut was brief, it nonetheless proved to be a turning point in his religious and political thinking because of Amyraut's death in 1664.

Amyraut's greatest effect on Penn was his unequivocal advocacy of religious liberty and toleration. Amyraut's opus, *La Morale Chretienne*, established him as one of the most creative Protestant theologians of seventeenth-century Europe. By the time of Penn's arrival at Saumur, Amyraut had done more than any of his counterparts to restore a spiritual vitality to Protestantism, a quality that decades before had disappeared, replaced by adherence to rigid Calvinistic dogma and empty form. Amyraut believed Protestantism needed to end its present sterility and literalness and resurrect its earlier dynamism. First and foremost, Amyraut believed, it was time to reject predestinationist thinking. The Divine will, he declared, did not select favored souls; rather, it yearned to save every person. Thus every individual was a free, self-determining entity capable of "supreme good," especially if that person accepted God's redemptive grace. Piety was not enough, however; charity was also needed, for an individual's responsibility to others was part of his definitive morality. As a result of his exposure to Amyraut's ideas, when Penn came into contact with the Quaker creed, the message was not unfamiliar; the Quaker's equally uplifting and emancipating gospel only further reinforced his earlier embracing of Amyraut's liberating new theology.

William Penn returned to England in the summer of 1664. He appeared to be a changed personality, "a most modish person, grown a fine gentleman," according to Mrs. Samuel Pepys. Her husband, Samuel, who became Restoration England's most noted chronicler and social critic, believed likewise, adding that young Penn perhaps affected "too much the vanity of French garb, manner of speech and gait." Pepys also served as secretary to the naval board and his wife was one of Lady Penn's closest friends. Although to many individuals Penn appeared to have become overly French in behavior and costume, such acculturation, despite its superficiality, pleased Sir William. At least in appearance and manner, the Admiral's son had returned from France the gallant gentleman he had hoped a sojourn abroad would unveil. Besides the Pepyses' observations, other contemporary accounts describe Penn as witty, courtly, haughty, very athletic, above average in height, and a good swordsman. Penn's intellectual prowess was also impressive: He was fluent in both Latin and French, and his capacity for discourse on a variety of topics, ranging from the classics to contemporary literature, was equally erudite and captivating. There is only one known portrait of William Penn as a young man, painted soon after his return from Europe. It is a depiction of young Penn in armor, and if the image is a true likeness, then it certainly confirms the Admiral's pleasure at the figure his son now cut. The Penn portrayed looks every bit the perfect cavalier: handsome, with stylishly long, flowing hair, wide, bright eyes, a sensitive mouth, and a firm chin. Most important, it projects the image of a young man about to embark on a military career. At the age of 19, he was all a proud parent could possibly expect.

No sooner did William return from France than he found himself being drawn deeper into the Admiral's network and influence. Apparently, Penn's outward appearance and behavior convinced his father he was ready to assume his responsibilities as heir, and thus some legal training was necessary, especially if young Penn were being groomed for some sort of government service. Learning law would also be an invaluable foundation for a business career if young Penn chose to go that route instead. For such purposes, the Admiral chose the law school of Lincoln's Inn, London. Sir William's real intention of sending his son to Lincoln's Inn had little to do with young Penn's becoming a lawyer. Sir William, like most of his class, regarded law school as the final "educational" polishing of a gentleman. Equally important were the social contacts one would make for future referral. If Penn acquired a little law on the way, so much the better. The Admiral did not have to worry on that score, for only the most devoted pedant could have learned anything in that playboy fraternity. Attendance at classes was never checked, and students were allowed to hire proxies to do their assignments and take their exams.

Two events interrupted Penn's attendance at Lincoln's Inn: a second war with the Netherlands and the advent of the plague. In 1664 the new Anglo-Dutch war broke out, triggered by England's capture of the Dutch colony of New Netherland in North America. In charge of the seizure was the king's brother James, Duke of York, to whom Charles had given the colony (with the proviso that he take the province from the Dutch) as a personal gift. No sooner was war declared than Admiral Penn removed his son from Lincoln's Inn and took him aboard his ship, the *Royal Charles*. Although young Penn's stay with his father lasted for only a few weeks, it nonetheless gave him the opportunity to watch his father in action. As a result, Penn gained an understanding and appreciation for what Sir William had accomplished both for his family and for England while placing his own life in constant peril. After three weeks at sea,

Young William Penn.

during which William experienced some combat, the Admiral sent his son home as a personal messenger to the king, a brilliant first step in introducing the two.

William's coming to terms with the aging Admiral, as well as his feelings of guilt for having believed his father had "abandoned" him during his childhood, is revealed in a letter Penn wrote to Sir William upon his return to England. "I pray God, after all the foul weather and dangers you are exposed to, and shall be, that you come home as secure. And I bless God, my heart does in any way fail, but firmly believe that if God has called you out to battle, He will cover your head in that smoky day. And, as I never knew what a father was till I had wisdom enough to prize him, so I can safely say, that now, of all times, your concerns are most dear to me."

After delivering his messages to the king, who was "most anxious to hear all the news about the fleet," and who asked about the Admiral "at three several times," young Penn returned to his law studies at Lincoln's Inn. As he traveled back and forth from his home and school he witnessed the direct affects of the Clarendon Code. Dissenters were placed in stocks and pelted with missiles of garbage, even rocks, by mocking crowds. Troops or mobs raided and pillaged their places of worship, arresting all in attendance. Penn even heard of brutal tortures inflicted especially on the Quakers, who refused to meet in secret. Such tenacity and courage in the face of such persecution impressed Penn, deepening his attraction to their faith and his empathy for their cause.

Not only did Penn see the effects of the Clarendon Code on dissenters, he also observed firsthand London's second bout of the plague, which reached epidemic proportions by the summer of 1665. Ironically, because England's economic prosperity was based largely on overseas trade, the ships carrying goods from all over the world also brought to port the rats that carried the infected fleas. Families with plague cases boarded themselves up in their homes for weeks without sufficient food and water. Door upon door bore the great placard with its red cross and the plea, "Lord have mercy on us." The spotted death swept through the city, killing so many so rapidly that there weren't enough burying grounds. Great pits had to be dug wherever there was waste ground, and bodies were brought by the wagonloads. The madness of pain and fever and mass hysteria ruled London life that summer. Regulations, preventions, and treatments, all designed by the medically ignorant, more often caused the disease's spread rather than its cessation. There were no real nurses, only the hags and crones so desperately poor that they would take care of plague victims for a fee and a chance to rob the corpse. The Great Plague claimed an estimated 70,000 Londoners before it receded.

Young Penn lived in the midst of such tragedy and desolation. He had been briefly introduced to the Quakers' humanitarian doctrine in Ireland, and he had only a few months before left the classrooms of Moses Amyraut, who had said piety was not enough; that an individual's responsibility to others was part of one's ultimate morality. It was the Quakers who most impressed Penn, for their courage seemed to quicken by human need. He watched them go about the city administering what relief they could, taking food to the self-quarantined and helping to gather the dead. They went into the homes of the stricken, giving ministry and physical aid. Even though hundreds of Quakers either died from the plague or were arrested, they went on about their errands of mercy. As Penn watched the Quakers' selflessness, courage, and unrelenting humanitarianism, he could not help but feel repulsed by the foolish gaiety, affected manners, and ornate dress that appeared all around him among his peers at Lincoln's Inn as well as at home among his parents' friends, and most of all at Whitehall.

It was at this juncture, after witnessing the plague and the Quakers' perseverance in the face of unremitting persecution, that Penn began to expurgate his own courtly affectations and dress, and to question whether he wanted to be part of such a decadent, narcissistic world. For the moment, however, he kept such qualms to himself for fear of once again upsetting his father. In his heart and mind Penn knew that his uneasiness with his father's world was due to his being spiritually unsettled. Regardless of how hard he tried to embrace his expected role, he knew that his actions were a façade, artifices designed to prevent incurring his father's wrath. He was beginning to accept the fact that by temperament and "nature" he was more suited for the spiritual life, especially that of the Quakers, which he had seen expressed so unselfishly and courageously during the plague.

While William Penn witnessed the plague and the Quakers' persecution, his father and the Duke of York were busy defeating the Dutch. Although James had limited sea experience, he was given the office of Lord High Admiral, and the following year he assumed command of England's sea defenses. In June 1665, off Lowestoft in the English Channel, James and Admiral Penn defeated a larger Dutch force. The victory, however, came under subsequent criticism when it was learned that James had failed to pursue the retreating Dutch and annihilate them. The Admiral intervened, shouldering the blame, and critics, leery of offending the king's brother, were glad to oblige. The carping, most of it unfair, ended his active career; the Admiral retired to a desk job in the naval office. Moreover, Sir William's health was beginning to fail. Too many years of drinking and overeating had finally taken its toll, as severe gout set in. Although the Admiral was no longer able to be the swashbuckling hero, his retirement from active service had its benefits. Being confined to a chair with his gouty foot on a cushion, meant Sir William could give more attention and thought to his son, who turned 21 in October 1665. In addition, for years thereafter James, in appreciation for the Admiral's loyalty, repaid Sir William with secret favors, both to himself and to his son. King Charles too seemed to have understood the obligation. When, many years later, the king granted William his American province, he cited among the reasons his gratitude for the Admiral's aid and understanding.

Sir William decided his son's attendance at Lincoln's Inn was no longer necessary, and that it was time for him to experience local politics. One of the first political opportunities Sir William secured for his son was that of one of the commissioners for charitable uses for Buckinghamshire. Initiated during Elizabeth's reign and placed under the jurisdiction of the Church of England, the commissioners were responsible for supervising and monitoring the dispensing of local aid, or "charity," to the poor and needy. The agency was a kind of nascent welfare system devised to help the down and out, especially during times of crises, which the plague engendered throughout the greater London area.

One of Penn's most important tasks as a commissioner was to investigate complaints about the system's abuse, either by recipients or by the dispensers of aid, and determine the appropriate punishment for violators. In many ways, the commissioners acted as local justices of the peace. Although he was aware of his father's motivation in securing him the appointment, Penn nonetheless liked his job, for it allowed him the opportunity to experience not only local politics but also to witness firsthand the plight of England's dispossessed and to try to help alleviate some of their suffering. Such exposure increased Penn's admiration for dissenting groups like the Quakers, who practiced charity toward others at all times, despite their own persecution.

Penn served as a commissioner for less than a year when Sir William decided that he needed his son to go to Ireland to handle the many complications that had arisen over the family's Irish holdings. Upon Charles II's accession, Irish royalists began to file claims for the return of lands confiscated by Cromwell. Charles, wanting to keep Ireland at peace during his reign, believed it wise to reward such allegiance. Consequently, Sir William's lands at Macroom were among those returned to their original owners. Sir William, always eager to please his king, accepted the restoration, and Charles, not wanting to alienate the Admiral, granted Penn extensive estates (totaling 7,000 acres) in Shangarry, Kinsale, and Cork. Kinsale, fourteen miles from Cork, was particularly valuable because it was a crucial seaport for the navy's victualling as well as an entrepot for trading beef and butter to the West Indies and tallow and hides to England. Because of his gout, Sir William sent his son to work out all the legalities of the acquisition, and to establish amicable relations with the local tenants and residents.

Also motivating the Admiral to send William to Ireland was his son's increasingly somber countenance, which Sir William believed was the result of Penn's exposure as commissioner to the adversity of his charges. Because of the Admiral's status, Penn would have access to the Viceregal Court in Dublin, a small replica of London's Court, which Sir William hoped would help divert his son from his growing introspection and spiritual seeking.

Despite such inner turmoil, Penn was still capable of performing to his father's expectations, demonstrating remarkable political and social savoir faire. He still sported a wig, fancy attire, and a sword. Most important, in May 1666 Penn helped put down a mutiny at the garrison of Carrickfergus in County Antrim. Not being paid for nine months had caused the soldiers to revolt. Penn, skilled with both musket and sword, served under the Earl of Arran in restoring order to the fortress. The event was Penn's one brief record of military service. He handled himself so conspicuously well and revealed such officer-material qualities, that many enthusiastic letters were sent to the Admiral about his exploits. The Duke of Ormond was so impressed by Penn's abilities that he wanted to appoint Penn Captain of the Foot Company at Kinsale. The Duke urged Sir William to "send a resignation to that purpose" immediately.

No doubt the Duke's compliments pleased Sir William. However, to many individuals' surprise, the Admiral did not want his son to pursue a military career. Although he understood his son's "youthful desires" to please a parent, Sir William advised "sobriety on the matter," telling William that since he planned to "fix in Ireland" (retire to Ireland) himself, he needed his son to "continue in your present business so as no damage may befall us there." No doubt an infirm Sir William would need his son's assistance in managing the family's vast Irish holdings. However, it was also possible that the Admiral knew Penn's desire to pursue a military career was momentary; the result of being flushed with pride and exhilaration at proving his mettle in combat. He had demonstrated a manly prowess of which his father thought him incapable, and in so doing, proved that he was indeed able to fulfill all his father's expectations.

The Admiral knew his son was not suited for a military career and supporting such an idea could lead to further resentment and estrangement. They had reached a point in their relationship at which there was a sense of mutual respect and affection, and that was something neither father nor son wanted to jeopardize. Thus, Sir William, through the Duke of Ormond, had Penn appointed victualler at Kinsale; that is, Penn would be responsible for provisioning all the ships leaving that busy port.

It was during the year 1667 that young Penn converted to Quakerism when attending a meeting in Cork. Ironically, Penn's "convincement" was circumstantial; he happened to be in Cork on business and while there went into a store to purchase clothes. During the course of conversation with the shop's owner, much to his joy Penn learned that the Quaker minister, Thomas Loe, whom he had heard speak as a boy, was in town to attend a Friends' meeting. Remembering how impressed everyone had been by Loe when he came to the Penns' home at Macroom nine years earlier, Penn wanted to attend the meeting and hear Loe again. The shopkeeper insisted that Penn spend the night in her home with her family so he would not miss the meeting. Penn was amazed by such hospitality, but as he later learned, such was the Quaker way. Retiring to a plainly appointed home among simply dressed folk, feeling self-conscious about his expensive fabrics and lace ruffles, his elegant wig and clanking sword, Penn felt captivated once more by an atmosphere of giving that questioned not, judged not, and asked for itself no degree or rank.

The meeting next evening was probably in a private home, for even in Ireland the Clarendon Code applied to all dissenters except the Catholics, and thus sects like the Quakers were forbidden to meet and worship publicly. Penn stepped inside with his companions and sat down in silence with a great deal of curiosity as he surveyed the attendees. Penn was unaffected by the first speaker who rose to break the silence, but when Thomas Loe spoke, Penn heard a testimony that spoke deeply to his condition. Loe found the indefinable melancholy growing within Penn, the increasing sensitivity to human need and suffering, and the nebulous new direction he had been drifting toward for many years but hesitated to embrace, for fear of upsetting his father. Loe brought a blurred image into focus and showed it to Penn, and once Penn had seen it he could never forget.

The image had been assembling piece by piece since his first religious experience at Chigwell. It became less inchoate as he absorbed the teachings of Moses Amyraut and witnessed the sufferings of plague victims and the ministering of the Quakers amid their own persecution. With Loe's guidance, all the related fragments came together in a new pattern of living. That spark of God in every man expanded to a great fire in Penn. As Penn later recalled his convincement that day, he was "ready to faint concerning my hope of the restitution of all things, it was at this time that the Lord visited me with a certain sound and testimony of His eternal word." As Penn experienced his revelation of the Inner Light, he could not express in words what was transpiring within; he simply wept, and so decided to let his tears be the only evidence of his convincement. After standing for several minutes crying, Penn sat down and when he did he knew himself to be a Seeker. From this moment on Penn immersed himself deeper into this exquisitely simple yet transfixing new faith. He sat with friends in silent worship to be absorbed by their mystical powers; he listened to members rise and speak who were moved by a power that the meeting brought alive within them. He acquired a new style of companionship, traveled in a new world. The belief of the Friends in the power of the Inner Light of Christ to guide them and the right of the individual alone or with a group to communicate directly with God fascinated Penn. He wanted more of the Friends' companionship, more of their meetings, more of their messages, more of their literature.

Within a few weeks of his first convincement, Penn personally experienced the harassment Quakers had been enduring for years and which Penn had witnessed on several occasions both in England and Ireland. The incident proved pivotal to Penn's conversion process, for his arrest and subsequent treatment by the magistrate roughly coincides with Penn's public embracing in toto of Quakerism. At another meeting in Cork, a soldier blundered in with the deliberate intent of creating a disturbance. Finding himself affronted by the ruffian, Penn did what came naturally to him; he picked the intruder up by the collar and was about to hurl him down the stairs when Friends stopped him, telling him to be gentle, for retaliation, especially the use of physical force, was not the Quaker way. Penn let go his hold, allowing the soldier to depart. Unfortunately, the soldier returned with reinforcements and all nineteen in attendance, including Penn, were arrested and brought before the mayor. Mayor Christopher Rye took one look at Penn's attire and declared that Penn's arrest must have been a mistake for by dress and manner he obviously was not a Quaker. Penn was free to go. It was in that moment that Penn set aside his privileges of birth and present status, declaring that he was indeed a Quaker and insisted on being treated the same as his comrades.

With Penn serving as counselor, the group wanted to know why they had been arrested. The mayor responded by telling them they had all been present at what was termed a "riotous and tumultuary assembly." The magistrate further informed Penn that if he did not give bond for his good behavior he would be imprisoned. Penn wanted to know the mayor's authority for such a sentence, since it was clear that without a Parliamentary act to back such action, the mayor would be guilty of "too much officiousness." Penn's comment enraged the mayor, who ordered Penn and his companions off to prison.

William Penn, still a Cavalier, had a subtle sense of the dramatic, which he never lost. The grand gesture had become part of his personality. Although striving all his life from the time of his convincement to achieve the modesty required by Quaker doctrine, there always seemed to be that countervailing force of aristocratic pretension that simply would not go away and which Penn willingly exhibited, especially if he desired an audience response. Such was the manner in which he gave up his sword—perhaps the most important physical symbol of the Cavalier gentleman. Just before crossing the threshold of the Cork prison, Penn paused, unbuckled his sword, and handed it with a bow to a bystander, announcing that henceforth he would walk unarmed in an armed world. William Penn had become a Quaker.

CHAPTER

3

"I Owe My Conscience to No Mortal Man"

Admiral Penn's son became a Quaker at a time when it was most costly in terms of social ostracism, economic hardship, and personal suffering. Although designed to scourge every trace of Puritanism from England, the Clarendon Code was especially applied to the Quakers, who, as one of them later declared, "were the bulwark that received the shot." The Code's purpose was to reestablish Anglican uniformity, episcopacy, and discipline, all under Parliamentary initiative and authority. Of the code's four decrees, it was the 1664 Conventicle Act (the forbidding of nonconformist religious meetings of more than five persons) and the 1665 Five Mile Act (the prohibiting of dissenting ministers from preaching within five miles of a town), that was most widely used to harass and persecute the Quakers. Since Quakers refused to go underground or hold their meetings in secret, they became easy marks for magistrates abetted by paid informers. "They [Quakers] go like lambs, without any resistance," wrote Samuel Pepys, who added compassionately, "I wish to God they would either conform, or be more wise, and not be catched [sic]." Over the course of Charles II's twenty-five-year reign no less than 15,000 Quakers were imprisoned. Four hundred and fifty died in jail. Such was the potential fate that awaited William Penn after surrendering his sword to his jailer.

Fortunately, William Penn's first incarceration for being a Quaker was brief. Thanks to his father's intercession as well as to his own friendship with the Earl of Orrery, Lord President of Munster, Penn's stay in the Cork prison lasted but a few days. Not only was Penn released, but so were the other Quakers arrested and imprisoned with him. No sooner was Penn freed than he plunged passionately into the Friends' activities. His brief moment of martyrdom fed his ardor and made the Quakers his brothers. Now that he had experienced their life and caught an inside glimpse of their sufferings, he respected them more than ever. However, before he could commit all his energy to the Quaker movement, he had to return home and confront an angry father and try to make him understand what had happened and why he had become a Quaker. Helping to persuade Penn to meet the Admiral face-to-face was another "man of good family," Josiah Coale, who also endured the wrath of his father after his convincement. Penn found Coale a "tremendous source of strength," and with Coale by his side, Penn returned to England to try to "reason" with the Admiral.

Penn arrived back in London in December 1667. His parents no longer lived in the city, having moved back to Wanstead the past summer. Before going to see his father at Wanstead, Penn and Coale spent several days in London commiserating with fellow Quakers. Many who knew Penn before his convincement, such as Samuel Pepys, noticed how he had changed since his return from Ireland. According to Pepys, Penn appeared "in a condition of perpetual melancholy," and "cares for no company, nor comes into any, other than those who are Quakers. His attire is that of the plainest person and he speaks like a commoner as well. No doubt his being abroad so long is the cause. His father will not be pleased."

Pepys was correct, Sir William was not at all pleased when he saw his son but held his temper even when young Penn and Coale addressed him with the familiar *thee* and *thou* and refused to remove their hats in his presence. The Admiral wanted to know why young Penn used *thee* and *thou*, for surely he knew, because of his upbringing, that the plural *you* had to be used when speaking to those older or of higher rank, which applied to Sir William in both instances. Penn told his father he meant no disrespect and that "'Twas obedience to God," for according to the Quaker faith, God considered all men equal, and "to honor that," they therefore adopted the language of the common folk. Sir William was not mollified by his son's explanation and insisted that he must address the king, the Duke of York, and himself in the courteous plural. William was sorry, but henceforth he refused all acknowledgment of rank, regardless of the person, including the king and his brother. The Admiral's temper mounted as father and son broached the subject of hat homage—the removing of one's hat as a sign of respect for recognized elders and superiors in status. Fortunately for young Penn, his father kept his anger in check, simply telling his son that they would discuss these issues further in an early morning carriage ride and it would be just the two of them.

The Quakers' flouting of social conventions may seem merely quaint today. However, in seventeenth-century England "hat-honor" dress code and the proper forms of address to one's social superiors was paramount, as it signified one's place in society. The Quakers' use of "thee" and "thou" indiscriminately demonstrated defiance of social authority, structure, values, and respect for one's superiors, such as William's father and the king. According to one amusing legend, in one of his first visits to Charles II's court, Penn wore his hat, unlike the other courtiers. Upon noticing Penn's rejection of such protocol, Charles removed his own hat, wryly declaring to the Quaker that "only one person wears a hat here." The episode is telling because it illustrates the significance of hat propriety, Charles's wit, and Penn's stubborn independence.

When the coach arrived the next morning, Sir William ordered the coachmen to drive them into the park, for the Admiral wanted to have a private conversation with his son that no one could overhear. Ever the astute politico, Sir William knew how fraught with political dangers nonconformity was to both of them; it could cost the Admiral the King's and the Duke's favor, and it could cost young Penn his freedom, perhaps even his life. Sir William was still seething with anger at his son's "betrayal." The elder Penn could not understand how his son could become a Quaker, for the Admiral had "trained you [young Penn] up in learning and other accomplishments for a courtier or for an ambassador or other minister." Young Penn's response was simple and direct: "'Twas in obedience to the manifestation of God in my own conscience."

Although a dissenter and possessing an open mind when it came to many nonconformity issues, Sir William could never embrace a sectarian faith as radical as Quakerism. To do so would have meant political and social suicide for a man who had spent his entire life pursuing status and the privileges associated with it. Unable to resolve their quarrel, the Penns returned to the Wanstead house, which was large enough that Penn and his father could avoid each other most of the time. A kind of temporary truce settled down on the Penn family, but neither Sir William nor young Penn would acquiesce to the other's wishes. The air of unresolved rancor that marred his relationship with his father did not deter William Penn from attending Friends' meetings in and about London and becoming more deeply entrenched in their world.

Penn not only attended Quaker meetings, but more importantly "came forth in the work of the ministry . . . to recommend to all that serenity and peace of conscience himself had felt: to walk in the Light, to call others out of darkness. . . ." Once embarked on such a calling, Penn quickly became, after George Fox, his faith's most energetic, eloquent, and zealous propagator. He traveled about the countryside visiting meetings, evangelizing for new members, until the inevitable happened: the authorities broke up a meeting at which he was present, scooped him up with the others, and brought him before the local magistrate. Fortunately for Penn he still had a cavalier's bearing. The constable not only recognized Penn but also knew Sir William, whom the official did not want to upset by sending his son off to jail. Instead, the magistrate sent Sir William a note telling the elder Penn of the "tumult" his son had been making.

Sir William ordered Penn home but remained too distracted and exhausted by increasingly poor health and by problems in the navy department to severely reprimand his son for his continued defiance. The Admiral's enemies had launched impeachment proceedings against him; high-placed intrigue had been closing in around him for months. He was accused of embezzling prize goods during the Dutch War. Although ultimately exonerated by both Commons and Lords, the ordeal nonetheless took its toll on an already distraught Sir William, his distress caused by his son's Quaker "escapades." Penn came home to an upset household, one with an enraged father and a saddened mother. The Admiral insisted his son disavow his conversion, while William remained steadfast in his commitment to the faith. Both father and son remained intransigent, neither willing to concede. From the depths of humiliation at his son's betrayal, Sir William ordered Penn to pack his belongings and leave the house. In a statement reflecting complete dismay and exasperation with his son's behavior, the elder Penn caustically remarked that William "should dispose of his estates [his clothes and other personal items] to them [the Quakers] that pleased him better."

William Penn left his father's house without hesitation and without money, to devote all his energies to the Quaker movement. Although without means, Penn knew he would be all right. In accordance with their tenets, other Quakers were bound to help take care of Penn until his funds could be restored. While staying in the home of Isaac Pennington, a prosperous and influential London merchant, Penn met his future wife, Pennington's stepdaughter, Gulielma Maria Springett. "Guli" was 24, just a few months older than Penn when they first met. Like Penn, she was descended from

Puritan dissenters and had become a convinced Friend. Educated, cultured, and possessing a gentle, temperate personality, Guli captivated Penn from their first encounter that lasted only a few minutes, but nonetheless Penn was so smitten that he later declared he was destined to marry Guli, for it was "A match of Providence's making."

Penn had seen beautifully fashioned ladies, bedecked with satins and feathers and their faces painted with beauty spots, in the courts of France, England, and Ireland. Undoubtedly, many such women wooed Penn into courtship and marriage, for he would be quite the appropriate catch because of his close association with the Stuarts. However, it would be the unadorned and modest Guli who captured his heart and soul.

Although no longer able or even wanting to enjoy the cavalier lifestyle, Penn was not completely without funds, thanks to the clandestine efforts of his mother, Lady Penn. At least once a month Lady Penn, without her husband ever finding out, sent her wayward son enough money to maintain, according to Samuel Pepys, "a decent and respectable manner of living." In the meantime, Sir William had recovered from the gout that had debilitated him for several months. The Admiral had also overcome the political embarrassments caused by his son's conversion to Quakerism. By June 1668, he was back in the social whirl, dining at Whitehall with the king and the Duke of York, taking carriage rides and long walks with Samuel Pepys in Hyde Park, and attending the theater with Lady Penn.

Although forsaking his father's world of court politics and the attendant social niceties and prescribed protocol for the Quaker way of "being," Penn quickly realized that he could not eschew such an environment altogether no matter how much he disdained it. If he did, he would be abandoning his fellow Quakers at a time when he could be of the greatest service to them. He needed to use his own status as the son of a court favorite, to gain access to the individuals (the king and Duke of York included) who could help protect Quakers from further persecution at the hands of an intolerant and vindictive Parliament. Penn knew that historically he could never expect help from Parliament, for that body had proven itself to be the most intolerant institution when it came to minority sects. Penn knew that any hope of a reprieve for minority sects rested with the king and the court favorites who influenced his thinking and made policy. Such contacts could also help Penn promote the cause of religious liberty for all Englishmen, which became as passionate a cause for Penn as his devotion to the Quaker faith. One of the great ironies or contradictions of William Penn's life was that, no matter how much he disparaged his father's world and tried to escape it, he remained throughout his life an inextricable part of his father's milieu. Penn simply could not have accomplished all he did for England, for its North American colonies, and for his fellow Quakers, had he severed ties to the men who wielded power in Restoration England.

Penn's first forays into becoming a liaison between these two worlds occurred in 1668. In that year he met first with the second Duke of Buckingham, George Villiers, who was one of the most favored and powerful men in Charles II's court, and then later with Sir Henry Berwick, Secretary of State. Penn had little difficulty gaining an audience with either man, for after all he was the son of a personal friend of the king. In both instances Penn's principal objective was to appeal to individuals in Charles's court who not only had the king's attention but who also wielded sufficient power independent of the monarchy within the government, including Parliament. Both Buckingham and Berwick had such status. Such individuals, Penn hoped, could persuade both the king and members of Parliament to support a Declaration of Indulgence for all nonconformists.

Penn asserted that the Quaker's persecution, "the stocks, whips, dungeons, fines, sequestrations, and banishments," were completely unjustified because the Quakers observed "peaceable dissent in matters relative to faith and worship." Penn reminded the noblemen that Charles, in the Declaration of Breda, had offered an indulgence for "tender consciences," as long as such individuals did not "disturb the peace of the kingdom." Penn assured Buckingham and Berwick that the Quaker faith not only preached pacifism but respect as well for the right of "all tender consciences" to worship freely. After several hours "engaged in honest conversation," the best that Penn could extract from either man was an expression of support for the cause of liberty of conscience.

Undoubtedly affecting the aristocrats' attitude toward Penn was his refusal to observe Court protocol: the removal of his hat before one of higher rank and his use of the too familiar *thee* and *thou* when addressing the noblemen. Although his first mission to Whitehall on behalf of the Friends' cause proved fruitless, Penn was not to be deterred, for he knew that in the end, the Quakers' only hope for a redress of their grievances rested with the king and with those whom he favored.

It was incumbent on Quaker "preachers" to not only encourage others to come to their Light, but to answer as well every challenge, every theological attack, and every denial of their liberty with their own best eloquence. In these roles, William Penn proved early on to be one of his faith's most zealous defenders. Whether it was vindicating his beliefs publicly before hostile crowds or writing Quaker broadsides, Penn committed his remarkable skills, as both a writer and a speaker, to the cause of liberty of conscience. Over the course of his life, Penn produced 150 books and essays, most of which were Quaker apologies. In his later years, however, Penn ventured into a variety of other topics, ranging from the writing of purely secular political treatises to offering a blueprint for future world peace.

One of Penn's first opportunities to defend his faith publicly while demonstrating his erudition and oratory skills came in the fall of 1668, when he and George Whitehead agreed to debate the Presbyterian minister Thomas Vincent in the town of Spitalfields. Prompting the eventual debate was Vincent's anger at losing two members from his church to the Quaker Light. He accused the Quakers of proselytizing the "most erroneous and damnable doctrines." At his next sermon Vincent told his entire congregation that if he heard of anymore of his people attending a Quaker meeting, he would "give you up, and God will give you up, and you will [be] damned!" He then called William Penn a "Jesuit," the most damaging imputation of one's character in Protestant England.

Penn believed he had to respond to both Vincent's personal affront as well as to the minister's attacks on his faith. As Penn saw it, the two newly convinced Friends were being denied liberty of conscience, which Penn believed he could not "for the Truth's sake let pass in silence." Penn, with Whitehead's support, wrote Vincent a letter requesting to meet him in public debate to refute "the UnChristian and Untrue character put upon Us [Quakers and Penn personally]." Vincent initially was reluctant to debate Penn and Whitehead. A confrontation with Penn especially worried the minister because Penn was more than just a Quaker: he was the son of a war hero–nobleman and, potentially most troublesome, one of the king's favorites. The Presbyterian minister could not dismiss Penn as a harmless fanatic whom no one cared about. Indeed, Vincent feared that if he agreed to debate Penn publicly the encounter would surely get the Admiral's attention and in order to protect the family name, Sir William would use his power and influence at Court to discredit Vincent. However, Vincent had little to fear from the Admiral. Once Vincent heard of the Penns' estrangement, he agreed to the debate, for he no longer agonized about incurring Sir William's wrath.

The debate took place in Spitalfields at Vincent's church on Saturday, November 14, 1668. The discussion was to begin at two in the afternoon but Vincent told his brethren to arrive at one so he could whip them into an appropriate anti-Quaker frenzy. As Vincent calculated, when Penn and Whitehead arrived, a hostile gathering greeted them. No sooner did the Presbyterians catch sight of Penn and Whitehead than the hissing, laughing, and shoving began amid the shouts of "impudent villain" and "blasphemer." As Penn began to speak, Vincent cut him off, declaring that *he* would examine the intruders with questions and their answers would be the basis of the "debate." Penn and Whitehead had no choice but to agree to this format if they hoped to explain and defend their faith. For over three hours, Vincent, with his congregation's gleeful support, railed at Penn and Whitehead, hurling one personal invective after another while deprecating Quaker beliefs. The minister gave Penn and Whitehead only a few minutes to refute his charges, while he repeatedly and peremptorily cut them off after a few sentences while his congregation shouted them down. Through the verbal trickery of the syllogism and the use of complex verbiage, Vincent tried to intimidate and bewilder the Quakers. Vincent's harangues, however, failed to fluster or daunt the two Quakers. Both Penn and Whitehead remained calm and confident throughout the entire ordeal, trying to answer their inquisitor's questions as best they could amid the constant laughing, shouting, and ridiculing.

As the audience grew increasingly unruly and menacing in their jeers, Vincent rightly sensed the "debate" should end before violence erupted. Thus, as Penn was about to tell Vincent there was no need for him to use "such high language and words, for God spoke to man in plain language," the minister abruptly declared it was time to pray. At the prayer's end Vincent adjourned the meeting and left his pulpit as Penn and Whitehead remained standing before a still very agitated crowd, whose rage finally erupted into physical abuse as several men hauled Penn and Whitehead from the platform and "escorted" them out of the church.

Such "rough hands" emotionally affected young Penn. He had seen other Quakers being physically assaulted, but until Spitalfields, he had been spared from such abuse. It made his blood boil with anger and filled him with a desire to retaliate. Indeed, as he and Whitehead were thrown out of the church, Penn, still affecting Cavalier "manners," unconsciously reached for his sword, ready to draw the blood of those who had so egregiously disrespected him. Whitehead calmed his hot-headed young companion, telling him that such treatment was customary, and reminding Penn that physical retaliation against those who so violated Quakers was not the Friends' way. Penn agreed, promising Whitehead that in the future he would refrain from such displays of "foul temper and malice in my heart."

Penn, however, could not dismiss the unresolved arguments from his mind. He believed more intensely than the majority of his comrades, that it was a Quaker's "sacred duty" never to allow any misunderstandings or false accusations about Quaker doctrine to go unanswered or unchallenged. If the Spitalfields Presbyterians, and no doubt others, would not heed a Quaker voice, perhaps they would respect a Quaker tract. It was out of Penn's first public exposure to the outright scorn and contempt that most Englishmen had for Friends that he wrote one of his most important early Quaker tracts, *The Sandy Foundation Shaken*.

The Sandy Foundation Shaken was not Penn's first written apology for the Quaker faith. His earlier, shorter pieces, *Truth Exalted* and *The Guide Mistaken and Temporizing Rebuked*, although filled with great passion and devotion to the Quaker cause, were not nearly as sophisticated in eloquence or argument as *The Sandy Foundation Shaken*. The early pamphlets revealed a brash, impassioned young man out to share his new faith with the world. Nonetheless, Penn's first two tracts reflected his complete devotion to Quakerism and belief that it was the only true religion in England.

In his early years as a public defender of his faith, Penn was persistently contentious. Beginning with his 1668 disputation with Vincent, over the course of the next ten years, Penn engaged individuals of every religious stripe, from conservative churchmen to rather mad sectarians, in often rancorous, vitriolic debate. Regardless of the consequences, he was always ready to go head-to-head with anyone who excoriated his faith. He even courted arrest in order to extend the controversy he engendered into the civil sphere. Penn purposely used words and language to agitate his enemies and he clearly relished the quarrel, becoming powerful in the use of the invective. For example, in a public debate, Penn unleashed a most graphic and vicious verbal condemnation of the fanatic Ludowick Muggleton, who believed he had been personally chosen by God to save or damn people (and he damned more than a few Quakers). Borrowing from the Book of Revelation, Penn told Muggleton, "Boast not, thou Enemy of God, thou son of Perdition, and

Confederate with the unclean Croaking Spirits reserved under the Chaines [sic] of Eternal Darkness. . . . On you I trample in his Everlasting Dominion, and to the bottomless Pit are you sentenc'd [sic] . . . where the Endles [sic] wormes [sic] shall gnaw and torture your Imaginary Souls to Eternity."

To comprehend Penn's writings better, it is essential to understand the way most seventeenth-century Englishmen read the Bible: English society was steeped in the scriptures. A great boon to such familiarity was the printing in the previous century of English-language Bibles and their ready availability to the common folk. For many Englishmen, the Bible was the only book they read. More important was the fact that those who read the Bible believed it to be an accurate history of the Hebrews and of early Christianity. However, the naïve literalism of seventeenth-century Englishmen cannot be compared with twenty-first century scriptural literalism. Theologians of Penn's time did not have to contend with evolution, modern science, or biblical criticism; they were not rejecting another way of interpreting the scriptures. As a result, Penn could quote a passage, or even a few words, and assume his readers, especially those as well educated as himself, would identify the reference and know its context.

Penn's 1668 publication of *The Sandy Foundation Shaken* not only earned him a prolonged prison term but Quaker sainthood as well. Until its printing, no Friend, not even George Fox or George Whitehead, had put forth a more forceful and erudite defense and assertion of Quaker beliefs. After the pamphlet's release, there was little doubt that William Penn could claim the status of one of the Quaker movement's most articulate, popular, and powerful leaders. Penn's principal purpose in writing the tract was to clarify and define the fundamental precepts of the Quaker faith. Penn, twenty-four then and with only a year in the movement, was confident his essay would be sufficient in logic, erudition, and theological legitimacy to substantiate Quaker beliefs. He also hoped his pamphlet would show that Quakerism posed no threat to the nation's social and religious order.

After recounting in a Preface the rude treatment he and Whitehead received, Penn, showing off his knowledge of classical scholars, asked "Would Socrates, Cato, or Seneca, whom they call heathens, have treated us with such unseemly carriage?" Penn then plunged into his three main topics: Quaker refutation of orthodox Protestant interpretations of the Trinity, Christ's atonement, and the doctrine of justification. Of the three themes, the most important and most dangerous politically was Penn's denial of the existence of the Trinity. Penn based his negation of the Trinity on Scriptures, which he believed "declare One to be God and God to be One." Penn further asserted that, "If God, as the Scriptures testifie, hath never been declar'd or believ'd but as the Holy ONE, then it will follow, that God is not a Holy THREE, nor doth subsist in THREE distinct and separate Holy ONES." Penn further argued that Trinitarian belief was not only contrary to Scripture but illogical as well, "since the Father is God, the Son is God, and the Spirit is God, then unless the Father, Son, and Spirit are three distinct nothings, they must be three distinct substances, and consequently three distinct Gods. . . . If each person be God, and that God subsists in three persons, then in each person are three persons or Gods, and from them three, they will increase to nine and so ad infinitum. . . ." Since Trinitarians "pretend to credit those holy testimonies," they had made "their kind of trinity a fiction." In Penn's mind (and heart), the Scriptures made it clear from "the days of the first covenant and prophets," there was "but One Holy God, and God but that Holy One."

Penn's essay's second theme was the issue of Jesus's divinity. If the Trinity was not valid, as Penn implied, was Jesus of divine essence? Penn professed an interesting fusion of Socinian and Unitarian doctrine, which reflected a degree of uncertainty in his own mind about whether Jesus was divine. Penn asserted that Jesus was the logos: He was the "Word of God" who enlightens everyone; He was God's interpreter; the appointed mediator but he was not God, only deified man. According to Penn, Jesus was "of the seed of Abraham and David after the flesh and therefor truly and properly man, like us in all things, and once subject to all things."

Since Quaker doctrine preached private judgment and the rejection of authority and the insistence on the free use of reason, Penn believed such tenets made Jesus's divinity suspect. Although for Penn and the Quakers the Bible was everything, it had to be interpreted by the light of reason. Penn thus thrust aside "the mystery" of Jesus—his divinity, which he believed the Bible did not sufficiently or "reasonably" substantiate. Penn fortified his contention by quoting the English Socinian John Crell, who declared that "Mysteries are indeed exalted above reason, but they do not overturn it; they by no means extinguish its light, but only perfect it." To Penn it was relatively simple: If God was but One and the Father, logically the most Jesus could be was a great religious teacher or someone inspired by God to live an exemplary life and to spread

God's word like the prophets of old. To give Jesus any other status would be to deny God's "unity, eternity, omnipotence, justice and wisdom; His immensity, infinity, and omnipresence." For the time being, Jesus's sanctification remained, for Penn, an unsubstantiated "mystery." Jesus was to be exalted but not hallowed as a deity and certainly not on a co-equal basis with God in any capacity.

The third theme of Penn's essay was to establish God's infinite capacity for mercy and forgiveness. Penn's and the Quakers' God was not the wrathful, vengeful deity of most other Puritan sects, but rather a God of perpetual benevolence and absolution, who through Jesus's agency, conveyed an understanding of the universal and saving light graciously available to all persons. That Jesus suffered, Penn admitted freely. It was the purpose of that agony that he was eager to interpret. Penn asserted that Jesus anguished and was executed for his beliefs, not as the savior or messiah, but as the perfect example of holy resignation to divine will. Penn was thus challenging the orthodox Christian belief that Christ suffered and died for mankind's sins, to atone for centuries of transgressions, to redeem humanity. To assert such a notion, Penn believed, was to sanctify Jesus as Redeemer, and consequently to affirm the efficacy of the sacraments, which the Quakers disavowed. In Penn's view, being purely man, Jesus "did not work out our Redemption in the sense of satisfying for our sins, and we cannot regard the sacraments as instruments whereby the fruits of that redemption are applied to man." Penn thus asserted that the Passion of Christ was merely an example to mankind and a pledge of forgiveness.

Finally, Penn refuted categorically the notion of original sin and predestination. To Penn both of those notions "insulted," a merciful, forgiving God, who granted salvation to anyone who repented for their transgressions and asked for His grace through their Inner Light. Reason and freedom of choice as well, God's two greatest gifts to humankind, were also proscribed "by such arrant creeds." Moreover, contrary to both Catholic and Protestant doctrine, sin came not by imputation from Adam; rather, according to Penn, each individual decided for themselves, in the here and now, whether or not to follow God's Word, revealed in the Scriptures and reinforced by Jesus's preaching of the righteous life. Penn believed every individual had within themselves the light of goodness; all one had to do was recognize that Light. Such a revelation would come about if one opened his heart (and mind) to God's Word. If one did that, then God's grace would fill their souls and all would be right with the world and with God, for salvation would then be attainable.

No sooner was Penn's treatise published and circulated for public consumption than its inevitable condemnation took place. The writing, publishing, circulating, resulting furor, and Penn's arrest and imprisonment, all occurred within less than a month's time. In early November Penn and Whitehead debated Vincent; on December 12, 1668, Lord Arlington, Principal Secretary of State, issued a warrant for Penn's arrest and "to keep him close prisoner till further order." Although apprehended and charged with violating a civil law—alleged complicity in his printer's failure to obtain a publishing license from the Bishop of London—everyone knew his "real" crime was blasphemy. It was Penn's refutation of the Trinity and Jesus's divinity that resulted in his incarceration. Indeed, his essay rapidly became labeled as "a blasphemous book against the deity of our blessed Lord."

Penn's arrest and imprisonment for failure to obtain a printing license and blasphemy, seems, by current standards, to be an unreasonable, egregious infringement of basic civil liberties. Today, freedom of speech and press, as well as freedom of religion, are guaranteed and protected by law in both Great Britain and the United States. However, in Restoration England such was not the case. After Arlington arrested Penn he obtained the Privy Council's approval to confine Penn in the Tower "until the King's pleasure should be further signified." As Penn recounted in his autobiography, he was "committed [to the Tower of London] the beginning of December, and was not discharged till the fall of the leaf following [July 1669]; wanting about fourteen days of nine months."

Penn's close to nine-month tower experience was grueling. He was separated from the world in a tiny room under the roof, which was poorly heated in the winter and baked by the summer's heat. His hair that had grown back after his infantile bout with smallpox fell away. He ate only "prison fare," which was "most wretched and foul in smell, and lacked sustenance enough to keep one barely alive." He was permitted almost no communication with the outside world and allowed no physical exercise. Only 24, Penn was isolated from family and friends and books (except for the Bible), with no hope of release in sight. Yet, Penn knew that his Tower room was far better than most of the prison cells in which other Friends had been kept. If they could stand it, so could he, for like them, he believed he was experiencing "the exquisite privilege of surrendering up my life to the bidding of the Light within my heart."

Penn's arrest and confinement in the Tower was just one more humiliating episode in Sir William's life with regard to his wayward son. The Admiral was certain that his son's latest gaucherie would eclipse what little influence he might still have at Whitehall. Fortunately, Sir William still had the Duke of York's favor, who granted young Penn communication with the outside world. The Duke persuaded his brother Charles to allow the Admiral to contact his son via an intermediary, Sir William's personal servant, Francis Cooke. Penn's first contact with Cooke saw the servant bring an ominous message from the Bishop of London: the Quaker could "recant in Common Garden at an appointed time before the Fair of all the City," or he would "be a prisoner during his life." Penn must have concluded that an arrangement between his father and the Bishop had taken place, for his reply was "Thou mayst tell my father, whom I know will ask thee, these words, that my prison shall be my grave before I will budge a jot, for I owe my conscience to no mortal man. I have no need to fear. God will make amends for all. They are mistaken in me. I value not their threats nor resolutions, for they shall know I can weary out their malice and peevishness and in me shall they behold a resolution above fear, conscience above cruelty and a baffle put on all their designs by the spirit of patience. . . ."

As Penn adjusted to prison life he realized he had to find within himself the emotional, psychological, and spiritual sustenance essential to persevere. It forced him to pause and take stock, to examine his own faith, to tap depths within himself that might never have been discovered. Thus, out of Penn's first prolonged withdrawal from the violent persecutions of the Quaker movement and the hurly-burly of London life, came one of his most important early works, *No Cross, No Crown*.

There are two versions of Penn's work, the one he wrote while in the Tower and a later, greatly expanded and revised version, almost a new book of nearly six-hundred pages, which was published in 1682, just as he was establishing his "holy Experiment" in North America. The later rendition reflected the sophistication and erudition of an inveterate, seasoned pamphleteer, while the Tower conception represented the effort of a rapidly maturing novitiate. Penn simply used the title twice because his intent was the same in both instances: to try to clarify and present to the "world" what Quakers believed and why they believed what they did. At the same time, Penn hoped that by writing a full explication of the Quaker faith, he could disarm those who saw the Quakers as radical dissenters, propagating heretical ideas and subverting social order and stability.

In the Preface to the Tower version, Penn implored his readers to examine his text with a serious and impartial mind. Penn then explained in three chapters, Quaker rules of behavior. In each chapter he gave several reasons why Quakers rejected hat honor, titles, and the vanity of apparel while defending the use of *thee* and *thou* when addressing one another, regardless of status. Naturally, Penn plumbed the Scriptures to bolster his arguments. Quoting James 2:1–11, he urged people to look beyond a person's exterior, and not to accept anyone just "for his gay cloathing, rich attire, or outward appearance." As far as the doffing of hats and respect for titles was concerned, Penn reminded his readers that "Honour was from the beginning, but hats and most titles, here of late; therefore there was true Honour before hats or titles, and consequently true honour stands not therein." In addition to Biblical reinforcement for Quaker beliefs (he used nearly four-hundred Scriptural quotations and verifications, with exact citations noted in the margins), after each chapter Penn cited a variety of authorities whose writings testified to his views. Martin Luther, John Calvin, Erasmus, Plato, Socrates, Aristotle, Augustine, Cicero, Ignatius Loyola, Grotius, John Donne, and Sir Francis Bacon, were just some of the sixty-eight "great minds" he used in his book.

More important than Penn's impressive recitation from memory of Biblical chapter and verse or the works of the ancients, was the fact that his essay, first and foremost, was a trenchant Puritan commentary on the follies, immoralities, and unabashed worldliness of Restoration England. Pride, avarice, and luxury—these were the chief enemies of the soul in Charles II's kingdom. The greatest of these, according to Penn, was pride, for "Whoso then would bear the Cross of Christ and win the eternal crown must wage ceaseless war on these besetting temptations." Penn insisted that the spiritual warfare against sin could not ever be won by retreating from the battlefield. At this point in his essay, Penn unleashed a scornful invective about monastic life, which he condemned as "lazy, rusty, unprofitable self-denial." He who would carry Christ's cross must shoulder it as a full participant in daily life; he must be in the world, though not of it. "True godliness," Penn proclaimed "don't [sic] turn men out of the world, but enables them to live better in it, and excites their endeavors to mend it."

As reflected in the above sentence, Quakers, unlike most other Puritans, did not despair of the world; it was full of sin and suffering, to be sure, but these could be ameliorated. Penn, as well as his Quaker brethren, refused to accept the Calvinists' easy rationalization that poverty and misery were the visible signs of God's displeasure, the stigmata of damnation on the lazy and indigent. If one believed such notions, then there was no use in trying to improve the lives of the downtrodden. Penn would not accept that; he was a man of compassion and social conscience. He envisaged a time when there would be "no beggars in the land," when "the cry of the widow and the orphan would cease." To Penn it was the worldliness of the rich that was responsible for the misery and suffering of the poor. He thus intimated that some sort of levy on the wealthy—perhaps an excise tax—should be put into effect to help uplift the poor. To Penn, it would be money used for a worthy cause rather wasted on frivolous and expensive self-indulgence. *No Cross, No Crown* became the first coherent guide on Quaker behavior.

After overcoming his initial mortification caused by his son's arrest and imprisonment, Sir William spent the next several months trying to procure Penn's release. After weeks of lobbying both Charles and James, the best Sir William could extract from them was permission to visit his son virtually anytime he wanted. Suffice it to say that at their meetings the Admiral used every wile he could possibly think of to get his son to retract the assertions made in *The Sandy Foundation Shaken*. After several visits in which "much shouting" was heard coming from Penn's attic room by Sir John Robinson, Lieutenant of the Tower, Sir William, totally exasperated, finally gave up, stormed out of Penn's cell, never to return. Apparently, the Admiral was willing to leave his son's fate to the "tender mercies" of the king and his brother, hoping the Stuarts' affection for Sir William would ultimately lead to his son's release.

While his father stewed (and schemed), Penn decided that he would try himself via a letter, to convince Secretary of State, Lord Arlington, that what he had said in his treatise was neither blasphemous nor treasonous; that he was an "innocent man" found guilty by "men esteemed Christians," who "discours[ed] [sic] down" his reputation "by the most foul aspersions, black characters, and exasperating imputations." Penn "beseeched" Arlington "to intreat the King on my account, not to believe every man to be his enemy" because, like himself, they refused to let their consciences be "shaped by the narrow forms and prescripts of men's inventions." Penn then argued that he believed his punishment was "without any legal cause, or just procedure," and was "contrary to the privileges of every Englishman." Finally, Penn asked Arlington if he would be allowed "the favor of access to the King," to whom he would "freely and justly answer to all such interrogatories as may concern my present case." Penn was confident that if granted such an audience, Charles would readily see that "to prolong" Penn's "restraint" would be to "deprive an inoffensive Englishman of so great and eminent a right as liberty."

Arlington was so moved by Penn's letter that he granted him an interview. However, as was expected, the nobleman, although sympathetic to Penn's plight, told the Quaker there was nothing he could do personally to help obtain his release. That decision was up to the king and his Privy Council, of which he was but one voice and one vote. By this juncture, Sir William had regained his composure and was ready to try again to get his son released from the Tower. Once again he called on the Stuarts for help. Apparently, both Charles and James were growing weary of the "Penn affair," and felt sorry for the Admiral for having to endure such protracted humiliation. Charles thus agreed to send his own chaplain, the Bishop of Worcester, Dr. Edward Stillingfleete, "to discourse" with Penn and to help him find a way of "clarifying" what he "really" meant in the treatise that had caused such a whirlwind of controversy. After several days of intense discussion, Penn and Stillingfleete concluded that Penn did not ever deny Christ's divinity either in or out of *The Sandy Foundation Shaken*. Stillingfleete then suggested that Penn write another essay explaining his exact views; in short, an apologia for *Sandy Foundation*. If the king and Council would not see Penn, perhaps they would read a tract. Penn agreed and within a week's time produced his second Tower essay, *Innocency with Her Open Face Presented by Way of Apology for the Book Entitled, The Sandy Foundation Shaken*. Penn cleverly put the word "apology" in his title, which could mean either apologia (explication) or apology (retraction).

In *Innocency*, Penn wrote carefully and in detail, reminding his readers (who were principally the king, his brother James, and the Privy Council) that his recent dispute was with some Presbyterians, not with the Anglican Church. Penn realized that his refutation of the Trinity had been interpreted as him also denying Christ's divinity. To Penn, such a charge was "a most untrue and unreasonable censure. I conclude Christ to be God; for if none can save, or be styled properly a Savior but God, and yet that Christ is said to save, and properly called a Savior, it must need follow that Christ the Savior is God." Although acknowledging or "clarifying" that he believed Jesus the Christ and divine, Penn still embraced anti-Trinitarianism. He declared "unfeignedly" belief in "one holy, just, merciful, almighty and eternal God, who is the Father of all things." Penn's God, as expressed in Christ, remained a God of remission and forgiveness, a God of love and gentleness and boundless understanding.

At this juncture in Penn's life as a Quaker, it is interesting to speculate why so militant, irreverent, and irascible a convert as Penn was willing to compromise on issues in which he so fervently believed. Was it because he simply buckled to the pressure being applied by his father and the royal family to recant? Possibly, for no doubt Sir William, Charles, and the Duke of York, worried that the prolonged imprisonment of the son of so revered a hero as the Admiral, who was so intimately connected with the king, could escalate into a scandal of sorts. Indeed, some contemporaries maintained that because of the close relationship between Sir William and the Stuarts, Charles was keeping young Penn in the Tower to protect him from further public wrath. Did young Penn realize this potential? Difficult to say, although Penn was always acutely aware of his status as the Admiral's son and was not afraid to use it to gain access to Charles's court.

Did Penn disavow his original position on Jesus's divinity simply because he could not stand, physically or emotionally, to be confined in the Tower any longer? While this may have been a factor in his concession, Penn was made of sturdier stuff both physically and spiritually, and thus, it is difficult to justify such capitulation. Perhaps the best explanation was that he realized he could do virtually nothing, in any capacity to help the Quaker cause if he remained in the Tower indefinitely. If Penn's primary goal was to gain toleration for Quakers, then he had no choice but to "reinterpret" his original premise on Jesus's exaltation. In the final analysis, it was this realization more than anything else that moved Penn to modify his position on Jesus's divinity. Also in that context, it was possible that Stillingfleete, after hours of intense reflection with Penn, was able to convince him of the more orthodox view of Jesus. Penn's acceptance in *Innocency* that Jesus was God was genuine; he had, thanks to the King's chaplain's exhortations (or admonishments), "come to Jesus," and was now willing to accept him as divine. Interestingly, despite his public recantation, the label of deist stuck to Penn for much of his life.

Apparently the double entendre of *Innocency* mollified the king and the Privy Council, for on July 28, 1669, Charles signified his approval of the tract. He then sent an order to the Lieutenant of the Tower to release Penn to his father's custody, which to Penn meant that he would soon be back into the mainstream of Quaker life.

Indeed, Penn's stay in the Tower combined with the publication of his two controversial tracts, catapulted him into the limelight of the Quaker cause. He was now recognized as one of the movement's most cogent spokesmen and most admired martyrs. Wherever he went, Friends flocked around him, ready to give him support, while the newly convinced were eager to hear his messages in meetings and at other Quaker gatherings. However, before he could once again immerse himself in the Quaker cause, he had to return home and try one more time to reconcile with his weary and infirm father.

4

"I Matter Not Your Fetters"

Penn was released from the Tower on July 29, 1669. As he made his way from London to his father's estate in Wanstead, he was certain he would once again incur the Admiral's wrath for his latest transgression. However, much to Penn's surprise and great relief, Sir William greeted him "with none of the anger of voice or demeanor" that had "marked all our previous conversations & encounters." No doubt contributing to Sir William's more benign attitude toward his son was the father's ill health. The Admiral suffered from severe gout (as well as incipient alcoholism), an affliction so debilitating that it forced him to retire from the navy board. The Admiral was simply too weary and infirm to muster enough energy for a tirade. It was also possible that Sir William had finally accepted the reality that his son was not going to pursue the career path he had hoped and that no matter what he did or said, his namesake was committed heart and soul to the Quaker way. Sir William believed it was time to reconcile with his son before death, which was more imminent than anyone knew, even the old warrior. Within less than a year, Sir William Penn died.

For the moment, however, the father and the son talked not of religion or politics but of business. Penn was to go to Ireland immediately to make sure that Sir William's lands and interests there were being properly managed and that the revenue being collected was sufficient to provide for the family after the Admiral died. Three weeks after his release from the Tower, Penn left for Ireland. However, before departing from Bristol, Penn took a "side trip" to Amersham, to the home of Mary and Isaac Pennington, parents of his future wife, Gulielma Springett.

Penn intended to stay only a day and a night with the Penningtons, but was so captivated by seeing "Guli" again that he remained in Amersham for five days. According to contemporaries, Guli was equally attracted to Penn, and would be quite "a catch," for she reputedly was a strikingly beautiful woman who "was crowded with suitors." However, she "gave encouragement or ground of hopes to none until he [William Penn] at length came, for whom she was reserved." By the end of their five days together, there was no doubt they would marry. Before such an event could take place, Penn told Guli he had much work to do for both his father and the Quaker cause. Being a Quaker, Guli understood. Her fiancé was the sect's newest hero, who now had responsibilities to a greater calling than the fulfillment of personal desire. Before he left for Ireland, Guli assured Penn she would wait patiently for him, for to do otherwise would be to defile "the Honour of a Man busy about the World doing God's work." At the time neither Penn nor Guli realized that "doing God's work" would postpone their marriage for three more years.

There was little doubt that Penn and Guli had great affection for each other. Helping to bolster their intimacy was the fact that they were not only religiously compatible but equals as well in family, education, class, and wealth. Guli was an heiress whose father, Sir William Springett, a rich Puritan London merchant, died on the battlefield while serving in Cromwell's New Model Army. Springett not only left his widow and daughter a successful business (which Mary Springett sold before marrying Isaac Pennington) but a substantial estate in Buckinghamshire as well, where Guli and her mother lived after Mary's marriage to Pennington. Guli Springett, like her future husband was a "weighty Friend," the term used to describe the minority of wealthy Quakers within the faith. Despite his embracing and advocacy of Quaker simplicity, thrift, and egalitarianism, Penn was an ingrained elitist, who never would have chosen a wife from among the majority of Quaker women whose "pedigree" was that of tradesmen, shopkeepers, and farmers.

It was also while at Amersham that Penn met and employed as his personal accountant, fellow Quaker, Philip Ford, who, in later years caused Penn great financial distress and humiliation. Ford was to assist Penn in his father's affairs in Ireland. Soon after his Irish sojourn, Penn entrusted Ford with the handling of virtually all of his personal business accounts, ranging from the paying of servants' wages to providing pocket money for the Penn family.

Although sent to Ireland to ensure the security and income of his father's estates, no sooner did Penn set foot on the island than he immersed himself in the plight of his fellow Quakers rather than immediately attending to Sir William's affairs. Upon arriving in Cork he needed only one glimpse of that city's prison to confirm that his father's business could wait. Incarcerated were eighty Quakers, including children, many of whom were in stocks. The Friends' cell was so small that they literally slept on top of each other, and the stench from such close, unsanitary conditions made Penn vomit. He found all to be malnourished and suffering from all manner of illnesses caused by lack of sufficient food and water. As Penn recorded in his *Irish Journal*, "The judge went out of town and left the prisons full, and Friends were fined L195 besides fees; one Friend was beaten in the court but was not regarded [no one stopped the abuse] by judge or jury. A wickeder judge has not been in the city of Cork since Truth came."

It was while attempting to free his brethren that Penn for the first time exploited his status and influence on behalf of the Quaker cause. No sooner did Penn leave the Cork prison than he wrote letters to the men whom he knew would be receptive to his entreaties; individuals for whom the Penn family name was respected and individuals who knew Penn personally from his previous "stay" in Ireland. In fact, Penn wrote to some of the very same men—the Duke of Ormonde, the Earls of Arran and Orrery—who were personally responsible for securing Penn's release three years earlier from his first incarceration for having become a Quaker.

Penn knew, however, that a show of leniency toward radical sects such as the Quakers could easily cost one the loss of personal power or "favor" at Court, for such was the tenuous and ruthlessly competitive nature of Stuart politics. The Crown was the fountain of power, and its ministers were well aware that they were merely the conduits through which royal patronage flowed. Favorites served at the king's pleasure and could be employed one year, dismissed the next, and then employed again. Courtiers who were "in" (for the moment), were always looking over their shoulders to see who from the "outside" was conspiring to replace them. Royal fickleness or a changed situation in Parliament usually determined who was "in" or "out" at Court. During the Stuart Restoration, the question of religious toleration for sects such as the Quakers became the lightening-rod subject maximized by all factions to either maintain or regain power at Court. For such reasons, Penn's high-placed contacts dragged their feet on acting on his petition for the Quakers' release.

Thanks to his father's tutelage, Penn understood Court machinations and knew that even in "far-way" Ireland his patrons could not escape the long arm of London politics. Indeed, Penn, beginning with his Quaker-Irish experience, became a keenly sensitive weather vane, picking up the slightest breeze of change at court. He thus knew that the Irish magnates' initial hesitation to help him was posturing: the result of not wanting to appear weak or compromised and thus run the risk of losing the king's favor.

Penn was not to be deterred. He persistently, painstakingly, wore down one man after another. He flooded their respective offices with letters, went to their homes for private meetings, cornered them at social functions, and even hosted dinners for his "befeathered and beruffled friends." At all such encounters Penn unleashed upon either his guest or host, a litany of moral, religious, and even political reasons why currently imprisoned Quakers should be released and continued persecution of the sect stopped immediately. Penn was fast learning the tactics of court maneuvering while simultaneously developing and sharpening the diplomatic and political skills that would prove, over the years, indispensable to protecting both himself and his fellow Quakers from official reprisals. After months of relentless solicitation, Penn's convincing arguments, filtered through a multitude of channels, finally produced the desired results. In June 1670, Penn wrote in his *Irish Journal* that James Butler, Duke of Ormond and Lord Lieutenant of Ireland "promised to release our Friends and did so by order of Council. All our Friends were released with great love and civility from the judges."

It was Penn's relationship with influential power brokers such as James Butler, and a host of other prominent aristocrats that allowed him such weight in the Stuart court. As the release of his fellow Quakers confirmed, if Penn wanted a favor it was accomplished through the intercession of these individuals. These court managers were men of broad experiences, too cosmopolitan to be bound by religious orthodoxy, which many of them loathed to enforce and privately condemned. For this and other reasons they strove to remain above the parochial and increasingly partisan nature of Parliamentary concerns, choosing instead to support the initiatives of their most important patron—the king. Whether he was championing the Quaker cause or protecting the interests of his colony in North America, Penn possessed the remarkable ability to retain the good graces, if not the firm friendship, of a variety of politicians whom he could call on for help when needed. Those with whom he felt most comfortable—as well as those who proved most effective in assisting him—were not party politicians but the monarch's managers, the individuals who acted as brokers between the Crown and those who sought its favors.

With a deep sense of satisfaction Penn could now tend to his father's business, which he had sorely neglected for several months, consumed by his determination to secure the release of his fellow Quakers. Penn's first stop was Shanagarry, where a former captain in Cromwell's New Model Army, named Boles, "holds land for my father and I found it well improved." Penn then went to see Sir William's fort at Kinsale, where he paid the soldiers "two cobbs or plate pieces" for having "well-maintained the place."

Not all of the Admiral's lands were well attended by tenants who paid their rents. Indeed, the opposite was true more often than not, and thus Penn spent much of his time trying to collect quitrents, renegotiating or determining fair, annual rental charges, and dealing with stubborn tenants who would not "give way" on terms offered. Penn was getting a small taste of what he would encounter on a much larger scale in Pennsylvania. The same issues he was currently handling for his father would become his alone, magnified by a hundredfold, 3,000 miles from England. Penn demonstrated a firm hand with recalcitrant tenants; but at the same time, those willing to negotiate amicably often found Penn rather magnanimous, willing even to reduce some folk's rent "who barely had enough to go to market." Overall, Penn could report to his father that the majority of his Irish tenants were loyal, paid their rents, and "maintained their houses and gardens with great solicitude." All the while he was in Ireland, Penn and his father kept a running correspondence about the Admiral's Irish tracts. In June 1670 Penn wrote in his *Journal* "My father's business is done."

Penn's letters to his father relieved the Admiral of much worry regarding his Irish estates. Perhaps more important, Sir William wanted Penn back in England, for his letters indicated a desire for reconciliation. The Admiral admitted that he was "in decline" and needed Penn to come home "to attend to all the business here." Penn knew from his mother's letters that his father's health was failing. In one such missive, which Penn noted was "full of tears," Lady Penn described in detail her husband's condition. The old sea dog was "very ill of a dropsy scurvey [sic] and jandies [sic jaundice] and hath a very great belly and full of water and the fisick was to get out the water if possible, but the doctor had given over and had said that the fall of the leaf would put him hard to it, and that if not then the first of the winter would carry him away. He seldom walks in the garden and not at all abroad." After receiving such a dire report Penn immediately set sail for England, leaving Philip Ford in Ireland to handle his affairs.

English history had ground on in Penn's absence. Hard-line Anglicans still controlled Parliament, objecting strongly to Charles II's desire for leniency toward Catholics and Dissenters. Thus, with increased fervor, Parliament determined to enforce the full weight of the Clarendon Code, especially the Conventicle Act, which was the most widely used measure to persecute and harass the Quakers. Ironically, at this juncture in English history, the real fear was Catholicism, yet it was the Quakers who still incurred the full wrath of Anglican hostility and bigotry because of their refusal to meet secretly.

It was the Quaker leader George Fox who first tested the act's renewed enforcement by publicly preaching to a gathering of Friends *outside* their new meetinghouse on Gracechurch Street. Guards had been placed at all the entrances to their new place of worship, so Fox decided that he would hold their first monthly meeting (May 1, 1670) out of doors, where he "expected the storm was most likely to begin." The streets were crowded with the curious, with many anticipating, if not hoping for an outbreak of violence, eager for an excuse to join in a melee. As predicted, no sooner did George Fox begin to speak than a constable accompanied by musketeers dragged Fox from the podium, charging him with violation of the Conventicle Act.

Fox was brought before London's Lord Mayor, Sir Samuel Starling, who, to the shock of many, released Fox after hearing the Quaker's plea that he and his followers were a peaceable, loyal people, who had gathered to worship and not to incite insurrection. Apparently, Starling was more than a little afraid of Fox's potential to cause a greater "disturbance" than just gathering together peaceful Quakers for worship or of attracting curious onlookers. The Quaker leader's appeal transcended the confines of the Society of Friends; he was tremendously popular among many dissenters, who admired his courage and perseverance in the face of such constant harassment. Starling was well aware of Fox's stature among nonconformists, whose ranks seemed to be swelling despite government repression. The last thing Starling needed was for Fox to use his homely eloquence to rouse the masses, which the Quaker founder's passion and oratorical talents could easily have incited. The Lord Mayor thus implored Fox to "be instrumental to dissuade them [the Quakers] from meeting in such great numbers." Starling knew Fox and the Quakers would never abide by the Conventicle Act, and thus was not surprised by Fox's response to his request: "If Christ had promised to manifest His presence in the midst of such an assembly where but two or three were gathered in His name, then how much more where two or three hundred are gathered in His name."

William Penn arrived back in London three months after Fox's experience at Gracechurch Street. He naturally agreed with Fox's interpretation that the Conventicle Act should not be applied to the Quakers, for their only purpose in assembling was to practice their faith, nothing more, and certainly not to conspire against the government. Unfortunately government officials did not see the Quakers in that light and rigorously enforced all the laws designed to punish dissenters. Quaker meetinghouses were policed and boarded up and their membership carted off to jail.

Penn was incensed by what was happening to fellow Friends and thus decided it was time for him to personally challenge the law, which he did on August 14, 1670. Penn knew that regardless of his pedigree, he would be arrested if he spoke to Friends gathered in the street in front of the barred and guarded Gracechurch Street meetinghouse. As Penn predicted, no sooner did he begin to speak than the constables came to arrest him and one other, William Mead, a recently convinced Quaker and former captain in Cromwell's New Model Army. Apparently not all the people assembled in front of the meetinghouse were Quakers; also in the crowd of several hundred were many "rude people who came mostly to gaze." It was the presence of so many non-Quakers that alarmed authorities, for they made the meeting disorderly, thus giving the soldiers the excuse to arrest Penn and Mead on charges of fomenting a riot, which could not have been further from the truth.

Nonetheless, Lord Mayor Sir Samuel Starling, who earlier had released George Fox from the same complaint, showed no such toleration for Penn. Indeed, Starling made "much mockery" of Penn and Mead. Perhaps Starling had been reproached for his previous show of sympathy and was now being pressured by the ultra-Anglicans in Parliament and Charles's court to prove his loyalty to king, church, and country (Parliament) by enforcing the antidissension laws to their fullest. He thus accused Penn and Mead of "preaching seditiously and causing a great tumult of people on the royal street to be there gathered together riotously and routously."

In many ways, Starling's harsh treatment of Penn reflected the jealousy among many secondary officeholders of the Penn family's close ties to the Stuarts. It appeared to such individuals that no matter what illegal activities young Penn indulged, neither he nor his father ever lost favor with the royal family. No doubt such partiality grated on those officials who, despite their unswerving loyalty, had no such status. To show that he was indeed a hard-line conformist, Starling initially wanted to send Penn and Mead to infamous Newgate Prison, where they would join the likes of murderers, thieves, and highwaymen. Starling, however, had a "change of heart," apparently realizing that to place a friend of the Stuarts in the foul confines of Newgate perhaps would not bode well for his future. Instead, he allowed Penn and Mead to "lodge" at the Black Dog Tavern, which overlooked Newgate Market, one of the seamiest places in all of London, where the venders of flesh, fish, and fowl haggled daily.

Fortunately for Penn and Mead, the Conventicle Act contained a clause providing for the right to a trial by jury to determine whether they were guilty of allegedly inciting a riot or fomenting insurrection. Both men decided that they would together exercise their right to a trial by jury and thus refused to pay their fines. Although Penn initially believed the charges against him were "harmless," after the reading of the indictment, he was less sure of his fate. Penn and Mead were accused of "unlawful and tumultuous assembly" for the purpose of "the disturbance of the peace of the said Lord the King [Charles II]." According to the official complaint, Penn's "preaching and speaking" had caused "a great concourse and tumult of people in the street." Supposedly, despite attempts to silence Penn, he continued "in contempt of the said Lord the King, and of his law; to the great disturbance of his peace, to the great terror and disturbance of many of his subjects. . . ." Insult was added to injury as both Penn and Mead were further punished—fined—"forty marks apiece upon your heads"—for contempt of court for refusing to remove their hats. Although being held for contempt, Penn was assured that "no advantage shall be taken against you," and that he and Mead would "have liberty; you shall be heard"—a jury trial.

Penn's trial opened at the Old Bailey on September 1, 1670, and ran for four days. To the surprise of many officials, the public took a keen interest in the proceedings, largely because of the notoriety of the defendants, especially that of William Penn. Indeed, Londoners liked a court wrangle as much as they liked a cockfight, and for four days they were treated to one of the best court battles to visit the Old Bailey in many years, as the verbal dueling between Penn and government officials became one of the most memorable in English legal history. After several witnesses testified, none of whom could confirm what Penn was saying at the meeting at Gracechurch Street, Penn then spoke, declaring that every word he uttered was "to preach, pray, or worship the eternal, holy, just

God, that we do believe it to be our indispensable right duty to meet incessantly upon so good an account, nor shall all the powers upon earth be able to divert us from reverencing and adoring our God who made us." In Penn's mind, since he had violated no law, he refused to plead "to an indictment that hath no foundation in law." After several heated exchanges in which the court asserted repeatedly that Penn was not "here for worshipping God but for breaking the common law," Penn still maintained that the question before the court was not his guilt but the legality of the indictment, for as Penn asserted "If it [the indictment] contain that law you say I have broken, why should you decline to produce it, since it will be impossible for the jury to determine, or agree to bring in their verdict. I say again, unless you show me, and the people the law you ground your indictment upon, I shall take it for granted, your proceedings are merely arbitrary." Suffice it to say, the court did not take kindly Penn's *indictment* of the proceedings. After being called "sawcy [sic]," and "troublesome" by the Recorder, John Howell, Penn further infuriated an already incensed court by accusing its officials of "denying me an acknowledged right, and evidence to the whole world your resolution to sacrifice the privileges of Englishmen to your sinister and arbitrary designs." Penn's last remark sent the Recorder and the Lord Mayor into a rage, with the latter ordering Penn to be taken away to the "bale-dock"—the cupboard-sized cylindrical enclosure in a corner in the courtroom, where prisoners were confined for contempt of court and were not allowed to speak or appear again before judge and jury until they "repented."

From the beginning of his bouts with the law, Penn was unable to suffer passively, especially when he knew the law was being perverted or arrogated by corrupt individuals in order to subvert justice for their own personal power and vindication. Applying his belief that "true Godliness don't turn Man out of the World, but enables them to live better in it, and excites their endeavors to mend it," Penn believed acquiescence, let alone withdrawal, in the face of iniquity or tyranny, was a dereliction of duty to God and man. In Penn's view, this was especially true in a country like England, where God had brought his countrymen far enough in the direction of the kingdom of heaven to give them a constitutional government and some sense of a social contract. They thus had, as true Christians, a responsibility to exercise and preserve their political rights and to ensure that the fundamental laws of the land operated justly and fairly. When they were not, then it was the obligation of all Englishmen (but singularly Quakers), to protest against such discrimination and vitiation.

In the meantime Mead was subjected to the same questioning as Penn, and he too refused to plead to the indictment, telling the court that both he and Penn were innocent of the charges of allegedly inciting a riot. Mead was as bold as Penn in defying the Recorder and Lord Mayor, telling the jury that since neither of those officials would tell them "what makes a riot, a rout, or an unlawful assembly," he would, by citing the great seventeenth-century English jurist Lord Edward Coke, who, according to Mead, "tells us what makes a riot, a rout, and an unlawful assembly. A riot is when three, or more, are met together to beat a man, or to enter forcibly into another man's land, to cut down his grass, his wood, or break down his pales." No court official took the linen draper seriously; the sheriff sneered "He talks at random." Mead then surprised the court by responding to the insults in Latin! At that point, the Lord Mayor once again lost his temper, telling Mead "you deserve to have your tongue cut out." Starling then had Mead dragged away to join his companion in the bale-dock.

With Penn and Mead confined to the bale-dock, Howell charged the jury, reminding them that they had heard the indictments against Penn and Mead and now they must decide whether the Quakers were guilty as charged. As Howell was about to finish his statement to the jury, Penn shouted from the bale-dock to the jurors for them not to render a verdict, either guilty or innocent, for to do so would make a mockery of English law, for "the proceedings of the court are most arbitrary, and void of all law, in offering to give the jury their charge in the absence of the prisoners." To Penn's plea the Recorder sarcastically remarked, "Why ye are present. You do hear. Do you not?" At this juncture, Penn's temper got the best of him, and in a harsh tone he declared "No thanks to the court and you of the jury take notice that I have not been heard. You cannot legally depart the court before I have been fully heard, having at least ten or twelve material points to offer in order to invalidate their indictment." Mead seconded Penn's condemnation of the court, declaring the proceedings to be "barbarous and unjust." For their brickbat Penn and Mead were taken away and locked in a "stinking hole" to await the jury's verdict.

While Penn and Mead sat in the stinking hole, the jury debated the two men's fate. After about an hour and a half of deliberation, the jury assembled before the court, and much to the justices' scarlet chagrin, Penn but not Mead, was found guilty of only "speaking" at Gracechurch Street but not for the purpose of inciting a riot or of fomenting insurrection. An enraged Starling asked jury foreman Edward Bushel that by his use of the word "speaking," he certainly meant that the gathering was "an unlawful assembly and you [Bushel] mean he was speaking to a tumult of people there?" Bushel replied "no," for that was all he had been "in commission" (instructed) to state by the other jury members. Thus, as far as the jury was concerned, Penn was innocent of all the more serious charges brought against him. Much to the shock of the jurors, Howell refused to accept the verdict and ordered the twelve men to "go and consider it once more that we may make and end of this troublesome business."

This time it only took the jury half an hour to decide, and once more, to the court's seething anger, the jury delivered the same verdict: "We the jurors, hereafter named, do find William Penn to be guilty of speaking or preaching to an assembly met together in Gracechurch Street, the 14th of August last, 1670, and that William Mead is not guilty of the said indictment." At this juncture, court officials, especially Howell and Starling, were so infuriated that they let their ire get the better of them and in an illegal act, not only rejected the recent verdict but, *imprisoned* the jurors until they delivered the *right* verdict: Penn's conviction for sedition and fomenting insurrection. As Howell told the jurors, "you shall not be dismissed till we have a verdict that the court will accept; and you shall be locked up, without meat, drink, fire, and tobacco. You shall not think thus to abuse the court. We will have a verdict by help of God or you shall starve for it." The jury was returned to its chamber and placed under lock and key.

Penn was so outraged by this blatant mockery of English law and justice by the court that he once again lashed out at its defilers. "It is intolerable that my jury should be thus menaced; their verdict should be free and not compelled. Is this according to fundamental law? Are not they my proper judges by the Great Charter of England? What hope is there of ever having justice done when juries are threatened and their verdicts rejected? I am concerned to speak and grieve to see such arbitrary proceedings." Starling was once again so nonplussed by Penn's audacity and poignancy that all he could do was threaten Penn with physical punishment. "Stop his mouth," shouted the Mayor. "Bring fetters [shackles] and stake him to the ground." To such intimidation, Penn majestically replied, "Do your pleasure, I matter not your fetters."

By forcibly detaining the jury and by trying to coerce a verdict satisfactory to the court, Starling, Howell, and the other justices were transgressing sacred legal ground. They believed, however, that since Penn was a dissenter as well as an alleged rabble-rouser, their highhandedness would go unnoticed. Although Penn indeed was a dissenter and a rebel, the justices' refusal to accept the jury's verdict made Penn the center of a controversy far more important than whether a Quaker had violated the law; the issue was now the sanctity of the jury system itself, and Penn became its current champion. His trial for violating the Conventicle Act was fast becoming less important than the illegal, forced detaining of his jurors for their refusal to convict an individual they believed innocent. Indeed, Penn was no longer defending himself but a fundamental right entitled to all Englishmen since the days of Magna Carta—the right of a man to a free and uncoerced judgment by a jury of his peers.

Despite constant admonishments from the justices to deliver the "right" verdict, as well as another night's detention, the jurors, when asked the next day, "What say you? Is William Penn guilty or not guilty?" the foreman replied again "Not guilty." Since the jury acquitted him again Penn naturally demanded his liberty. The Lord Mayor rejected Penn's request, charging him now with contempt of court, for which he was to pay a fine. Penn refused to pay the fine and was hauled off to Newgate Prison. Starling's frustration with the jurymen now became so great that he decided to fine them forty marks apiece for not convicting Penn. The jurymen refused to pay and they too were carted off to Newgate to join Penn until they paid their fines. Eight of the twelve soon capitulated, paid their fines and went free; but the other four, Edward Bushel, John Hammond, Charles Milson, and John Baily, resolved to become a test case and they remained in prison for two months until they were released on a writ of *habeas corpus*.

No sooner were they free than they hired counsel and sued the Lord Mayor and Recorder for illegal punishment. Their case hung fire for about a year, but all the while it was "business of great consequence to his Majesty's Government." The "Bushel case" (named after the jury foreman Edward Bushel) finally was heard by England's highest court, the House of Lords, who decided that a jury must have the right to hand in a verdict based on the facts as they saw them without coercion from the bench. A judge, the court said, "may try to open the eyes of the jurors, but not to lead them by the nose." Little did Penn know that when he was arrested for preaching the Quaker message on a street corner, that his trial would become one of the most celebrated in his country's legal history. Henceforth, the independence of the jury was beyond question in English (and American) courts. William Penn's courageous defiance of persecution in Gracechurch Street provided the occasion, and his cogent defense of English rights in the courtroom the inspiration for this notable triumph. For Penn the cause of liberty was a holy crusade and any victory in its behalf was exultation for the spirit of man, which was the candle of the Lord.

Beginning with the Penn–Mead trial, Penn tried to prove in court that the laws being applied to Quakers were either unconstitutional or inapplicable. In this case and in subsequent ones, Penn's acts of civil disobedience reflected more than his faithfulness to Quaker teachings. They were a stratagem in the war to transform society. In Penn's mind, defiance led to legal confrontations, hopefully in public forums such as courtrooms, in which he could assert the fundamental rights every Englishmen should possess. One of those essential rights was liberty of conscience. Penn's conflicts with royal officials thus became campaigns not only to protect Quakers from the imposition of unjust laws but to establish as well the right of all his countrymen to worship as their consciences dictated.

The Penn–Mead trial also brought Penn widespread respect for his able championing of dissent. From this point on, both Crown and Parliament took Penn seriously, for he was someone who had significant influence with the separatists; someone who through persuasion of speech, status, and obvious commitment to a cause, could rally to his calling sufficient numbers of nonconformists to possibly plunge England into religious and political unrest. Indeed, Penn's ability to incite the masses was fast approaching that of his mentor George Fox. Fortunately for Restoration England, neither Penn nor Fox realized their potential for "disruption." Despite his temper and contentiousness, which fellow Quakers constantly reminded him he had to restrain, Penn embraced Quaker pacifism. He "turned his cheek" and worked assiduously through peaceful, diplomatic and political channels to obtain his objectives of religious toleration for all English Protestants and a refuge for his fellow Quakers, a "holy experiment" in North America called Pennsylvania.

When William Penn passed under the iron-spiked gate of Newgate Prison, he had no idea whether he would ever see his home or father again. Newgate could have been his last resting place, for it had never lengthened anyone's life. The lurid and revolting conditions inside had been somewhat ameliorated, only because the Great Fire had damaged a portion of it, forcing officials to make new those areas that had been razed. The old vices, however, were still there, as drunkenness, prostitution, and all manner of other sordid behavior stalked the corridors. Penn knew his father would be even more despondent than when Penn was confined to the Tower, for compared to Newgate, Penn's "room" in the Tower was a luxury suite. He knew the Admiral would do all he could to once again secure a release. Penn, however, did not want his father to free him, for he believed to do so would "mock" all he had just accomplished in the courtroom. Moreover, Penn believed he "could scarce suffer on a better account, nor by a worse hand, and the will of God be done. . . . I intreat thee not to purchase my liberty."

Penn should have known there was no way his father would allow him to languish in such an awful place as Newgate, even if Penn believed his imprisonment was for a righteous cause. The Admiral was dying and he wanted his son with him in his last days. He thus paid both his son's and William Mead's fines, and the two men were released. Penn came home to a wasted, bedridden man within whom an amazing tolerance and acceptance had been awakened. Sir William was at last reconciled to the reality that his eldest son was not going to follow in his footsteps, that his heir had chosen instead an entirely different life path, one that was the complete antithesis of his. Sir William had been a warrior; indeed a destroyer of life, while his son embraced a faith and a calling that cherished life and saw the good rather than the evil in humankind. Like his father, Penn too believed he had a duty, but it was not one that called upon him to lay waste but to help build, in God's name, a better world, one founded and held together by peace, love, and the brotherhood of all people.

Much to Penn's surprise and great joy, the Admiral told him that not only had he come to accept his son's desire to devote his life to the Quaker cause and to doing good works for his fellow men, but was adamant that he pursue it well. "Let nothing in this world tempt you to wrong your conscience," Sir William told Penn, "I charge you do nothing against your conscience. Whatever you design to do, lay it justly, and time it seasonably; for that gives security and dispatch. . . . Son William, if you and your friends keep to your plain way of preaching, and keep to your plain way of living, you will make an end of the priests to the end of the world."

William Penn returned home on September 9, 1670, and for the next week he watched his father sink rapidly. The Admiral, however, rallied long enough to do one more thing for his son, one more real effort to protect him: He wrote to the king. Much to Sir William's relief and serenity, both Charles II and his brother the Duke of York wrote back, sending their profound solicitude as well as a promise to continue "to favor" young Penn. A day after receiving such comforting news from the Stuarts, on September 16, 1670, Sir William died. In accord with his wishes his body was carried back to the port city of Bristol, from where he had embarked on several occasions to lead English fleets to great victories at sea. The Admiral was buried in the churchyard of St. Mary Redcliffe. In a final burst of filial piety, Penn erected a monument to his father at St. Mary Redcliffe, including all his military panoply and naval pennants. Penn's tribute to his father was most un-Quakerly, for he was honoring a man whose entire adult life had been about war and destruction. Yet, Penn believed that regardless of how violent and disturbing his father's life had been and how he chafed against it since childhood, if his father could finally accept him then he certainly, as a good Quaker, could embrace his father and ennoble his memory.

The Admiral's last will and testament—of which William Penn was the sole executor—was dated January 1670, suggesting that he must have forgotten that he once told his son in one of his tirades against Penn becoming a Quaker, that he would "dispose of his estates to them that pleased him better." Interestingly, even if Sir William remained angry and unforgiving of his son's "betrayal," he could not, because of the law of primogeniture, leave his estates to anyone but his eldest son. Thus, all of the Admiral's lands went to Penn, as well as a sentimental gift—the gold chain and medal bestowed upon the old warrior by Cromwell. Sir William's other children as well as Lady Penn were not left impoverished. Indeed, Lady Penn received 300 pounds sterling and all his jewels and the use and occupancy during her life of his plate, household stuff, coaches, and horses. Margaret Penn lived at Wanstead the rest of her life with her son's consent. To his son Richard went 4,000 pounds sterling, a diamond ring, and all his swords, guns, and pistols. There was certainly no quarreling among the brothers over who got Sir William's firearms, for his elder son would not have wanted weapons of war. To his daughter Margaret went 100 pounds sterling.

The great Admiral Penn was no more. The line had passed on, and his heir, who stepped into the responsibilities of estate and station, was no longer the "son of Sir William"; he was William Penn.

5

"A Larger Imprisonment Has Not Daunted Me"

Soon after his father's passing, Penn left Wanstead, leaving behind the poignant memories of canings, quarrels, estrangements, but in the end, reconciliation. Penn decided to travel to Amersham, seeking peace after the strains of trial and imprisonment and family grief. He was in pursuit of a refuge and knew he would find one in the affection of his fiancée Guli Springett and her family. After a few weeks respite, in which he and Guli reaffirmed their love for one another as well as their plans to marry, Penn believed he was replenished enough to resume his role as Quaker apologist and minister.

No sooner did Penn become actively involved in Quaker affairs than he found himself in a familiar setting: a public debate with a local Baptist preacher named Jeremy Ives, who from his pulpit had been thundering abuses against the Friends, declaring the universality of the divine Light to be blasphemous, even heretical. Ives must be confronted, just as Thomas Vincent and others had been challenged when they impugned Quaker beliefs. Penn thus arranged to debate Ives publicly. Ives agreed, and the meeting was to take place on February 10, 1671 at West Wycombe in Buckinghamshire. Although the feisty Penn relished the opportunity to verbally combat Ives, his close friend Thomas Ellwood counseled against it, telling Penn that, "I have rarely found the advantage equivalent to the trouble and danger arising from such contests."

Ellwood's forebodings fell on deaf ears, for no Friend, not even George Fox was as fervid as Penn when it came to publicly engaging those who excoriated Quaker beliefs. To Penn, such harsh attacks seemed not only mean-spirited but also illogical, for the Quaker creed proclaimed a loving, forgiving God, who's Divine Light was within everyone, predisposing them to do good in the world. How could anyone disdain and condemn those who followed such an uplifting, righteous, and peaceful faith? Sadly, few of Penn's fellow Englishmen, not even other sectarians such as the Baptists, saw Quakerism in such a context. It would take Penn nine more years to realize that no matter how often he challenged those who reviled his faith and the laws that persecuted Quakers, neither his countrymen nor his government would allow the Quakers to practice their beliefs freely and openly. If Quakers hoped to have such freedom they would have to leave England, an idea Penn could not even remotely fathom in 1671.

Jeremy Ives spoke first, arriving with a "stock of syllogisms ready framed for his purpose," according to Penn. After a lengthy discourse, he tried to trick Penn by leaving the platform immediately, hoping his action would break up and disperse the meeting. Much to Ives's chagrin, the people remained, waiting to hear Penn, whose notoriety as a champion and martyr for liberty of conscience for all Englishmen gave him great appeal among non-Quaker sectarians. The audience was so rapt by Penn's convincing elocution, that Ives returned in an "angry railing manner." He was too late; Penn had won the day. The majority of listeners walked away, embracing much of what Penn said and, most important, secure in their minds and hearts that the Quaker message posed no threat to other denominations and that the tenet of the Inner Light was not blasphemy. A relieved Thomas Ellwood could report to Isaac Pennington that, "Truth hath prevailed, the enemies did fly; we are in safety; praise to God on high."

Inspired by his vindication at West Wycombe, Penn began traveling about England, preaching the Quaker Truth. November 1671 found him at his alma mater, Oxford, where university faculty still harassed the sectarian students, especially the Quakers. Penn was so disturbed by what he heard and saw that he wrote a letter to the Vice Chancellor, telling the administrator that not only was he incurring God's "fierce wrath and dreadful vengeance" for his "illegal persecution of His poor children," but that he was a "poor mushroom" for doing so. Penn further insulted the chancellor by declaring that because the Oxonian was of such "low Creation" (a mushroom), "better thou hadst never been born." Friends were surprised that Penn had gotten away with such forceful denunciations without official reprisal. All were waiting for the other shoe to drop, which it did when an emboldened Penn went to London to preach.

It was while speaking at a Quaker meeting on Wheeler Street near Spitalfields, that Penn was arrested once again for violating the

Conventicle Act. No sooner did Penn begin to speak than soldiers pulled him from the platform and led him out into the street, where a constable and his assistants were waiting to take him to the Tower. After spending three hours in the Tower, Penn found himself once again face to face with his old nemesis, Samuel Starling. Joining Starling to interrogate and charge Penn were Sir John Sheldon and Lieutenant-Colonel Josiah Ricroft. Penn freely admitted to speaking to an assembly at Wheeler Street but insisted, as he had before, that he had broken no laws, particularly the Conventicle Act, which he declared "doth not reach me." Much to Penn's surprise, he had not been apprehended for violating the Conventicle Act but rather for contravening the Oxford Five Mile Act, which forbade nonconforming clergymen to come within five miles of any city or town for the purpose of preaching their doctrine in any conventicle. The penalty for disobeying the act was six months in prison without bail.

Penn couldn't believe the court had the audacity to charge him with violating an act that he declared, "can't concern me. For first I was never in Orders [ordained a minister], neither episcopally nor classically, and one of them is intended by the preamble of the Act." His inquisitors disagreed, asserting that the Oxford Act applied to anyone who even *spoke* in unlawful assemblies, which they contended Penn certainly had done. Penn naturally refuted the charge, reiterating that since he had never been ordained a minister the act did not apply to him. Moreover, since the measure did not define an unlawful assembly, then that allegation as well was inapplicable. As Penn told the court, they could "not borrow a piece of law here and a piece there" in order to indict him.

Starling and company knew that if they tried to indict Penn on such specious grounds they would have a replay of the Old Bailey experience. However, there was more than one way to catch a Quaker. Sir John Robinson, Lieutenant of the Tower, required Penn to take an oath, an act he knew Penn's faith forbade. Moreover, the oath Penn was to swear was absurd: that it was unlawful to take up arms against the king. Why did he have to make such a fatuous proclamation when it had nothing to do with the laws he allegedly violated and, most important, which his faith disavowed? Nonetheless, the magistrates believed they had a case against him in his refusal to take an oath. Penn refused to swear to such foolishness and predictably, exchanges deteriorated into personal insults as officials called Penn all manner of vile names. To their derisions Penn responded "Thy words shall be thy burden and I trample thy slander as dirt under my feet. You are grown too high to consider the plea of those you call your forefathers for liberty of conscience."

In desperation, the magistrates accused Penn of sedition; that his and Friends' real intention at the Wheeler Street meeting was to conspire to overthrow the government; to stir the people to sedition. Penn argued that such accusations were even more ridiculous than having to swear an oath that it was unlawful to take up arms against the king. Exasperated, Penn told the court "We have the unhappiness to be misrepresented. As for the King, I make this offer; that if any living person can make it appear, directly or indirectly, from the time I have been called a Quaker that I have contrived or acted anything injurious to his person, or the English government, I shall submit my person to your utmost cruelties." Even if the charges against him were trumped up, Penn knew he was a condemned man and thus was not surprised when told he would be confined to Newgate for six months. A defiant Penn responded to his sentencing by asking, "Is that all? Thou well knowest a larger imprisonment has not daunted me."

Penn entered Newgate on February 5, 1671, and would not be released until July. He possessed the financial means to pay the extortionist rates for better accommodations but chose instead to stay with fellow Quakers in the more loathsome common quarters. During the day prisoners were permitted to walk about the prison confines with minimal restrictions on their mobility, but at night they were all herded into one room—a huge, circular space with a great oaken pillar in the center that supported the chapel above. Prisoners strung their hammocks from the central pillar to the wall in three tiers because there were so many inmates, and those on the top tier had to climb up to bed first. The sick and dying lay on pallets scattered about the floor. In such an environment Penn finished one of his many seminal treatises, *The Great Case of Liberty of Conscience Once More Briefly Debated and Defended*, a tract he began writing while in Ireland and would now complete, inspired by his surroundings and the issues that landed him in Newgate. He addressed his essay "To the Supreme Authority of England"— Charles II—and signed his cover letter "From a Prisoner for Conscience-Sake, WP."

Penn opened his tract by defining, in "plain English," what he believed to be liberty of conscience: "By liberty of conscience we would be understood to mean is this; namely, the free and uninterrupted exercise of our conscience in that way of worship we are most clearly persuaded God requires us to serve Him in (without endangering our undoubted birthright of English freedoms), which, being matter of faith, that if we neglect it for fear or favor of any mortal man we sin and incur divine wrath." Penn warned his countrymen that if they continued "in such an anti-Protestant and truly anti-Christian path as that of persecuting honest and virtuous Englishmen only for worshiping the God that made them in the way they judge most acceptable," then as God "destroyed Sodom and laid waste Gomorrah by the consuming flames of His just indignation," a similar fate awaited England "and not leave a hiding place for the oppressor." God already had sent warnings—the plague of 1665 and the Great Fire of London the following year—that He would "scourge this land [England] for their cruelty to the conscientious."

Penn believed that if he based his case against persecution on purely religious and Scriptural grounds, it would fall on deaf ears. He knew that the men in power whom he must persuade were worldly individuals, influenced by rational and pragmatic considerations, not by jeremiads or Biblical citations. Penn thus devoted the lion's share of his essay to proving that persecution was contrary to nature and reason, concepts beginning to grab hold of men's views the way dogma and Holy Writ had dominated vistas for centuries. Penn was writing at a time when English society was becoming increasingly more secularized. Many of the leading proponents of the Scientific Revolution were Englishmen, including Francis Bacon, William Harvey, Robert Boyle, and ultimately Isaac Newton. All helped bring to England a revolution in mind and spirit. Although God continued to reveal His purpose through Scripture, there were now new sources of divine light that influenced people's views. Men's minds were slowly beginning to embrace the idea of change in all areas of human interest and speculation. The hand of God was being pushed back by the mind of man as educated Englishmen were coming to believe that everything that happened in the natural world had a rational explanation and that humans were capable of finding it. Man's power over nature, not God's grace, would henceforth be his salvation.

Penn did not accept this new worldview in toto, for it obviously had little room for God. Yet, he understood that many of the men to whom he was appealing did accept it, and thus he crafted his essay along more secular, rationalist contours. According to Penn, human nature consisted of corporal and intellectual senses, which were given by God to enable men to discern "things and their differences" and to judge, by means of reason and faith, the evidence gathered by the senses. Penn thus asserted that to force conformity was to deny man his faculty of judgment relative to his own knowledge and sense of God. To Penn, deprivation of this intellectual power—God's great gift to man—was enslavement of the mind and reduced men to the level of beasts.

Penn was well aware that the major obstacle to religious toleration was not moral or religious, but political: the notion that religious uniformity was necessary to political stability. To Anglican antitolerationists, the idea of the separation of church and state was unthinkable; separation would inevitably lead to the end of monarchy and revolution in England. Many in power still believed that the conflict of the 1640s resulted from the toleration of dissent. Penn agreed that a foundation in Christianity was essential for a stable society. He protested, however, that Christianity need not take only one outward form and that dissent was not antithetical to good citizenship. Penn thus had to prove in his treatise that the basis of government was civil, not ecclesiastical, and that the imposition of one form of Christianity was not necessary to political stability.

Penn concluded his tract with an entire chapter devoted to intellectual, literary, and historical evidence for his premise. All of Penn's writings were thick with historical references, for he believed knowledge of past events helped draw conclusions about the present. He referred to the tolerant practices of the ancient Jews, Romans, and Egyptians, as well as certain modern nations, most notably the Netherlands, which he rightly observed was "so improved in wealth, trade, and power" because of decades "of indulgence [religious toleration] in matters of faith and worship." To Penn, one of the most beneficial results of toleration was the promotion of national prosperity. If Englishmen continued to force conformity and persecute dissenters like the Quakers, then "farewell the interest [the nation's economic well-being] of England," for "Plenty will be converted into poverty by the destruction of so many thousand families as refuse compliance and conformity. . . . Such laws [the Conventicle Act and other restrictions on liberty of conscience] are so far from benefiting the country that the execution of them will be the assured ruin of it in the revenues and consequently in the power of it. From where there is the decay of families, there will be of trade, so of wealth, and in the end, of strength and power." In the end, Penn hoped he had convinced his readers that it was persecution, not dissent that destroyed government, religion, prosperity, and peace.

Penn's incarceration came to an end in late July 1671, and he headed straight for his fiancée in Amersham, just in time to join a Quaker entourage to see George Fox off to America. Fox was journeying to the New World in search of new converts, a mission started within a few years of the sect's founding. The first two evangelizing Friends were women, Mary Fisher and Ann Austin, who, in 1655 landed and preached first in Barbados and then unwisely traveled to openly hostile Puritan New England, where the moment they stepped off the ship they were viciously abused. They were immediately imprisoned, their books publicly burned, and they were stripped naked and examined for signs of witchcraft. After enduring several weeks of such indignity, they were placed on an outgoing vessel and sent back to Barbados. Although Friends suffered extreme cruelty in New England, meetings flourished in Barbados and other Caribbean islands as well as in tolerationist Rhode Island, which became a refuge for Quakers literally whipped out of Massachusetts.

In 1658 Penn's mentor Josiah Cole traveled with Thomas Thurston on foot through the wilderness from Virginia to New England, visiting Quaker settlements in Flushing and Long Island, New York. In 1665 John Burnyeat went to America, establishing Quaker communities in the Chesapeake area. Thus, by the time George Fox arrived he could attend Yearly Meetings in Maryland, Virginia, and Newport, Rhode Island. Interestingly, at this juncture in his life Penn showed no interest in a New World sojourn. He believed it was more important for him to remain in England, where his pen and his public preaching would be of greater service to the Quaker cause than traveling 3,000 miles across the Atlantic to the wilderness of North America. His mission was to stay in England and fight for liberty of conscience for all nonconformist Englishmen and for the end of Quaker proscription.

Penn remained in Amersham with the Penningtons and Guli for about a month before leaving for continental Europe, not as a man of leisure on a Grand Tour as he had done ten years earlier, but for the purpose of bringing the Quaker Light to Europeans. Joining Penn on his mission was Thomas Rudyard, and once they arrived in Rotterdam, the Netherlands, the wealthy merchant expatriate Benjamin Furly, who had made that Dutch city his home for several years. The three men formed a formidable evangelizing Quaker triumvirate. Furly was an especially important member not only because he was extremely wealthy, but also was a well-educated linguist who was fluent in Dutch, German, French, Latin, and Greek.

His personal library contained over 4,000 volumes. One would never guess that Furly possessed such a pedigree. True to the Quaker way, he dressed in plain, often worn-out clothing, in which he looked constantly disheveled, and he spoke in such common language that at first glance it would be easy to mistake him for a lowly artisan or mechanic.

After spending a few days in Rotterdam preparing for a trip that would take them all through the Low Countries and into Germany, the three Friends traveled up to Amsterdam, one of the freest and most affluent cities in Europe, the result of several decades of Dutch domination of the global carrying trade. Although impressed by Dutch wealth, Penn believed such material success had made the Dutch "Creaturely, worldly, and wanton." He called Amsterdam a Gomorrah and claimed that God's wrath would soon visit the Netherlands and its people, humbling them "as a thief in the night" for alleged debauchery and decadence. Apparently, in his fit of juvenile righteous indignation, Penn forgot that for almost a century the Netherlands had provided a safe haven for persecuted minorities, both religious and secular, and for independent thinkers from all over Europe. Only in the Netherlands were Penn and his fellow Quakers free to express themselves and travel about the countryside proselytizing without fear of harassment. Not even in his own country, supposedly the most enlightened in Europe, was Penn allowed such liberty.

Perhaps more important than convincing others to embrace the Quaker Light, were the close personal relationships Penn established with several powerful sectarian women, including Elizabeth, Princess of German Palatine, who at age 48 renounced her title to the Palatine thrown and became abbess of the Protestant convent of Herford. Radical sects attracted well-born and well-educated seventeenth-century women since some of the denominations tended to be more open to religious experience and participation than were the more structured, patriarchal traditional churches. Upper-class women found in sectarian theology a religious complement to their greater independence in other walks of life, and Quaker men viewed women as indispensable companions in their work. Between these women and Penn there were no barriers of authority or class, and they could establish good rapport. Indeed, within hours of his first meeting Elizabeth, Penn opened his heart and life, telling the abbess the story of his conversion and the tribulations that followed.

The only man in Penn's life for whom he had similar respect and affection was George Fox, who became a substitute father. In his relationship with Fox, Penn was willing to overlook differences in social station. However, with the majority of his Quaker brethren, his friendships acquired a patron-client character, and most of his "clients" came to deeply resent Penn's haughtiness and condescension. Penn was a devout Quaker but an ingrained elitist. Penn expected honor and obedience from his social inferiors—which meant all other Quakers. Easily disappointed, Penn often wallowed in self-pity, believing himself misunderstood and unappreciated by many common Friends. Because of his patrician background Penn had great difficulty establishing true friendships with those who were coreligionists but not gentlemen. Nor could he develop relationships with men of his own class, for only a minority were sectarians and none were Quakers. Few, if any, lived a life of simplicity and virtue; quite the opposite, the majority were notorious profligates. That was hardly a world in which a young Quaker convert could feel comfortable. The effect was that Penn lived most of his adult life insulated from others, unable or unwilling to develop friendships with either peers or fellow Quakers.

Penn was an incredibly restless individual, constantly traveling. He often referred to himself as "a wayfareing man," and viewed his life as a pilgrimage for God; he was to go whenever and wherever he must to deliver the Quaker message and help bring his fellow man to the Quaker Truth. Penn's peripatetic nature could be considered the quintessential Anglo-American characteristic, but it was also one he shared with his sailor father. Penn's passion for travel began with his Grand Tour after he was expelled from Oxford and continued with his trips on family business to Ireland. Even when at home, he was constantly leaving for days and weeks at a time not only to preach or to help Friends in distress but also to take care of personal business or to attend court. Until his debilitating series of strokes in 1712 at the age of 68, there was not a year in Penn's life in which he was not on the road for months at a time, moving from place to place in England then darting off to either Ireland or the continent and ultimately to North America.

Penn arrived back in England in October 1671 but spent the next four months traveling about England on behalf of suffering Friends. He returned to Amersham in January 1672 and appeared with Guli before the Monthly Meeting to declare their intention to wed. After four years of courtship Penn and Guli married on April 4, 1672. They retired for their honeymoon to Basing House in the village of Rickmansworth. For the next five months, Friends saw little of them. They had waited a long time for this hiatus; they had been in love a long time; they had bided the months faithfully and devotedly through arrests, imprisonments, foreign assignments, and all the other vicissitudes of seventeenth-century dissenters. Until the healing respite of his honeymoon, Penn had not spared himself for the Quaker cause. As Penn declared in a letter to Friends in the Netherlands, he was for the first time since his convincement "at peace with all men."

Soon after Penn and Guli married, Charles II issued a Declaration of Indulgence, suspending the Clarendon Code against dissenters and the Elizabethan penal laws against Catholics. It was a popular-appeal tactic, easily achieved while Parliament was not in session, and it offered relief and freedom to many. Informers and persecutors momentarily withdrew into the background; meetings assembled without molestation; and in May 1672, Charles issued a special pardon freeing from imprisonment nearly five hundred nonconformists, most of them Quakers.

Unfortunately, Charles's munificence lasted less than a year. When Parliament reassembled, it forced the king to rescind his Declaration of Indulgence. The men who still dominated Parliament, especially the House of Commons, were as fiercely anti-Catholic and anti-Dissenter as ever. Parliament presented the king with a choice: either a Test Act requiring all Crown officials, both civil and military, to swear an oath against the doctrine of transubstantiation—a requirement no loyal Roman Catholic could honestly meet—and a grant of 1.2 million pounds with which to fight the Second Dutch War or his Declaration of Indulgence and a bankrupt state. Always one to choose cash over religious principle, Charles retracted his declaration and signed the Test Act. By signing the act, Charles abandoned his brother, James, Duke of York, a recent devout convert to Catholicism. Charles knew the statute's main purpose was to deny his brother the throne. James was forced to resign his position as lord high Admiral, for he refused, as a Catholic, to take the oath. The Test Act also affected dissenters. Although Quakers did not pursue positions in public office, Friends knew that the loyalty oath would be applied to them. It rendered every Society member susceptible to imprisonment for the slightest offense.

During the brief respite from persecution under the Declaration of Indulgence, Puritan sects—most notably the Baptists and Presbyterians—exercised their freedom by once again attacking the Quakers, accusing them of all manner of blasphemy and heresy. Their relentless assaults ranged from an alleged series of *Dialogues*, written by the Baptist Thomas Hicks, between a Christian and a

Quaker, making the Quaker appear to be the intellectually and religiously inferior conversant, easily befuddled and overwhelmed by his adversary's obvious theological superiority, to tracts labeling George Fox an impostor and Friends heretics for their supposed denial of Jesus's divinity. Penn naturally responded to every falsehood ascribed to the Quakers.

Penn's most trenchant response appeared in *The Spirit of Truth Vindicated*, a 50,000-word essay that became part of Penn's second or revised version of *No Cross, No Crown*, published in 1682, just as Penn was setting up his North American commonwealth. *The Spirit of the Truth Vindicated* was one of Penn's more personally revealing treatises, as well as one of the most cogent expostulations of Quaker beliefs. In *Spirit of Truth*, Penn saw the history of God's interactions with humanity as the story of continuing divine revelation, made known to all people in all ages through the work of the Light within each individual soul. Central to God's dealings with humanity was the theory of apostasy. Briefly defined, this idea asserted that in each age God gathered a people and revealed a measure of truth to them. In each instance, for a time they would remain truthful to that revelation but inevitably they would fall away from it. Apostasy would supplant true religion, as people substituted their own ideas for those they had received from God. Penn believed this was what had happened in England among the various sects, all asserting they knew the Truth when in reality they had perverted the Truth in order to proclaim that their particular denomination now possessed the Truth and that all other beliefs—such as those of the Quakers—were heretical.

Penn argued in *Spirit of the Truth*, that it was those sects currently attacking the Quakers for their beliefs, who had become the apostates. They felt threatened by the Quakers because the Quakers had replaced them as God's chosen to finish the work of cleansing Christianity that the Reformation had begun but failed to complete because the Protestant movement had fallen into apostasy. In Penn's view, apostasy was particularly inevitable whenever the church is directly linked to the state, allowing the use of civil power to force people to deny their consciences and to submit to the dictates of an established church. Such had occurred in England, thus making the Quakers the targets and victims of apostasy because they refused to succumb to such religious, political, and moral corruption and tyranny. Penn believed it was now incumbent on Quakers, as God's favored, to lead England out of apostasy and into the Quaker Light of liberty of conscience.

In the midst of the constant barrage of letters attacking his faith, Penn rejoiced momentarily with Guli over the birth of their first child, Gulielma Maria Penn born on January 23, 1673. Their joy was short-lived; the baby died only seven and a half weeks later. Death struck a second time that spring, claiming Penn's 18-year-old brother Richard. Penn remained in a state of mourning and semi-retirement for several months, burying himself in his writing in order to forget the loss of his daughter and brother.

It was George Fox's return from America that ended Penn and Guli's withdrawal from the larger Quaker world. Fox had been in North America for almost two years, traveling through all of England's seaboard colonies as well as to the West Indies islands of Barbados and Jamaica. He was in constant communication with Friends at home, so when he returned in June 1673, Penn, Guli, and scores of other Quakers went to Bristol to welcome home their prophet. Fox returned spiritually invigorated and exultant, for as he told his followers, "Glorious, powerful meetings we had there." Indeed, Fox had returned to England fired with the idea of establishing a purely Quaker colony in North America, where Friends could live in peace, far away from the persecution and vagaries of Restoration England. Although always inspired by Fox, Penn still had little enthusiasm for Fox's idea of establishing a New World refuge for Quakers.

Any joy Fox's return brought Penn quickly dissipated when he heard the news of Fox's arrest in Worcester County "upon a pretence of exercise of religion otherwise than what is established by the laws of England." Officials knew such a charge would not stick, for Fox had been arrested *after* a meeting had adjourned. Instead, they used the law with regard to the loyalty oath to incarcerate Fox for over a year. The news of Fox's arrest disturbed the Quaker community, motivating Penn, to put his grieving behind him and place himself at the forefront of the effort to free George Fox.

While Penn and his comrades worked through legal channels to secure Fox's release, they also believed it essential to use whatever influence they had at Court. It had been six years since Penn's last visit with the Stuarts. However, unlike his first visit to the Stuarts, which resulted in little more than an "introduction," this time Penn found a much more receptive ear, especially from the king's brother, James, who, like the Quakers, had become a victim of religious bigotry. In addition, James had a deep, personal attachment to the late Sir William Penn and was more than ready to grant the Admiral's son an audience. Upon hearing of Penn's presence, the Duke "came immediately out of his closet [a small private chamber] to greet us [William Mead accompanied Penn to Court]." The reunion of Penn and the Duke of York was momentous. Most uplifting for the Quakers was James's declaration "that he was against all persecution for the sake of religion. That it was true he had in his younger time been warm, especially when he thought people made it a pretence to disturb government, but that he had seen and considered things better, and he was for doing to others as he would have others do unto him. . . . When he had done upon this affair, he was pleased to take a very particular notice of me, both for the relation my father had had to his service in the navy, and the care he had promised him to show in my regard upon all occasions."

Although both Stuarts still felt obligated to Penn's father, additional factors contributed to their willingness to see the younger Penn on his own accord. Charles and James may have seen that Penn's plea for toleration of Quakers and other nonconformists would benefit Roman Catholics as well. James was a practicing Catholic and Charles was more than likely a "closet" worshipper of the Church of Rome. Papal splendor and Quaker simplicity were ecclesiastical opposites, but they had mutual interests in the fear-ridden world of Restoration England. Moreover, both of the royal brethren found Penn a more interesting companion than the mindless, fawning sycophants who usually surrounded them. Thanks to Penn's friendship with the Stuarts, George Fox was released from prison in February 1675.

In the midst of his battles with the Baptists and with royal officials to secure George Fox's release, Penn and Guli lost two more children, twins, William and Mary, born in February 1674. William died that same May, and Mary the following February. While Mary was still alive, Penn and Guli's fourth child was born, a boy, they named Springett, who would be the first of Penn's children to live to early adulthood.

Fox's imprisonment convinced Penn that it was time for Quakers to realize that their acts of civil disobedience had become a stratagem in a war to transform society. Disobedience led to legal confrontations in which Quakers could assert fundamental English rights to rid England of unjust and unconstitutional laws. To the chagrin of many elder Friends, Penn introduced this idea into the Quaker movement. In 1675, Penn, Thomas Ellwood, and William Meade organized the Meetings for Sufferings, a committee for the legal defense of indicted Quakers. The committee's purpose was to help Friends decide when they were suffering beyond the limits required by law, and if they believed they were, they could either continue to suffer passively or Penn and others would help them sue for their rights. The Meetings for Sufferings met the last Thursday before each law term and in executive committee weekly during court sessions. In this new capacity as counselor, Penn's legal knowledge acquired at Lincoln's Inn proved invaluable. It not only helped free fellow Quakers but, perhaps more important, it made Penn a more effective manager of Quaker relations with Parliament. Penn knew that it was that body that ultimately would determine the Friends' destiny.

In March 1678, Penn appeared in person before a committee of the House of Commons. He had come to represent his faith's appeal for toleration. Penn's presence before Commons was the fruitful result of months of flooding the House with petitions, pleading that the real issue with Quakers was the loyalty oath, not their allegiance to king and country. Penn asked that a clause be inserted in the law allowing Quakers to give their word instead of having to take an oath. Penn then reminded the committee that the law was originally designed to punish Papists, not fellow Protestants. However, it was the Quakers, not the Catholics, who were being the most damaged by excessive fines and imprisonment. Indeed, "many industrious and prosperous men and their families have lost all because of a law that should not be applied to so loyal and beneficial a people to this country."

Penn next addressed what Quakers meant by "freedom of conscience." Penn told the committee that many in Parliament as well as other government officials had charged Quakers with being Papists because of their commitment to liberty of conscience for all Englishmen. If Parliament were willing to grant liberty of conscience to other Protestant sects and to Catholics, then so much the better, although he was arguing first and foremost on behalf of Quakers. Penn remained personally suspicious of Catholics but he nonetheless opposed "whipping them for their consciences." As he told the committee, "We must give the liberty we ask, and cannot be false to our principles, though it were to relieve ourselves, for we have good will to all men, and would have none suffer for a truly sober and conscientious dissent on any hand." Penn's sincerity and integrity convinced the committee that perhaps the time had come for Parliament to consider some sort of "relief cause"—toleration—for dissenters such as the Quakers. Such a measure passed the House of Commons, but before it could work its way through the House of Lords, Charles once more prorogued Parliament.

Much to Penn's surprise, he was viciously rebuked for having the audacity to advocate the right of Catholics to worship according to their own consciences. Many Englishmen misinterpreted Penn's plea for liberty of conscience for Catholics, believing that he was asking his countrymen to support toleration *for Catholicism*. Penn was accused of being a Papist. As fellow Quaker John Gratton told him, "there is in the country a very malicious lie and false accusation cast upon thee so forcibly affirmed; they say thou art turned to be a Jesuit." Gratton wanted Penn "to write as speedily as thou can" letters explaining what he meant when he spoke before the committee about toleration for Catholics. Fellow Friends did not believe Penn asked for toleration of Catholicism, but other sectarian faiths did. For many such as the Baptists, this was the moment they had been waiting for to bring Penn down. No greater stigma nor more vile an epithet could be ascribed to someone of Penn's stature, than being a "Papist" or "Jesuit," for such labels connoted conspiracy, disloyalty, and treason in the minds of the majority of Englishmen.

Surprisingly, for the first time in his life as a Quaker, Penn did not respond in kind to the imputations leveled against him. Weary and incredulous, Penn wrote only a handful of letters to his Court connections, assuring them he was no agent of the Pope or of the Jesuits masquerading as a Quaker in order to bring about the "re-Catholization" of England. Receiving such missives were his long-time friends, including Robert Spencer, second earl of Sunderland, who had known Penn since their days at Oxford and was now privy councilor and secretary of state; Laurence Hyde, earl of Rochester, and privy councilor; and the diplomat Sidney Godolphin. All three men knew Penn well and knew the charges against him were absurd. These men had the king's ear, and they assured Charles that Penn's advocacy of toleration for Catholics did not mean he was promoting or supporting the Catholic faith. Penn was confident that his letters to such well-placed individuals was all that was needed to erase the charges of papism against him. He left London and returned to his home in Rickmansworth to enjoy time with his wife, son, and new daughter Letitia, born in March 1678, who would be the second of Penn's children to survive to adulthood.

In 1679 Penn led the Meeting for Sufferings into further political activity. The Meeting agreed to encourage Friends to participate in campaigns to support election to Parliament of pro-toleration candidates. Not only were Quakers to help get such men into office but secure from them agreements that, once they were in power, they would work for the end of persecution. Penn naturally became the most active of all Friends in this capacity. Because of who he was and whom he knew, Penn's services to a potential candidate could be the edge that the individual needed for victory. Penn's 1679 tract, *England's Great Interest in the Choice of this New Parliament*, made clear his political views. Paramount was religious toleration, and thus he argued for his brethren as well as for Englishmen in general to support the Whig party's political agenda.

By the time of the 1679 election, England's ruling elites had split into two hostile factions, or coalitions—the Whigs and the Tories—ushering in "the first age of party" in English political history. Tory ideology was based on the belief that the country fell into civil war and revolution because Parliament and radical religious sects had usurped power from the Crown and Church. In the Tory frame of reference, the key to avoiding future calamities was for king and church to reclaim their supremacy and to weaken, if not crush, their rivals. To ensure their preeminence, the Tories restricted office holding at both the local and national level to Anglicans, passing the 1661 Corporation Act and the 1673 Test Act, which allowed only those receiving communion in the Anglican Church to run for office.

In opposition to Tory policy and ideology were the Whigs, led by their founder, Anthony Ashley Cooper, the earl of Shaftesbury, who believed that absolute monarchy and a monolithic, established church threatened traditional liberties. The Whigs advocated a limited, constitutional monarchy and religious toleration as the best guarantors of liberty and prevention against revolution. Although willing to grant toleration to dissenters, such generosity was only for Protestants; Catholics were to remain *persona non grata*. The majority of Whigs were rabid anti-Catholics, determined to bar the converted Catholic James from inheriting his brother's crown.

In the Parliamentary elections of 1679–1680, Penn and his fellow Quakers supported the radical republican but tolerationist Algernon Sidney, whom Penn had known for several years, and with whom he shared some common political views; and another tolerationist, Sir Charles Worseley. Quakers sided with the Whigs without embracing their ideology in toto. Penn was not as fanatically anti-Catholic as were the more ultra Whigs, and he was neither antimonarchial nor in favor of the exclusion of the Duke of York from inheriting the crown. Despite Penn's and other Quakers' support, the two tolerationist candidates lost the election.

Quakers' activities on behalf of Whig candidates disturbed Quaker elders, especially as the campaign degenerated into one of the most slanderous and vindictive elections in Parliamentary history. When elders gained control of the Meetings for Sufferings they ordered Penn and others to cease all political activities and refrain from using "those reflecting, disgusting terms of distinction of Whig and Tory; or any such nick-names tending to provoke one neighbor against another."

Penn accepted the elders' mandate and stopped his participation. He too worried about the prospect of violence, caused by "so much extremity intended on this side, as well as on that of the other." Consequently, as he told Robert Southwell, Jr., Vice-Admiral of Munster, Ireland, "I resolve to withdraw myself from all manner of meddling since things appear to be violent and irreconcilable." Although initially believing the election portended to be "the great and notable day of the Lord, and the breaking-in of his eternal power upon all nations," Penn's bursting optimism in the Quaker's ability to move the mountains of English society was shaken by the vicious nature of 1679–1680 election campaign.

Compounding the ugliness of the 1679 election was the hysteria caused by a claim, accepted by Parliament that Charles's Catholic wife, through her physician, was plotting with Jesuits and Irishmen to kill the king (poison him) so that his Catholic brother could assume the throne. In the ensuing frenzy, known as the "Popish Plot," several clearly innocent people were tried and executed, and the Whigs tried to exploit the furor by attempting to ramrod through Parliament an Exclusion Bill barring James from the throne.

The Popish Plot became a great personal crisis for Penn, who was especially vulnerable because of his personal association with the Stuarts, his renewed visits to Court, and his statement to the Commons' committee that not even Catholics should be "whipped for their faith." He was torn between his embracing of Whigism because the party supported toleration for dissenters, and his deepening relationship with the Stuarts, especially James, whom the Whigs hated and feared. Ultimately however, Penn's integrity would not permit him to renounce a personal friendship because of political and religious differences. Time and again over the years when Penn went to either Charles or James, he came as a true friend, to plead with them to change dangerous policies or plans. That they so rarely heeded his advice and warnings was their own undoing.

The above events prompted Penn to write several new tracts, the most important of which was *England's Present Interest Discovered, with Honor to the Prince, and Safety to the People.* In this particular treatise, Penn hoped to show king, Parliament, and fellow Englishmen that much of the present unrest, suspicion, and hostility were the result of ongoing religious bigotry and intolerance, which Penn believed would bring England's downfall. He asked his readers, "What is most fit, easy and safe at this juncture of affairs to be done, for quieting of differences, allaying the heat of contrary interests, and making them subservient to the interest of government, and consistent with the prosperity of the kingdom?" Penn then answered the question: "An inviolable and impartial maintenance of English rights." Either men or laws ruled governments, but it was always infinitely better for people when the latter prevailed. Unfortunately for England, in recent years, selfish, power-mad, bigoted, and vindictive men had usurped power and the laws, and they were now ruling England. Since England was "a kingdom of many minds [and faiths]," the only way to secure the peace, property, liberty, and prosperity of all Englishmen was for the government, with king and Parliament "in harmony and unity," to grant liberty of conscience to all citizens. Penn was convinced that if liberty of conscience became a fundamental English right, it would end the "prate that hath made way for all the incharity and ill living that is in the world [England]." If Englishmen were allowed "their own consciences their edge would be taken off, their blood would be sweetened by mercy and truth," and thus in time all the ills currently affecting England would dissipate and all Englishmen would enjoy years of unprecedented "Peace, plenty, and safety."

Few, if any, Englishmen heeded Penn's entreaties. He was taking the whole evil political picture upon himself as his personal, cumulative burden. He increasingly viewed England as a place impossible for the pure in heart to live in "peace, plenty, and safety." It was perhaps time to reconsider George Fox's idea of an American refuge, which, for years Penn had discounted, believing the Quaker's Truth could transform England. By 1680 Penn no longer had such delusions. Friends must now look elsewhere for their own safety. Once Penn embraced the idea of a North American haven for Quakers, it became an obsession, driving him like no other undertaking in his life. The establishment of a North American Quaker sanctuary came to represent the ultimate manifestation of his witness for God's Truth. Like the Puritans of Massachusetts Bay, he decided that if the forces of the old order proved intractable in England, then it was time to turn to virgin territory for the construction of the model Christian society. Since Quaker exhortations failed to transform England, then more direct action was now needed in the form of an example, "a Society compleat in Him throughout, as well in body as in Soul and Spirit." Thus William Penn set his sights on America, where he believed "an example [society based on liberty of conscience for all] may be set up to the nations: there may be room there, though not here [England], for such a holy experiment."

The decade of the 1670s saw William Penn emerge as one of his faith's most important proselytizers, intellectual leaders, and martyrs. By the decade's end his name was a household word, not only within the Quaker community but among other groups as well, even within the House of Stuart, as his personal relationship with the Duke of York deepened. It was also during the 1670s that increasing numbers of Quaker leaders began to seriously contemplate establishing a New World refuge for their people. Penn initially resisted such a move, immersing himself in tract writing, politicking, visits to Whitehall, and even incarceration to prove that Quaker beliefs portended no harm for England. In his crusade to vindicate his faith, Penn ultimately transformed his purpose into something much larger and more secular than trying to stop Quaker persecution. Penn realized that this was the fundamental issue, and, until all Englishmen were guaranteed this right, neither his sect nor any other nonconformists would be safe from harassment and imprisonment. Once Penn embraced the idea of exile to the New World, he committed body and soul to the undertaking.

6

"Bless and Make It the *Seed of a Nation*"

Although at last resolved that it was time for Friends to emigrate to North America, Penn now faced the daunting task of not only convincing the Crown to give him a charter for such an enterprise, but of finding available, suitable land as well. By the 1660s, almost all the usable land along the Atlantic coast had been claimed. Moreover, land grants were political plums; consequently, the likelihood of such a politically unpopular sect as the Quakers receiving such a gift was remote. However, in 1674 a way suddenly appeared for such a possibility, as a colonial property dispute between two Quakers was laid in William Penn's lap for arbitration. The land in question was the western portion of present-day New Jersey.

At the outset of the second Dutch war (1664–1667), England captured the North American Dutch colony of New Netherland. No sooner did New Netherland fall into English arms than the king gave it to his younger brother James as his personal estate, and he accordingly renamed the province New York. The king's grant, known as a "proprietary," was designed to ensure greater royal supervision of England's burgeoning New World empire while allowing others to absorb the costs and burdens of colonial enterprises. The proprietary grant was made to a trusted individual or individuals (in this case the king's brother), who were expected to govern the colony according to the king's mandates, not Parliament's.

James's proprietary extended from the Hudson River to the Delaware River on the South, and from the Hudson to Lake Erie on the West. In 1665 he subdivided this unwieldy tract, conveying the stretch between the Hudson and Delaware Rivers (New Jersey) to court favorites, Sir George Carteret and Lord John Berkeley.

Berkeley and Carteret were interested in quick profits. In order to entice new adventurers, they offered in their *Concessions and Agreements*, religious toleration to all Protestants and no payment of quitrents for five years. Perhaps more important than granting freedom of conscience and free rent until 1670 was the political autonomy allowed to the colonists: an assembly elected by the province's freemen, which would share governance with an appointed governor and council. In order to gain the status of freeman, all one had to do was swear allegiance to the king and be a property owner, which most male colonists could do because of the proprietors' generous policies. Under Carteret and Berkeley's *Concessions*, virtually all, adult, white males, had the right to vote, in contrast to the 10 percent in England who enjoyed the same privilege. To make things even simpler, Berkeley and Carteret divided their tract, drawing a diagonal line from the Delaware River to the seacoast. Berkeley took possession of the western half while Carteret took the eastern.

Berkeley and Carteret's political liberality was actually usurpation. Their grant did not include the right to govern; it was simply a land conveyance. Thus, from the start the two men found themselves at loggerheads with the king on this question, who was eager to increase, not diminish, the Crown's political authority over the colonies. To make matters worse, despite the proprietor's waving of quitrents for five years, the colonists revolted when rents came due in 1670, and the Dutch temporarily recaptured the province in 1672. Even before the territory was restored to English control Berkeley offered his entire holding for sale in 1674, and two Quakers, Edward Byllinge and John Fenwick, snapped it up for 1,000 pounds. Since Byllinge and Fenwick were men of modest means, it seems likely they were simply front men for a consortium of Quakers.

A feud soon developed between Fenwick and Byllinge, requiring Quaker intercession, for Friends preferred to settle their differences without going to court. Penn was asked to act as an impartial arbitrator and succeeded in persuading the two men to accept his suggested settlement: one-tenth of West New Jersey awarded to Fenwick and nine-tenths to Byllinge. Byllinge, however, was in serious debt and in order to pay his creditors, conveyed his share to the care of three trustees—William Penn, Gawen Laurie, and Nicholas Lucas. After paying Byllinge's creditors, the trustees retained for themselves what was left. Fenwick also relinquished his share of the colony to the trustees. Consequently, by 1675, West New Jersey belonged to the Quakers, specifically, to three "weighty Friends," Penn, Laurie, and Lucas. After fifteen years of searching for a place to create an American colony, the Quakers suddenly found themselves on the threshold of opportunity.

From 1676 to 1681, Penn became deeply involved in the business of launching the Quaker venture. Helping settle West New Jersey became Penn's training ground in matters of colonization. Most important for the future, Penn's activities put him in contact with the whole upper stratum of English and Irish Quakers, men whose resources would provide the financial foundation for Penn's "holy experiment" of Pennsylvania six years later. Prior to this time, Penn had limited contact with weighty Friends. Most Quakers he interacted with were common folk—small farmers and unskilled to semi-skilled laborers. Penn must have been surprised by the amount of fluid capital available within this smaller but affluent community of Quaker merchants, craftsmen, shopkeepers, and large landowners. The hundred shares into which investment in West New Jersey had been divided quickly sold at 350 pounds each. That Quakers frequently invested such amounts indicated their eagerness to become venture capitalist participants in England's burgeoning overseas commercial network of markets in Asia and America.

Before any Friends left for West New Jersey, Penn believed it imperative to extract from the Crown a formal acknowledgment of the trustees' proprietorship and right to govern the province. He also wanted the dividing line between East and West New Jersey exactly defined to avoid future border disputes. Finally, he believed it essential to draw up a frame of government so colonists would know before leaving England what rights and privileges they could look forward to in the New World.

The *Concessions and Agreements* for the Quaker colony of West New Jersey was largely Penn's handiwork, with Laurie and Lucas assisting as editors. Most important, all the ideas Penn first laid out in the *Concessions* for West New Jersey provided the foundation for his own colony's *Frame of Government* five years later. As he would later establish in Pennsylvania, all who came to West New Jersey would "meet and choose one honest man for each proprietary, who hath subscribed to the concessions; all these men to meet as an assembly there, to make and repeal laws, to choose a governor, or commissioner, and twelve assistants to execute the laws during their pleasure; so every man capable to choose or be chosen." In essence, Penn called for the establishment of a representative government based on minimal property qualifications for all *Christian* male voters over the age of 21.

Penn also guaranteed every colonist the right to a trial by jury, liberty of conscience for all Christians (even Catholics!), and "no man" was to be imprisoned for debt. Debtors would "be set at liberty to work" to pay their obligations. The New Jersey Indians, who were merely to be treated "with humanity" under the Berkeley-Carteret *Concessions*, were given the right to bring grievances to the commissioners and to have an impartial trial before six of their peers and six settlers whether they were the accusers or the accused. As Penn wrote even before the document was published, his purpose was to "lay a foundation for after ages to understand their liberty as men and Christians, that they may not be brought in bondage, but by their own consent; we put the power in the people." After completing the *Concessions*, Penn submitted the document for review and final approval. One hundred fifty-one Friends signed the charter, confirming their acceptance of Penn's efforts.

Penn then set to work writing a "brochure," *The Description of West New Jersey*, promoting all of West New Jersey's most salient natural features—fertile soil, warm climate, bountiful fish and game, fresh water, and plenty of space and fresh air. The advertisement attracted wide interest; so much so, that in June 1676, 230 passengers, the majority of whom were Quakers, boarded the *Kent*, and set sail for the New World. The ship made its way up the Delaware River in August 1676, finally dropping anchor near the present site of Burlington, New Jersey, where the passengers went ashore.

Although of fairly hearty stock—most were yeoman farmers and tradesmen—they were nonetheless from a country that was far more developed and "civilized" than where they now found themselves. Greeting them were clouds of mosquitoes, hot, humid weather, and all manner of vermin, the likes of which they had never seen before. Indeed, many undoubtedly felt duped, for this was not what they had read in Penn's broadside. They found the land so wild that many believed it uninhabitable.

Nonetheless, the settlers persevered, building hasty shelters until they could erect more substantial dwellings. Compared to their earlier seventeenth-century arrivals, including the Englishmen who settled in the Chesapeake, the Quakers were far more capable of enduring the vicissitudes of wilderness living than most others. Many were skilled artisans who brought the tools of their trade with them. Many had brought English brick with them to build houses. The majority, however, were farmers, who, once they cleared the forests, uncovering rich, virgin, soil, produced more than enough for immediate consumption. Within a few years' time West New Jersey yeomen saw the crops of their fruit orchards and grain fields go aboard export ships at Burlington.

Soon after seeing Friends off to West New Jersey, Penn, for the first time in his life, found himself financially pinched. Penn's constant traveling around England and the Continent on behalf of the Quaker cause had finally taken a financial toll. Compounding the constant outlay for travel expenses were Penn's other activities for his Quaker brethren, ranging from helping to outfit a colonial enterprise to money spent for the defense of Friends in jail. Not only were his English holdings in disrepair, but so were his Irish lands. Penn was supposed to have received 2,000 pounds annually from these estates, but by the mid-1670s Philip Ford was able to procure only 1,000 pounds in rents from both Penn's Irish and English lands. Furthermore, the drop in income did not curtail Penn's spending, which according to Ford's accounts, totaled more than 2,000 pounds a year. In order to maintain his lifestyle, Penn decided to sell some of Guli's Kent and Sussex properties, about 1,000 acres inherited from her late father, from which Penn received 5,800 pounds. Penn also contracted 2,000 pounds in loans, on which he paid 6 percent interest. With the money received from the sale of his wife's properties, Penn bought for 4,500 pounds a 350-acre estate, Worminghurst Place in Sussex, about fifteen miles from the coastal city of Brighton.

The place commanded a magnificent hilltop view of the surrounding countryside, an area known as the Weald, in the seventeenth century covered with dense forests of oak and elm. The estate also had a park, gardens, and orchards. The grandiose manor house, surmounted by a long row of tall chimneys, was "very large, but ugly," according to Penn. Large indeed; there was room for twenty to thirty residents and spacious enough to hold Quaker meetings for two hundred worshippers. The meetings got the attention of two of Penn's neighbors, both of whom were justices of the peace and members of Parliament from prominent county families. When they prosecuted Penn, he took it as a social affront, protesting that he possessed "as good a stake in the Country as either of them."

The move to Worminghurst compounded Penn's financial problems. In order to maintain it he contracted a series of new loans totaling 8,700 pounds—in modern currency, over $1 million. As of 1680 he had paid back very little of this money. The interest charges alone amounted to more than 500 pounds annually. Why was Penn failing to make ends meet? A number of factors contributed, and some were beyond Penn's control, such as his tenants defaulting on their rents. However, Penn's aristocratic pretensions did not help matters. He was simply extravagant in his living habits. Although no voluptuary, Penn enjoyed the good life. To maintain his grand house, he employed a staff of six to eight servants and clerks. He bought expensive household furnishings and clothes in London; and ample supply of costly and exotic victuals, ranging from barrels of oysters and scallops sent to him by Ford, to venison, salmon, sturgeon, partridges, and larks, and viands of fruits and vegetables such as gooseberries, strawberries, cherries, asparagus, and arti-chokes, with brandy and whiskey to wash it all down. Such a lavish lifestyle was grist for the vitriol of Penn's anti-Quaker adversaries, such as the Presbyterian minister Richard Baxter, who labeled Penn a hypocrite for pretending to embrace the Quaker's simple and plain existence "while hee swims himselfe in wealth."

In this capacity, Penn lived every bit as fully as his father; indeed his figure began showing signs of such "prosperity," for it was at this juncture in his life that Penn started to become the rotund, benign-looking figure portrayed in Benjamin West's famous paint-ing, *William Penn's Treaty with the Indians*. As his financial pres-sures mounted, Penn realized that he badly needed a fresh source of income. When he petitioned the king for land in America, Penn undoubtedly saw expansion as a way of relieving himself of his debts and other financial obligations.

A month after settling in his new home, in July 1676, Penn decided on another ministerial trip through the Netherlands and Germany. Accompanying Penn were George Fox, George Keith, and Robert Barclay—four of the greatest names in the first genera-tion of Quakerism. Barclay, for example, in 1676 wrote what became the template for the ordering of Quaker doctrine, *An Apology for the True Christian Divinity*. Until Barclay's publica-tion, the Quakers had no systematic philosophy to follow. George Keith had emerged as the most dynamic and learned of the Quaker itinerant preachers. Educated at Marischal College in Aberdeen, Scotland, Keith was deeply introspective and intellectual, an indi-vidual Penn discovered on this trip to be moody and brooding, prone to temperamental fits and passionate outbursts. Penn, however, overlooked his companion's disturbing behavior, believ-ing naively that Keith's tantrums were merely manifestations of his "zeal" for his faith. Penn would come to regret being so understanding of Keith's "eccentricities," for the Scotsman proved to be one of his most troublesome colonists in his "holy experiment" of Pennsylvania.

From July until October 1676, Penn and his comrades traveled all through the Netherlands and Germany, visiting as many Quaker enclaves as they possibly could, holding meetings not only for the already convinced but also to attract new converts. Although most of the Friends they encountered were free to practice their faith, especially those living in the Netherlands, there were still many Quakers in the German states not allowed such toleration. Such was the case for Quakers in Dusseldorf, Cologne, and Mulheim, where local Lutheran ministers told Penn and his companions that "We have no need of Quakers here!" Persistent persecution and the scattering of Friends across Germany, the Netherlands, England, Scotland, and Ireland, convinced Penn that the time had finally come for him to personally assume responsibility for establishing a single place, large enough for all Quakers, even those already in North America (West New Jersey could not hold everyone), to have a safe haven, and Penn had just such a place in mind. The land across the river from West New Jersey possessed the same rich soil, the same abundance, and it was scantily peopled—a few Swedish, Dutch, and Finnish settlements. From the Delaware River it extended westward into raw, dense, and unexplored wilderness known only to the Native American tribes living there. On its southern flank lay Maryland, and to the north lay more vastness. It would be space enough for hoards of refugees, and most important for Penn's vision, the land was part of the grant given by Charles II to Penn's friend, James, Duke of York.

Also motivating Penn to have his own Quaker colony was the fact that by 1680, New Jersey, despite its economic prosperity, proved to be an unsatisfactory refuge. The questionable methods by which the Quaker consortium had gained control of the colony left much confusion as to who owned what and where. Most disturbing to Quakers was the governor of New York's abrogation of the political autonomy granted to them in Penn's *Concessions*. When James learned that Berkeley had sold his portion to the Quakers, he seized the opportunity to claim jurisdiction over the New Jersey government. This subjected Quakers to the authority of the governor of New York, one of James's closest friends and confidants, the high-minded and overbearing Edmund Andros. Absorption into the New York province invalidated the provision for an elected assembly promised to New Jersey settlers in Penn's *Concessions*. Andros ruled by executive edict and the Quakers' freedom of worship remained dependent on the whim of a staunchly Anglican despot living in far-off Manhattan.

Not only did Andros force arbitrary government on the Quakers, but they were subject to taxes on all imports and exports that came up the Delaware River. Andros simply assumed he had jurisdiction of the whole river, and since West New Jersey had no other access to the sea, he had little difficulty collecting the duties. In protests to Penn and the other proprietors, the New Jersey Friends declared that "We have not lost English liberty by leaving England," nor were they willing to "give up [our] right of making laws," which Penn had promised them the right to do in his *Concessions*. Anticipating the universal colonial cry against Parliamentary taxation without representation in the 1760s, the New Jersey Quakers announced that "we are assessed without law, and excluded from our English right of common assent to taxes." The New Jersey Friends naturally looked to Penn not only to carry their protests to the Duke of York but to intervene on their behalf as well and restore their right of self-government.

Penn knew that to push the Duke too hard on this particular subject could cause tension between him and James, thus straining their relationship and jeopardizing future, requests and favors, including, possibly, a grant of Penn's own. Penn believed the New Jersey entreaties would become moot once he secured from the Stuarts his own Quaker sanctuary. Nonetheless, Penn agreed to argue, in writing only (he refused to physically go to Whitehall and "visit" with James face-to-face), against the Duke's claim. In *The Case of New Jersey State*, Penn convincingly established that "the conveyance he [Berkeley] made us, Powrs & government are expressly granted, for that only could have induced us to buy it." In this essay Penn used the terms "natural rights" and "consent of the governed," phrases that reverberated down to the American War for Independence. Penn asserted that obtaining the right of government was essential to safeguarding the settlers' rights. Moreover, their rights as Englishmen, under English law, were being abused. They were part of a nation that conquered the wilderness, therefore to be treated as one of the conquered was against "natural right," and to be taxed without a say in the matter was the equivalent of having their goods taken from them without their consent. Surprisingly, and much to James's chagrin, Charles and the Privy Council agreed with Penn's assertions and removed New Jersey from the Duke's authority.

Why was there a decision in Penn's favor, supported even by the Duke's brother, which in effect allowed Penn to trump James? More than likely Penn's victory was the result of increasing Court antipathy for James's Catholicism, which the Duke impoliticly flaunted. Charles's Anglican courtiers would welcome an opportunity to curtail the Duke's power and wealth, and stripping him of extensive landholdings in North America served that end. Although a "troublesome" lot, the Quakers were at least anti-Catholic Protestants and such a magnanimous gesture might also encourage more of them to leave England. The New Jersey Quakers' problems made it apparent to Penn that until he had his own colony, political ventures such as self-government would never come to fruition.

A Quaker refuge in the Americas might serve as a laboratory for political experimentation. Ever since his religious conversion, Penn had toyed with radical political ideas. Particularly impacting Penn's political thoughts at this point in his life were the republican theories of Algernon Sidney.

In Sidney's political world, individuals had the right not only to create whatever type of government they preferred but also the responsibility to abrogate that government if it degenerated into a tyranny. Sidney also posited that the best governments came out of the combined judgments of many; they must never be left to the will of one man. Most important, Sidney believed no government was legitimate unless it had the consent of the governed, and at all times it must rule not in the interest of the governors but of the governed. "Power is not an advantage, but a burden," Sidney declared, and "There is no natural propensity in man or beast to monarchy." His dream for England was a republic with a monarch at its head whose powers were carefully limited by laws created by a universally elected Parliament. Most appealing to Penn was Sidney's advocacy of religious toleration. Inspired by such ideas, Penn dreamed of a New World utopia, where the people not only would have liberty of conscience but also a role in their own government.

After several weeks of deep reflection on a variety of issues and personal concerns relative to having his own colony, Penn concluded that in the end, what mattered most was that he would be serving God by establishing a Quaker refuge in the New World. Penn was certain that "God hath made it [the founding of Pennsylvania] a matter of Religious Exercize to my soule in getting and settling this Land. And it is the Lord and to his service do I dedicate my dayes in the helpe of his people [the Quakers] there." With such righteous self-assurance, on June 1, 1680, William Penn formally appealed to the king for a land grant west of the Delaware River between Lord Baltimore's proprietary in Maryland and Duke James's proprietary of New York.

No doubt the audacity of Penn's request shocked Charles's court, for Penn was one of England's most notorious dissidents and ex-convicts. At the same time Penn was soliciting the Crown for a colonial charter, Charles and imperial authorities were attempting to consolidate the empire under tighter royal supervision. For example, they were in the process of implementing a plan to deprive Massachusetts of its charter, bringing that obstreperous colony under control. Neither Charles nor his advisers wanted to make the same mistake Charles's father had made in 1630 when he allowed a syndicate of wealthy Puritans to obtain a royal charter as the Massachusetts Bay Company, and who then promptly relocated themselves with their capital, charter, and records, to New England. By the time of the Restoration, Massachusetts had become a completely self-governing, commercially successful enterprise, whose Puritan citizens refused to obey either the Crown or Parliamentary mandates. Charles II was not about to let any future charters "leave" England; he wanted no more Massachusetts in his empire. That either Charles or Parliament would permit another religious visionary to set up a social experiment in the American wilderness seemed highly unlikely.

Facing the rising threat of Whiggism, the Stuart brothers were cool toward the idea of granting land to a group of alleged Whigs, who many at Charles's Tory-dominated Court believed the Quakers, including Penn, had become. Penn was fully aware of the controversial nature of his request, for few insiders knew the king as well as he did. He had to find some face-saving approach for Charles that would allow him to give Penn his land without causing a political uproar. Penn's tactic lay in the large sum of money—16,000 pounds—the Crown owed Admiral Penn for services and outright loans. Beginning with James I, the Stuarts seemed unable to live within their means, and thus, in order to support their extravagant lifestyle, accepted (if not expected) "loans" from their favorites, such as Sir William, who, out of a sense of responsibility and devotion, readily gave. Indeed, the higher the title, the more generous the giving was anticipated to be. Aristocratic creditors never asked for repayment of their loans, and kings rarely if ever worried about making good their debts. Penn thus suggested a deal in which the king would make restitution for money owed the Admiral with a land grant to William Penn, Jr. Since Charles was chronically short of money, the idea of paying a debt with currently worthless wilderness land that might eventually bring profit to the Crown attracted the king's attention.

Although Charles never mentioned the debt specifically in his discussion with his councilors or Parliament, he did allude to the Admiral's "discretion with our dearest brother James," an obvious reference to the battle of Lowestoft during the Second Dutch War (1665), when Sir William took the blame for James's failure to pursue the retreating Dutch and annihilate them. An additional consideration that Charles could not mention was the issue of James's Catholicism. The attacks on the king's brother were intensifying, with the Whigs calling for the Duke's exclusion from the throne. A generous concession to an ultra-Protestant group like the Quakers could go far toward proving that the Stuarts were not popish bigots. The launching of a new proprietary colony in which liberty of conscience would be granted conformed to Whig ideology that religious toleration and limited monarchy were more conducive to commercial expansion than "popery and arbitrary power."

On the other hand, Charles had to assuage the concerns of a Privy Council dominated by hardcore Anglican Tories opposed to any concessions to nonconformists such as the Quakers. The shrewd Charles argued that exporting whole shiploads of these "Whig-affected" dissenters would weaken that faction by depriving the Whigs of Quaker support. Charles would be ridding his realm of troublesome fanatics much the same way his father had relieved himself of the Puritan nuisance. Years later, in a letter to Lord Romney, a member of William and Mary's Privy Council, Penn revealed his knowledge of this motivation: "The government at home was glad to be rid of us at so cheap a rate as a little parchment to be practiced in a desert 3,000 miles off from here."

Perhaps the most important issue relative to Penn's grant was strategic. The area requested by Penn was inland from the coast, encompassing lands once held by the troublesome Susquehannas, and standing athwart the ancient Iroquois warpath to the south. The new colony would be in a position to help New York with frontier defense, and it would act as a buffer for the Maryland–Virginia frontier. The colony required a proprietor who had experience as well as integrity, and Penn was an ideal choice.

Penn was in serious financial straits by the time he petitioned for his charter. In 1672, he had tried to recover the money owed to his father, but the Stop of the Exchequer allowed the government to default on its obligations to the Admiral. If Charles II had repaid

Sir William's money to his son in 1680, William Penn's financial worries certainly would have ended. Penn, however, knew that he had a far better chance of obtaining North American real estate than English specie. He recognized his charter as a means of enlarging his property holdings and his way out of personal debt, telling Secretary William Blathwayt in the Colonial Office that Pennsylvania offered him the opportunity to serve God, to honor the king, and to make his own profit.

Many within Charles's inner circle believed the king supported Penn's request out of a desire to once again protect Penn from the wrath of the ultra-conformists in his government, much the same way he had held him in the Tower when Penn was younger, and then insisted that the Admiral send him to Ireland as soon as he was released. Perhaps Penn was going into secret exile at Charles's request in order to save his life. In a 1682 letter to Henry Sidney, Algernon's brother, Penn revealed that receipt of his grant did indeed portend safety from possible violent retribution. "I perceive thou art resolved to keep out of harm's way. So shall I, too, when I am got to my new granted province in America, where the change of the voyage shall secure me from the revenge of my enemies." Subsequent events support this idea. Just before Penn left for his New World colony, Charles dissolved Parliament and then set about executing many prominent Whigs, including Algernon Sidney. Would Penn have joined his friend on the block had he not been leaving England? If Charles sent William Penn to America to save him from the royal purge, then Charles's affection and esteem for Penn was genuine. That Penn retained this profound respect is evident in his continued support for James II during the stormiest days of James's reign, when loyalty might be life-threatening.

Charles's fondness for Penn was further confirmed when he pressured his brother to cede to Penn the Lower Counties—now Delaware—of his New York province. Two letters from Sir John Werden, secretary to the Duke of York, to William Blathwayt, secretary to the Lords of Trade and Plantations, suggest that Charles had to persuade the Duke to be generous. In the first letter, written in June 1680, Werden informed Blathwayt that he had discussed Penn's boundary request (the acquisition of the Lower Counties) with the Duke, and James's response was "If this be what Mr. Penn would have, I presume the Lords will not encourage his pretensions to it." James was hesitant to give up the Lower Counties because that meant ceding to Penn the Delaware River, the main fur trade route into western New York. For Penn, control of the Delaware River was even more important, for without it he would have no outlet to the Atlantic and his trade would be stymied by duties imposed by whoever controlled the waterway. Penn needed to secure from the Duke rights to the Delaware River, particularly the western bank, where deep water enabled heavy ships to navigate safely.

Penn appealed to Charles for assistance, and over the course of the next several months, Charles convinced his brother to acquiesce to "dear friend Penn's desires." By October 1680, the Lower Counties became part of Penn's original grant. In another letter, Werden wrote Blathwayt that the Duke, after "several conversations" with the king was "now pleased to tell Mr. Penn, to expect favour from his Majesty [the Duke] touching that Request of His"—the Lower Counties. The Duke's willingness to cede the Lower Counties and the Delaware River may have been influenced by the fact that at the time of negotiations he was persona non grata at court on account of the Exclusion controversy. Because of his unpopularity James had left England for a while, exiling himself first to Brussels and then to Scotland. Wanting to mollify as many Crown supporters as possible (and few were as loyal to the Stuarts as Penn), Charles wisely saw that meeting Penn's request would go far toward ensuring the Quaker's loyalty. The significance of the Lower Counties and the Delaware River to Pennsylvania's success was confirmed two decades later in a petition by Philadelphia merchants, who told the Board of Trade that their city's claim as the richest, most profitable entrepot in North America was possible only because of Penn's acquisition of the Delaware.

Penn also needed access from the Susquehanna River into the Chesapeake Bay. There were several reasons for having an alternative passage. Penn knew that, while initial trade would flourish along the eastern part of the colony, ultimately, commercial activities would move west, requiring a water route down the Susquehanna. He also knew that the Delaware River froze in the winter, stopping commerce for several months while the salty Chesapeake did not freeze, providing clear access for shipping. Thus, it was economically imperative for his colony's commercial success to have access from the Susquehanna through the Chesapeake.

Acquiring access to the Susquehanna required another round of negotiation since the river's lower reaches were within territory granted to Lord Baltimore, Catholic proprietor of Maryland. Baltimore's faith made him like James, "suspect" at court, and thus he would have little support among Charles's ultra-Anglican councilors or the Lords of Trade and Plantations for his claim that Penn's grant infringed upon his province. Thus, in December 1680, when the Attorney General, Sir William Jones, rendered his opinion that Penn's patent, including access to the Susquehanna, did not encroach upon Maryland, Lord Baltimore was not surprised. However, this was only round one in a boundary dispute that was not resolved until the 1760s, with the drawing of the Mason and Dixon line. Penn and Baltimore continued locking horns on this issue for the next four years, until 1685, when the Lords of Trade again ruled in Penn's favor, declaring that the Susquehanna had never been part of Maryland, thus giving Penn full access and use of the river as well as the right of deposit of his colony's goods where the river flows into the Chesapeake. Indeed, no sooner did Penn arrive in his colony than he had Friends build a port, called appropriately "Port Deposit," at the Susquehanna's mouth.

With his boundaries secured and access to vital rivers ensured as well, Penn was confident that the relative ease by which he obtained such privileges portended well for his charter's final approval. Indeed, the speed and precision with which red tape was cut in Whitehall was nothing short of amazing; Penn received his charter in less than nine months. To date, no proprietor had ever had his patent go through the labyrinth of imperial bureaucracy with such rapidity. All previous petitions had taken at least two years of "consideration." The speed at which Penn received his grant demonstrates the strength of Penn's connections with the inside power brokers of the Restoration government. Indeed, the "Chits" (Sidney Godolphin, Laurence Hyde, and Robert Spencer) were more instrumental than even Charles in pushing through Penn's charter with such haste. Of this powerful triumvirate, it was Robert Spencer, Earl of Sunderland and Secretary of State, who proved to be the most invaluable court friend in Penn's life at this particular moment. Sunderland, according to Penn, "was the first in the business of my American country." Translated, it was Sunderland, who, more than any other member in Charles's government, worked the councilor machinery and halls of power, shepherding Penn's petition through with minimal opposition. Spencer and Penn formed a "dynamic duo," whose clever maneuvers made granting Penn a colonial proprietorship seem like a brilliant move politically, economically, and strategically, from which many would benefit in a variety of ways, including those who opposed such an enterprise.

When finally approved in April 1681, Penn's charter was generous. It declared Penn the "True and Absolute Proprietor" of an

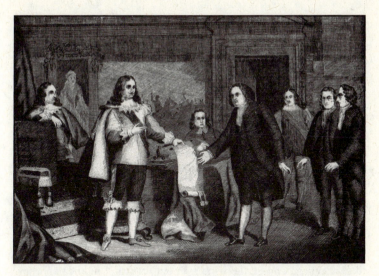

William Penn receiving his charter for Pennsylvania from Charles II.

empire of 45,000 square miles and to whom the colony's inhabitants were to render total obedience. No private citizen in English history had ever possessed as much land. Penn's charter gave him free and "undisturbed" use of ports, harbors, waters, soil, woods, mountains, all living creatures in the waters and forests, and all precious minerals and gems that may be discovered. For such bounty Penn was to pay to the king a fee of two beaver skins "to be delivered at castle Windsor on the first day of January every year." Just in case any precious metals such as gold or silver were found, the monarchy typically demanded one-fifth of such wealth. Penn was given the power to govern in conjunction with an assembly, and together they would make the colony's laws. The king could not impose trade duties without the proprietor's and the assembly's consent. Penn could also appoint all magistrates and establish a judicial system. In all cases (excluding murder and treason), Penn was the ultimate source of appeal, not the king. Indictments and writs would also be issued in the name of the proprietor instead of the monarch. In short, Penn could do "whatever else may be necessary for establishment of justice, provided it is not contrary to the laws of England." Penn also had the power to make war on enemies, levy customs, and dispose of lands as he saw fit. Finally, and most important, Penn was given the right to grant religious toleration to all *Christians* (even Catholics!) in his colony.

Although munificent, Penn's charter had a number of strings attached to it, which reflected London's rising concern for a tidier, more obedient empire. For example, even though Penn and his descendants were to be sole proprietors and governors of Pennsylvania, any deputy governor Penn appointed would have to be royally approved. The colony was specifically directed to obey the Navigation Acts, which guaranteed revenue to the Crown by requiring that the colonies trade only via English shipping and export their most profitable ("enumerated") goods, such as tobacco, timber, and sugar, exclusively to the mother country. Colonial ships were free to take their other produce where they wanted. The acts also stipulated that all foreign imports to the colonies first had to pass through an English port, where they paid customs duties. If Penn wanted a bottle of French wine, it had to come via England, rather than directly from France. More than likely Penn purchased the wine from an English "middleman" beverage merchant, who increased the price after paying the duties. Such a procedure gouged Americans, especially on non-English-made or non-English-grown goods. The wine cost Penn considerably more than if he had bought it directly from a Frenchman. Americans came to resent such profiteering at their expense, and engaged in bribery of customs officials and smuggling in order to get around this particular stipulation of the Navigation Acts. By the 1690s, Penn's future capital city of Philadelphia would become a hotbed of contraband activity, and both king and Parliament would call on Penn to stop such illegality or forfeit his colony.

Another stipulation was that every five years the colony's assembly had to submit its laws for royal inspection and approval. However, if the Privy Council did not act on the laws within six months, they would be automatically confirmed. Considering the Privy Council's busy agenda, any "temporary law" would more than likely become permanent without ever being reviewed by the Privy Council. The idea of Privy Council examination of colonial laws was new, reflecting once again the government's desire to try to manage the colonies better. However, in Pennsylvania and elsewhere it was easy for colonists or proprietors to outwit the Lords of Trade, who were responsible at this time for colonial policy. Penn, when negotiating his charter's particulars, no doubt included the five-years–six-months stipulation, knowing fully well that such a provision would make the clause ineffective. A final Crown mandate to ensure that Pennsylvania fulfilled its strategic objectives was a requirement to maintain a militia for defense against "pirates, thieves, or invading barbarians."

Penn tactfully accepted all directives. When the Bishop of London, Henry Compton, who had evidently missed the point about religious toleration, demanded that Penn allow Anglicans to worship in their own church, the proprietor readily agreed. The good bishop also suggested that Penn should purchase the lands he planned to settle from the Indians. That, like religious toleration, was redundant, since Penn and other Quakers had scrupulously observed Native American titles in New Jersey, but Penn thanked the bishop and publicly gave him "credit" for Pennsylvania's "enlightened" Indian policy. Penn's ingratiating behavior toward the Bishop of London reflected political savvy, not sycophancy, although Penn, the quintessential courtesan was capable, when necessary, of such fawning. Penn knew the prelate to be hostile toward Quakers, and thus to prevent the bishop from blocking the charter by claiming Penn was anti-Anglican, Penn prudently accepted the bishop's dictums. When it came to protecting his colony and his faith (which were symbiotic in his mind), Penn often used whatever un-Quakerly stratagem the situation required. Nothing was as important to Penn (not even his family at times) than the success of his "holy experiment" called Pennsylvania.

In a letter to the Irish Quaker merchant Robert Turner, who became an important recruiter of colonists in Ireland for Penn, Penn related the different permutations the name of his colony went through before King Charles insisted Penn call "my country Pennsylvania; a name the King would give it in honor of my father, whom he often mentions with praise." Penn originally wanted to call his colony New Wales because of his family's Welsh background. He did not want to use the name Penn at all because "it should be looked on as a vanity in me." However, "as a respect in the King, and to my father," Penn acquiesced and accepted Pennsylvania. Penn was certain that the hand of the Lord was upon the colony and that He "will bless and make it the *seed of a nation*."

Four days after receiving his charter, Penn wrote a letter to the current inhabitants of Pennsylvania, the thousand or so Dutch and Swedish settlers living in the southernmost part of his grant. Penn wanted to assure them that he was not establishing his proprietary "to make a great fortune." Most important to the colonists and for Pennsylvania's future was Penn's pledge that they would "be governed by laws of your own making, and live a free, and if you will, a sober and industrious people. I shall not usurp the right of any, or oppress his person." It remained to be seen how much power Penn would actually turn over to his people.

Without question Penn owed receipt of his charter to the debt outstanding to his father as well as to his own intimate friendships with both Charles and James Stuart. The speed with which Penn obtained his charter demonstrates how deep his court connections were. Motivating Charles was a variety of economic, strategic, and political factors, including the potential for a new source of income for the Crown from duties on trade; a defensive location; and both the Tories and the Crown's hope that Quaker migration would debilitate the opposition party by depriving it of the potential membership of "Whig-affected" dissenters. Tories also supported Penn's charter because it meant the possibility of ridding England of a most irreconcilable group of nonconformists.

Penn's charter was far more exceptional than customary. It was geographically and politically generous. His proprietary powers far exceeded those granted to any other individual or group of individuals. Neither Lord Baltimore of Maryland nor the Lords Proprietor of the Carolinas had such complete authority over their respective dominions. Penn was indeed the "True and Absolute Proprietor" of his colony. Perhaps what is most revealing is the fact that Penn was given such autonomy and personal control at a time when the Crown (and Parliament to a lesser degree) was trying to consolidate the empire by bringing it under tighter royal supervision. The generosity shown to Penn ran completely counter to what the Crown was doing elsewhere in North America. The autocratic rule of Edmund Andros in New York and the 1685 creation of the Dominion of New England are evidence of the Crown's efforts to bring all of the northern colonies under direct royal control. At that same time, the Pennsylvania assembly was well on its way toward becoming the ruling body in the colony without Crown interference. Both Charles and James Stuart remained confident that Penn would do nothing to jeopardize their mutually beneficial relationship.

7

"As Fit a Man
as Any in Europe
to Plant a Country"

As historian Gary Nash observed, for Penn, "Pennsylvania offered the rare opportunity to serve at once God, personal fortune, and fellow Quakers." However, in Penn's mind his principal motivation was religious. Indeed, that was the only motive he publicly admitted possessing. All his prior endeavors on behalf of the Quaker cause paled, for never had he felt so strongly guided to do the Lord's will as he did in the establishment of Pennsylvania. Penn believed "God had not cast my Lott here [Pennsylvania] but for a service to his Truth, and I know his hand was and is in it." Penn was equally certain that his undertaking would be "an example and standard to the nations" of the world of an ideal Christian community. In short, Penn's idyllic hope was that Quakers in America, free from the corrosive effects of Restoration England, would build a new, regenerated society in North America. Penn believed Pennsylvania was center-stage in history; the eyes of the world—England and Europe as well as the other North American colonies—would be on the young colony. Penn was determined to prove that Quakers were disciplined and industrious. He wanted England to take great pride in the certainty that Quakers were God's stewards, transforming the wilderness and its heathen inhabitants into a land of milk and honey, populated with God-fearing Christians.

Similar to the New England Puritans, who believed their colony of Massachusetts was a special place, "a City Upon a Hill," Penn referred to Pennsylvania in equally righteous terms: it was a "holy experiment." However, in stark contrast to Puritan Massachusetts, Pennsylvania had no tax-supported established church, not even for Friends. Penn certainly wanted his colony first and foremost to be a refuge for persecuted Quakers but he spoke in universalistic terms, of "a free Colony for all Mankind that should go hither." Penn thus welcomed (much to the dismay of many Friends) both non-Quakers and non-Britons, promising them all equal rights and opportunities.

Finally, Pennsylvania represented to Penn an opportunity to recast the family name and legacy, erasing the blemish he believed his father had placed upon it by the Admiral's years of destructive warfare. Penn hoped that by creating the "ideal Christian society" the Penn name henceforth would be associated with the preservation of life and the propagation of peace and the brotherhood of all men rather than the desolation of society and the killing of people. Penn wanted to be remembered as the creator of a better world accomplished by peaceful, Christian-inspired values. That Penn was successful in this endeavor is confirmed by the fact that the image most Americans today have of Penn and his fellow Quakers is precisely what Penn hoped for his posterity. Indeed, of all the Christian faiths that came across the Atlantic from Europe, thanks in large part to William Penn, none have had a greater impact on the creation of the American creed than the Quakers, whose fundamental principles and beliefs still inform much of Americans' collective national character and identity.

Yet, for all his righteousness, Penn knew he still had to live in *this world*, and thus it would be only fair for God to bestow on him some material rewards for his efforts. There is little doubt that Penn saw in Pennsylvania a means of recouping his sagging finances. He certainly expected the colony to return handsome profits through quitrents and land sales. Penn was honest about expecting to be compensated for his efforts, telling Robert Turner that, "Though I desire to extend religious freedom, yet I want some recompense for my trouble." Penn's plans for Pennsylvania thus reflected his dual identity as a Quaker and aristocrat, hoping to augment his own fortune while providing a haven for his persecuted brethren. Many fellow Quakers, however, believed Penn's motives were strictly pecuniary, for they doubted how much real service to God and the gospel could be accomplished in the wilderness. They accused Penn of pursuing worldly goals and of encouraging Friends to emigrate to the New World while the majority of their brethren suffered in England.

The image, treasured by generations of Americans, of God-fearing pilgrims, either Puritans or Quakers, dressed in simple, plain clothes, addressing each other with "thee" and "thou," piously turning their energies to the creation of a Christian paradise in "the place that God will show us to posses in peace and plenty," is far from reality. Not only did many of God's elect (including Penn) wear clothing in the height of Stuart fashion, but they also came to the New World for profits of the purse as well as those of the spirit. Colonial settlements were expensive, requiring long-term investments and confidence in the future to realize a return on the original capital outlay. Long before William Penn received his charter, Francis Bacon acknowledged this fact when he compared the founding of colonies to the planting of trees. "You must make account," he said, "to lose almost twenty years' profit, and expect your recompense in the end." Given this reality about colonial enterprises, few if any of Penn's associates, especially if they were businessmen or weighty Friends, should have been shocked or outraged by Penn's desire to be "recompensed" for all his efforts.

Penn placed a heavy burden on his brethren who came to Pennsylvania to live up to all his expectations, the most important of which was to prove that Quaker beliefs were compatible with good government. In this capacity Pennsylvania Quakers had to play their roles perfectly, for in England, Friends, more than any other group of dissenters, had been accused of disavowing good government and true religion. Penn's vision of Pennsylvania and early hopes for the colony reflected his faith's distinctive political radicalism and optimism. Pennsylvania was to be a largely noncoercive, consensual society, in which a deep spirituality pervaded every aspect of life, especially government, which Penn regarded as "a part of religion itself, a thing sacred in its institution and end." Indeed, Penn hoped that all government could be transformed into a spiritual rather than a coercive activity. Penn believed, and hoped to prove in Pennsylvania, that when governments are created by appealing to "that of God"—the Inner Light—in every individual, then there would be little need to maintain order and safety for all by threats and punishments. Only when dealing with evildoers should government become "more corporeal and compulsive." Otherwise a government must display "kindness, goodness, and charity" toward all its citizens. Those who asserted that a government's most important function was to maintain control of the population by force, "weakly err that there is no other Use of Government than Correction, which is the coarsest Part of it; Daily Experience tell us, that the Care and Regulation of many other Affairs, more soft and daily necessary, make up much the greatest Part of Government."

In Penn's concept of government, as in the Friends' meetings, controversial issues would be resolved through quiet deliberation. In Penn's view, his colony would be a place where freedom and liberties flourished, but within an ordered, stable setting. With such utopian visions in mind, Penn set to work drafting his *Frame of Government*. Penn gathered a council of advisers to help him draw his colony's political and social constitution.

Among those from whom Penn sought input were old friends Algernon Sidney and Benjamin Furly. The result was the publication of a remarkable document for its time in the fall of 1681. It reflected the pure distillation of Penn's philosophy, a composite of his reading of classical republican writers, his practical experience in the affairs of West New Jersey, and the political ideology of men like Sidney and other Commonwealth/Whig theorists such as James Harrington, author of *Oceana*. Although receiving almost absolute power from Charles, Penn deliberately divested himself of much of the control granted to him and his successors, for he never wanted to be accused of abusing his authority, or as he told Robert Turner, of "doing mischief." Penn wanted to design a government that would prevent "the will of one man" from "hinder[ing] the good of a whole country."

The *Frame of Government* went through several editions and revisions (there are twenty known drafts) before its final approval by the "First Adventurers" (those Quakers who invested in the enterprise and who came to Pennsylvania from the time of the colony's founding through 1685) and Penn. It consisted of two parts: a document with a Preface, signed by Penn in April 1682, and a body of forty laws, signed by Penn in May 1682. Penn blanketed them under the one long title, *The Frame of Government of the Province of Pennsylvania, in America, Together with Certain Laws Agreed Upon in England, by the Governor and Divers Freemen of the Aforesaid Province, to be Further Explained, and Continued There, by the First Provincial Council That Shall be Held, if They See Meet*. Interestingly, the *Frame of Government* became a work in progress because it was never completely satisfactory to anyone, especially Penn, who found himself constantly at ideological logger-heads with his more democratically inclined colleagues, Sidney and Furly. Thus, the document went through four developmental phases: the first from 1681, when Penn began to hammer it out, until he published it in 1682; the second as it was altered in 1683 after he had held discussions with his colonists; the third in 1696; and the final version in 1701.

Why so much roiling and churning over the constitution? The answer was simple: despite all of Penn's embracing of liberal Whig doctrine, when push came to shove and he was confronted with the reality of making good his supposed attachment to Whig/republican ideology, his aristocratic elitism prevailed, especially when it came to the issue of popular sovereignty. Such a disposition shocked Sidney and Furly, for five years earlier Penn was quite magnanimous when promulgating the *Concessions and Agreements* for West New Jersey, which delivered all legislative power to an assembly, chosen by the "inhabitants, freeholders, and proprietors" of the colony. As Penn told fellow Quaker Richard Hartshorne, at the time, he was willing "to put the power in the people."

What caused Penn to have such a change of heart when it came to Pennsylvania? Despite his embracing of Quakerism, Penn suffered great cognitive dissonance when it came to accepting his faith's political radicalism. No matter how hard he tried to reconcile the movement's more egalitarian tenets he could not extend himself very far in that direction, especially when it came to governing his *own* colony, for which, thanks to Charles's generosity, he alone was responsible. It seemed that once such a reality struck Penn, his ingrained elitism reemerged, revealing his essentially conservative thinking. Thus, he was committed to a political order based on property while concomitantly favoring a social system, which upheld "all reasonable distinction and those civil degrees that are amongst people." Even during his supposed "radical, Whig-affected" years of the 1670s, he wrote that freedom was endangered "by the ambitions of the populace which shakes the constitution." Penn never conceived of Pennsylvania as a radically egalitarian society. His concept of a non-coercive government was to operate within a hierarchy of social relations. When individuals became unruly—that is, unwilling to accept their proper place in society by challenging the "rightful" authority of superiors—the principle of noncoercion then had to give way to the imposition of order. Society's "natural" governors, the elite, would then take control, restoring the proper arrangement essential for the society's safety and preservation.

Penn was no starry-eyed utopian idealist, bemused and misled by an overly optimistic estimate of human nature. He had witnessed and personally experienced too much cruel intolerance and oppression to have such a naïve view of humanity. Moreover, his intimacy with the Stuarts, in which he had to use his own less-than-saintly un-Quakerly wiles to get his charter, confirmed that men naturally tended to "side with their passions against their reason," and that "sinister interests" too often override their attachment to the good—hence the need for the coercive power of government. Penn's elitist tendency was strongly reinforced by his confidence in his own superior wisdom and righteousness, which, over time, alienated many of his once more fervid supporters and friends.

Through revision after revision, the constitution, changing names with new versions, metamorphosed from a liberal document, the Fundamental Constitutions of Pennsylvania, in which an annually elected 384-member assembly, would alone propose and pass laws, to the final, more conservative Frame of Government, in which power was firmly under the proprietor's appointee, the governor, who ruled in conjunction with a 72-member council chosen from among the colony's wealthy elite. Governor and council would appoint all the officials, including judges, and draft the laws. The council was also to serve as the upper house of a bicameral assembly. The lower house, containing 500 members, had power only to approve or reject laws proposed by governor and council. It was not the initiator of legislation. In effect, the assembly was a sop; Penn's token gesture to placate the common folks' demand for a voice in government.

The council was also charged with preserving the colony's peace, safety, and financial stability as well as the right to determine the location of cities, ports, and market towns; regulate all matters relating to public buildings and roads, and decide the fate of convicted criminals. The proprietor, as governor, also possessed extensive powers. He sat as the presiding officer in the council, where he held a triple vote. Most important, Penn, or whomever he appointed as governor, held sole power of appointment of all proprietary, provincial, and county officers—judges, treasurers, masters of the rolls, sheriffs, justices of the peace, and coroners.

By contrast, under the Fundamental Constitutions of Pennsylvania, the council was to be a 48-member, purely consultative "second" branch of government, sitting with the governor, making *only* recommendations on bills initiated in the assembly. The council possessed no veto power. Moreover, the assembly chose from its own ranks council members to serve three-year terms. This was the "frame" of government that so excited republicans like Sidney and Furly, for it represented, although fleetingly, Penn's embracing of fundamental Whig political ideals such as balanced government and popular sovereignty. Instead, Penn concentrated political power in the hands of a small coterie of weighty Friends, who over time became an entrenched oligarchy of the colony's wealthiest merchants and landowners.

Penn's liberal meanderings not only disquieted his own inherent aristocratic sensibilities, but more important, they disturbed the men of substance upon whom he relied for leadership and financial backing. Such individuals would not exchange carefully cultivated estates and businesses in England for the uncertainties of a proprietary wilderness unless they were promised a very strong presence and say in running the enterprise. The majority of the colonists came to resent these "proprietary men," and by extension Penn, for they blamed him for having created a frame of government that allowed for such concentration of power in the hands of a few. It was through the initially emasculated assembly that the common folk expressed their discontent, ultimately forcing Penn and his weighty associates to grant that body the power Penn originally envisaged in the Fundamental Constitutions.

Most disillusioned by Penn's capitulation to aristocratic pretensions and elitism were Sidney and Furly, both of whom believed that Penn was as devoted to Whig political ideology as they were. They saw Penn's "holy experiment" not only as providing a refuge for Quakers and as a righteous experiment in Christian living, but as a political venture, as well, in representative government based on popular sovereignty. They felt duped and betrayed by Penn when they heard the news that the Frame of Government was to be the colony's constitution. Sidney called the document "the basest laws in the world, and not to be endured or lived under"; even "the Turk was not more absolute" than the Proprietor, claimed Sidney. Penn, concluded Sidney, exercised more power in government than the king in England.

Furly was equally dismayed, wondering "who should put thee upon altering them [the earlier, more liberal drafts] for these, And as much how thou couldst ever yield to such a thing. . . . Who has turned you aside from these good beginnings to establish things unsavory and unjust?" demanded Furly. Most alarming to Furly was the elimination of the assembly's legislative power, which, he rightly predicted, "in time to come will lay morally a certain foundation for dissention amongst our successors." The Rotterdam merchant further warned that the document's "patronizers" would soon be castigated for dispossessing Englishmen of "that naturall right of propounding laws to be made by their representatives." Furly was convinced that if Penn hoped Pennsylvania would be "the seed of a great nation," he was deluding himself, for this "divesting of the peoples representatives" was guaranteed to "tear asunder all ye good intentions" and plunge the colony into bitter factionalism and "mischief." Furly believed Penn needed to scrap the present constitution and go back to the drawing board and write one that befitted "a noble and virtuous and trusting people [the Quakers]," who expected to be treated "justly and fairly" by a government "of their representatives."

Although an elitist, Penn was no dogmatist, assuming instead a pragmatic, reformist position. Constitutions must not be so rigid that they cannot be altered as "some singular emergences" required. He thus included in his Frame of Government the first amending clause in any written constitution. Penn, however, defended his scrapping of earlier, more liberal plans, rationalizing that: "There is hardly one frame of government in the world so ill designed by its first founders, that in good hands would not do well enough. . . . Governments, like clocks, go from the motion men give them, and as governments are made and moved by men, so by them they are ruined too. Wherefore governments rather depend upon men, than men upon governments. Let men be good, and the government cannot be bad; if it be ill, they will cure it. But if men be bad, let the government be never so good, and they will endeavor to warp and spoil it to their turn." It was Penn's emphasis on the personnel rather than on the structure of government, the reverse of conventional Whig thinking, that permitted him to be swayed from initial plans for a more progressive political arrangement.

Although concentrating ultimate power in the hands of the few, in all other areas Penn's Frame of Government was far more democratically advanced than his critics were willing to admit. Inviolably secure was the cornerstone of religious toleration, the driving obsession of Penn's life since his convincement. Indeed, to Penn, his colony was first and foremost a "holy experiment" in religious toleration. The government would make no effort to dictate matters of conscience. However, Pennsylvania was not to be a prototype for total religious freedom; it was to be a safe place for *all Christians*, including Catholics, but especially for persecuted Protestant sectarians. Penn granted permission to worship or not to worship, as one pleased. A public officeholder had to be a Christian, but it was only necessary to "confess and acknowledge the one Almighty and eternal God," to live in the province.

Also firmly established were an enlightened judicial system and penal code. All courts were to be open and conducted in the English language, and a person was allowed to plead his own cause. Naturally, trial by jury was guaranteed, so was bail except in the case of capital offenses, and anyone wrongfully imprisoned was entitled to double damages against the informer or prosecutor. Prisons were to be workhouses and inmates were provided free lodging and food. Only two offenses were subject to capital punishment: treason and murder. Penn's charter gave him the power to pardon and abolish all crimes except murder and treason, so he eliminated the death penalty on all others. At the time, England still had a long list of crimes punishable by death other than treason and murder: piracy, arson, burglary, highway robbery, horse stealing, stealing from a person above the value of a shilling, rape, and kidnapping. The Frame also included a strict moral code to be adhered to by all colonists. "Offenses against God," such as cursing, lying, drunkenness, incest, sodomy, whoredom, duels, as well as such "other violences" as stage plays, card playing, dice, "may-games, masques, revels, bull and bear-baiting, cockfights, and the like, which excite the people to rudeness, cruelty, looseness, and unreligion shall be respectively discouraged and severely punished."

As far as citizenship was concerned, the Frame established that any Christian (including women) of 21 years who possessed 100 acres of land (50 acres if one had been released from indenture within the preceding years) or who paid scot and lot, a tax levied upon persons according to their ability to pay, was eligible to vote. Such criteria probably enfranchised about half the adult male population or one-eighth of all Pennsylvanians, including women but there is no record that any female tried to exercise the right. Although initially far from granting outright universal suffrage, Penn made it very easy for his colonists to obtain such a privilege. Indeed, by 1700, virtually all adult, white, male Pennsylvanians had the right to vote. Finally, a third of the provincial council would rotate yearly, and the whole assembly would be up for annual elections and voting for all offices would be by secret ballot. Although there was no established church, it was clear that Friends would dominate the government, frame the laws, and set the tone of Pennsylvania society. Others would be welcome but they would have to submit to Quaker principles.

In many respects the political machinery Penn designed proved cumbersome and unworkable. However, there were many features that showed Penn's good sense and his concern for democratic practice: staggered terms for councilors; compulsory rotation of offices "so that all may be fitted for government and have experience in the care and burden of it"; a provision for the establishment of schools and the encouragement of "useful sciences and inventions"; the division of the provincial council into four working committees, one of which had the responsibility for "manners, education, and arts"; and most important, the amending clause. Penn's commitment to the concept of constitutional adaptability was not just lip service; he agreed to several successive overhauls of the Pennsylvania charter. The last revision, the 1701 Charter of Privileges, signed by Penn just before he left America for the last time, proved so satisfactory to the colonists that it remained in effect for seventy-five years. Despite its failure to fulfill the republican dream of popular sovereignty, the Frame of Government was a charter its author was most comfortable with, allowing Penn to translate his noble vision into reality. Indeed, upon reading the Frame, Quaker James Claypoole told fellow Friend Samuel Clarridge that, "I do judge William Penn as fit a man as any in Europe to plant a country."

The endorsement of such weighty Friends as Claypoole and Clarridge boded well for Penn's holy experiment, especially when it came to soliciting capital for his visionary scheme. As an experienced colonial promoter, Penn knew his colony's success depended on his ability to recruit wide financial support. The lessons of nearly one hundred years of English colonization were clear: neither Puritan nor profiteer, pilgrim nor promoter could have built his temple or trading post without the wealth of England standing behind him. The age of colonial expansion was possible because it happened to coincide with an era of capitalistic and industrial growth in which money was available to finance seventeenth-century pioneering energies.

Penn was fortunate in that by the time he obtained his charter there had emerged within the Quaker community a considerable number of merchants and wealthy landowners. According to one contemporary, the "Richest Trading Men in London" were Quakers. To such individuals would Penn turn for the financial backing of his enterprise. Penn's status within the Quaker movement also helped his cause. As one of the sect's leading intellectual leaders he had circulated for years among the faith's more affluent members, establishing cordial relations with Quaker merchants in Dublin, Cork, Bristol, and London, as well as with Quaker gentry in the countryside. By the time of his New World venture, the name of William Penn was a household word among Friends. Penn thus reaped the benefits of years of work on behalf of the Quaker movement and cultivation of friendships with the sect's most prominent individuals. Every "Publick Friend," as the itinerant leaders were known, became potential spokesmen for Penn's undertaking. There were Friends, however, particularly among the movement's elders, who refused to promote Penn's enterprise. They still believed that the true site of any holy experiment should be England, not America.

It was in England that God's chosen people were being tested through persecution. In their view, Quakers such as Penn, who escaped this suffering by emigrating to the New World, betrayed their divine mission.

Like colonial promoters before him, Penn, if he wished to attract weighty Quaker investors, had to present his colony not only as a refuge for his persecuted brethren—a place to build a Quaker "city on a hill"—but also as an area ripe for economic exploitation. Between March 1681, when he received his charter, and August 1682, when he left for America, Penn devoted his every waking hour to trumpeting and selling his colony. Penn's promotional tracts, addressed to both investors and potential settlers, reflected his awareness that support depended on advertising his colony as a place of great potential economic development. Penn was already a seasoned booster, having written several promotional pieces to attract settlers to West New Jersey. Penn wrote his advertisements in a style quite different from that of his earlier Quaker apologetics. His audience then was quite different, and so was Penn's purpose. Penn was now older, more mature in thought and action, less rabid about his faith, and increasingly aware of how crucial to his colony's success it was to attract the right sort of people to invest in and to migrate to Pennsylvania.

In his promotional pieces Penn made no mention of his Quakerism; to Friends he did not need to. Other than to state that "an eye to the providence of God" should direct prospective settlers, Penn downplayed religious reasons for migrating. In this respect Penn's broadsides were quite different from those he had written for West New Jersey, where the intent was to attract only Quaker emigrants. However, for his own colony he was trying to attract non-Quakers as well, either as settlers or as purchasers/investors. Penn knew that the scope of his venture was simply too big for a small sect like the Quakers to sustain. Pennsylvania was to be as much a secular as a holy experiment, in which anyone could improve his or her lot regardless of religious or political persuasion. His tracts thus addressed practical issues such as Pennsylvania's climate and location, types of crops that could be grown there, price of land to be sold or rented, cost for a family to make the journey, and supplies needed. The voyage would cost 5 pounds, 10 shillings for individual males and females, and 5 pounds for servants. The fare for children under seven would be 50 shillings, though babies not weaned could travel free. Settlers should take with them "all sorts of apparel and utensils for husbandry and building and household stuff." Colonists should be willing to spend two to three years "without some of the conveniences they enjoy at home."

Penn also stipulated in his advertisements the kind of emigrants his colony needed. Although wanting to attract "industrious husbandmen [farmers] and day labourers," he specifically wanted "laborious handicrafts, especially carpenters, masons, smiths, weavers, tailors, tanners, shoemakers, shipwrights, etc." As can be readily seen from the list of the most desired type of skilled settlers Penn hoped to interest, it was clear he needed people who could build a colony from scratch. Contrary to popular myth, not even in colonial America's supposedly most humanitarian colony, were the huddled masses welcomed. The soliciting of such individuals was left to nineteenth-century propaganda. Penn provided little space if any on his ships for the unskilled poor or the destitute. The skilled were given preference. Penn did not worry whether the poor or desperate would swell the immigrant ranks. In seventeenth-century England the riffraff and ambitionless were generally unwilling to leave behind the "security" of the parish alms in exchange for the rigors of starting life anew in the American wilderness. Indeed, when Penn proposed to Robert Barclay, his Scottish agent and promoter, to transport some of Barclay's poor countrymen to Pennsylvania and "set them downe at easy raits," Barclay advised against such a move, telling Penn that "such is the humeur [sic] of that gang of people here" that none would "stir from home for such a journey."

Those who sought land and new opportunities in the New World were craftsmen and farmers in whom still burned the fires of ambition—a desire for betterment not extinguished by years of destitution. This was especially true among Quakers. Penn simply did not recruit from the ranks of impoverished Friends; his strongest appeal was to the skilled urban worker or shopkeeper and in the country to already established yeomen to whom he offered the potential of owning more land than they could dream of possessing in England. Eighty to ninety percent of nonindentured immigrants were of the artisan-yeoman class.

Nor did Penn make his colony out to be a natural paradise but an extremely inviting place to start afresh. He did, however, make much of his colony's commercial prospects in his first promotional, *Some Account of the Province of Pennsilvania*. If his principal audience was the burgeoning Quaker merchant class, he had to present Pennsylvania as the future center of overseas commerce in North America. He discussed the natural channels of trade to other mainland colonies and the West Indies, the fur trade, the rich timber resources, and the ripe prospects "for those that will follow merchandize and Navigation." Pennsylvanians would "send to the southern plantations corn, beef, pork, fish and pipestaves and take their growth and bring for England, and either sell them here or carry them out again to parts of Europe." A flurry of such mercantile boosterism followed, culminating in the 1683 claim that not only the Delaware River but all of its tributaries as well had "room to lay up the Royal Navy of England."

Although ultimately wanting Pennsylvania to be the empire's most dominant North American entrepot, Penn realized that before that could happen he had to populate his colony and develop the soil. Ever the country squire, Penn dreamed of a "greene country towne" serving the commercial needs of an agricultural society. He thus offered his land to prospective buyers at attractive and competitive terms with the realty market elsewhere in America. Penn's price was 2s. 6d. an acre, a bit more per acre annually than he was getting from his tenants on his Irish estates. He advertised his land in blocs of 5,000 acres for 100 pounds. By offering so much for so little, Penn hoped that weighty Friends would buy substantial tracts and send over servants and tenants to develop them.

Penn soon discovered however, that few of his sect's more affluent members were willing to invest as much as 100 pounds in the Pennsylvania wilderness. More than half of the 589 First Purchasers in the 1680s paid him only 5 or 10 pounds in order to buy small parcels of 250 or 500 acres. This was not what Penn had envisioned; he needed greater participation by weighty Friends. To entice such individuals Penn decided that the purchasers of the first 500,000 acres would receive bonus lots in his capital city, the future Philadelphia. These bonus lots proved to be among Penn's most enticing initiatives. The land in the capital city would be distributed by lot at the rate of 10 acres for every 500 purchased in the country. The greater the amount of hinterland purchased, the larger the dividend in the city. Naturally, city lots would appreciate more rapidly than the province's other real estate. Penn was clearly trying to attract wealthy buyers with the tantalizing offer of city realty.

His scheme worked. By April 1682 he had sold nearly 500,000 acres, primarily to weighty Friends—Quaker merchants from London, Bristol, and Dublin—yielding Penn, at least on paper, receipts of about 10,000 pounds. The other major investors were a potpourri of professional men, prosperous landowners, and Penn's relatives and personal associates, including Penn's steward, Philip

Ford, who was one of the first purchasers of 5,000 acres for 100 pounds. For some of the investors their purchases were purely for speculative reasons: venture capital advanced by men who had no intention of going to Pennsylvania. They either sent tenants to occupy their claims or even sold them to others. It has been calculated that two-thirds of the First Purchasers, 392 of 589, migrated to Pennsylvania. By 1685 these same 589 individuals owned 715,000 acres of Pennsylvania real estate.

Despite all of Penn's attempts to garner the financial support of his faith's more prosperous members, the majority of the First Purchasers—a combined 71 percent—were either craft workers or farmers, exactly the types whom Penn hoped would settle in Pennsylvania. Only 14 percent were wealthy merchants, 8 percent were of the "gentleman" status (independently wealthy because of inheritance, like Penn), and 6 percent were members of the professions. Although Penn cast his recruiting net wide, obtaining colonists from Ireland and Scotland in the British Isles, and from France, Germany, and the Netherlands on the continent, the overwhelming majority—88 percent—came from England, including Wales.

Penn not only attracted weighty Friends through land sales concessions but also by forming a joint-stock company. Named the Free Society of Traders, the consortium was primarily the work of a small group of London merchants, mostly Quakers, and most of whom were intimates of Penn. Under the leadership of James Claypoole, the company projected bold initiatives for Pennsylvania's economic development. As a start, 200 indentured servants were to be sent to the colony as agricultural laborers on the 20,000 acres purchased by the society's nine charter members. Hopefully these servants could quickly produce commodity surpluses on the land for market export. Further profit was anticipated from the lease of land to incoming settlers, who would pay quitrents to the Free Society while living under its administrative auspices. More sophisticated enterprises would be initiated after intensive land cultivation proved profitable. Extraction of whale bone and oil, hemp and linen manufacturing, mining operations, and fisheries were projected. A fur trade with the Indians was also to be launched and for that endeavor, the society allocated 2,000 pounds. However, the most remunerative efforts were to be the "factories" established in Philadelphia and on Delaware and Chesapeake bays. These were not to be manufacturing centers, but rather supply depots, manned by Society agents who would barter or sell an assortment of imported finished goods needed in the colony in exchange for tobacco, fish, grain, and other products brought in by the settlers.

From the outset Penn regarded the Free Society as an integral part of his plans for Pennsylvania's development. When he sold the company 20,000 acres as part of its "seed" money, so to speak, he agreed to forego quitrents on the tracts, allowing the company to maximize its return on the land. Politically, Penn granted the society three seats on the provincial council. Like the major land purchasers, the principal investors in the society were the same handful of rich Quaker merchants and prosperous landowners. Joining this coterie of affluent Quaker businessmen were Penn's relatives and close associates, such as Philip Ford, who invested 400 pounds in the society. Although the major investors were well-established Quaker entrepreneurs, the lesser subscribers were smaller merchants, shopkeepers, artisans, and yeomen, who, unlike the First Purchasers, remained in England. Perhaps most important to Penn and fellow Quakers, the formation of the Free Society of Traders allowed investment to interested parties regardless of their religious affiliations. Prior to the creation of the Free Society of Traders, most other companies required not only religious uniformity but the taking of an oath as well. Since the Free Society was Quaker-based, no oath was required of any of its investors or members. In short, the Free Society provided a chance for Penn and his brethren to do what they were prohibited from doing in England, where company membership was limited and monopolies flourished.

Readers of this biography may conclude that Penn was a hypocrite; that by giving economic and political control to the elite few who had invested most heavily in his enterprise, he violated his faith's more egalitarian tenets. Such assessment overlooks the reality of Penn's situation. Like any entrepreneur, he sought venture capital for his colony from among the wealthiest and most experienced members of the Quaker community. These individuals were shrewd, practical, successful businessmen, who expected a significant return for their financial backing of a risky undertaking. No matter how much Penn sang the praises of his colony's potential, there was no guarantee it would deliver the material rewards he extolled in his promotional tracts. His investors thus wanted as much of a say— both economic and political—as they could possibly extract from Penn in how Pennsylvania was to be run.

Although Penn and his wealthy Quaker brethren believed in liberty of conscience, and were certainly more tolerant in other areas than most upper-class seventeenth-century Englishmen, they nonetheless did not embrace political democracy in nineteenth, twentieth, or twenty-first century terms. Nothing could have been more natural to them than the transplanting of an ordered society in which positions of power belonged to those who had the largest stake in the venture. That equation—wealth equals power—still offends liberal, democratic sensibilities, for it smacks of elitism, egoism, and acquisitiveness. In essence, these key components of the conservative ethos are not at all what most Americans attribute to the Quakers. But if Quakers like Penn were truly hard-boiled conservative "wolves" in liberal "sheep's clothing," then even revered Founding Fathers such as Thomas Jefferson and James Madison, among several other republican egalitarians (most of whom were also men of extreme wealth and property), were conservatives. To a man, they too believed in societal deference and stability above all else, for such were the essential prerequisites for good government. So, too, in Penn's view, good government meant the rule of law, not of men. Only in an appropriately ordered society, in which all citizens knew their proper places and responsibilities, could the rule of law prevail. However, that is not to suggest that either the Quakers or the Founding Fathers opposed upward mobility. Both wholeheartedly supported personal advancement, and in fact believed that the two most important functions of government were first, the protection of property (wealth accrued by an individual), and second, the removal of restrictions blocking opportunities for individuals to improve materially.

Like the Quakers, the Founding Fathers also embraced progressive ideals such as representative government (albeit voting and office holding was restricted to property owners), liberty of conscience, amendable constitutions, and many other "Quaker-inspired" principles. Perhaps most important, the Quakers and the Founding Fathers believed in meritocracy; that is, one *earned* the right to make decisions for the commonweal by demonstrating abilities that were clearly superior to others at that particular (generational or historical) moment. When Penn drafted the Frame of Government and formed the Free Society of Traders, he was vesting power in his colony to those individuals whom he believed deserved to govern because of their accomplishments and willingness to support his vision, not because of their titles or pedigrees.

To dismiss Penn and his Quaker brethren as conservatives because they believed in ordered, deferential social arrangements managed by an elite of talented achievers, is a superficial assessment. Penn, in particular, was too complex an individual for such facile categorization. Penn was no doctrinaire thinker. Indeed, he was quite the opposite. His political thinking was fluid and above all, pragmatic. Penn was both a liberal and a conservative, a product of his faith as well as his upbringing as a member of the English upper class. In establishing a political system controlled by the richest investors in his colony, Penn reflected an inherent conservatism appropriate for his class and heritage. And yet, Penn was uncompromisingly devoted to making real in his colony his faith's belief in human equality; racial and ethnic pluralism; liberty of conscience, and a world without war. William Penn and his fellow Quakers offered a new concept of community, in which differences of birth, background, and belief are ignored or downplayed, allowing everyone equal opportunity to succeed.

William Penn was a man of thought in action—arguing, negotiating, cajoling, remonstrating, and compromising in order to launch a colony, populate it, and guide his *creation* through its crucial formative years. One of Penn's principal motivations in establishing Pennsylvania was his desire to create a better society, not only in a spiritual and moral sense, but also in a physical and corporeal context as well. Compelling Penn was his desire to erase his father's legacy as a destroyer of humanity and replace it with his own history as an architect of brotherhood. Even if Pennsylvania fell short of what Penn envisioned as a holy experiment in righteous living, it nonetheless was a place where men and women lived together peacefully, regardless of their differences in faith, skin shade, and place of origin. These ideals have come to inform the American creed more than their conservative counterparts, and thus the Quaker legacy and that of the man who brought it to North America, William Penn, endures.

8

"Not to Devour and Destroy One Another"

The thread of Penn's personal life ran through all his labors for Pennsylvania. In early March 1682, Lady Penn died at Walthamstow. Although once close, especially during Penn's turbulent adolescence when Lady Penn was an aegis against his father's tirades, in recent years mother and son had grown apart. Causing the estrangement was Penn's wanderlust, as well as Lady Penn's increasing petulance and demanding personality, which seemed to intensify after her husband's passing. She simply could not get enough of her son's attention. Penn rarely visited his mother at Walthamstow, and when he did he stayed for only a day and upon his leaving, Lady Penn upbraided him most venomously. However, maternal bonds run deep, and when Lady Penn died, Penn wept for days. Despite relegating his mother to a burdensome obligation, Penn paid her due homage, burying her next to his father at St. Mary Redcliffe in Bristol with all appropriate protocol and filial respect.

Causing Penn greater remorse was the thought of leaving his own family, which now included three surviving children out of six, Springett, age seven, Letitia, age four, and "Billy," or William Penn III, age two. Penn was to go to America first and Guli and the children were to follow later. In a long missive to both Guli and his children, Penn not only revealed his deep love for them all, but his "counsel" as well on how they should proceed with their lives if "I should never see you more in this world."

Ever the task master and patriarch, Penn enjoined his wife to live within her means, even though he was unable to, and as far as the children were concerned, he was most anxious about their education, instructing Guli "to be liberal for their learning. Spare no cost but let it be useful knowledge." Interestingly, Penn did not want his progeny formally educated in the sense of attending all the "right" schools, which he believed, based on his experiences at Oxford were places where "too many evil impressions are commonly received." Instead, Penn wanted his children to be home schooled, telling his wife to "keep an ingenious person in the house to teach them."

Penn not only wanted his children to be taught at home but for their learning to be "practical" as well, for he confessed to his wife that much of what he learned at Oxford "hath not been of great service to me in managing my daily accounts nor my estates." He wanted his children to acquire specific skills, such as "building houses or ships, or surveying" but farming was particularly in Penn's "eye; let my children be husbandmen and housewives; a country life and estate I like best for them." Finally, Penn reminded his children that since "Pennsylvania and my parts of East Jersey" would some-day be theirs, allow "the law free passage. Though to your loss, protect no man against it; for you are not above the law, but the law above you." After finishing his letter, Penn gave it to Guli and told her not to read it until after he had left for North America.

After several months of preparation, by August 1682, Penn was at last ready to embark for North America. However, two days before he was to sail, his steward Philip Ford and his wife Bridget, visited him and presented him with a bill for 2,851 pounds, which the Fords claimed was money they had laid out on Penn's behalf. Preoccupied with his voyage, Penn signed this account without inspecting it—his usual habit. Penn also signed in haste two other documents at Ford's request, both of which came back to haunt Penn in later years: a conveyance of 300,000 acres of Pennsylvania land to Ford and his heirs unless Penn paid 2,851 pounds in two days, and a double indemnity bond of 6,000 pounds guaranteeing payment of the almost 3,000 pounds. At the time, the Fords' claims did not trouble Penn, for he believed that they were merely "for-malities" requiring his signature. Moreover, Penn was confident that the debt of almost 3,000 pounds owed to Ford would be easily liquidated when Ford sold more Pennsylvania lots. Penn then signed a power of attorney, authorizing Ford to handle his English affairs while he was in America. Penn would one day pay dearly, both emotionally and monetarily for his cavalier attitude toward his financial obligations, especially when it came to his commitments to Philip Ford.

Penn arrived at his colony on October 27, 1682. Pennsylvania was a year old and on the surface, it appeared to be well on its way to becoming the profitable and righteous enterprise Penn envisioned as he sailed into Delaware Bay. Indeed, between December 1681 and Penn's arrival, twenty-three ships had brought over 2,000 colonists to Pennsylvania. A year later, twenty more ships brought another 2,000 immigrants. By 1686, Pennsylvania's population exceeded 8,000. The first settlers were a varied lot—yeomen from Wiltshire in southern England, artisans from Bristol in the west, tradesmen from London, and gentry from Ireland and Wales. The majority of emigrants were naturally Quakers but because Penn had granted religious toleration to all Christians, the colony also attracted English Anglicans, German Pietists, Dutch Calvinists, and even a smattering of English and Irish Catholics. Like the New England Puritans—but unlike the Chesapeake colonists—most early Pennsylvanians came in freedom as families of middling means, simple folk, many arriving with only the barest essentials they could haul in one trunk, but with a deed of sale, paid for in England, for a freehold in the uncharted expanses of the new "Promise Land" of Pennsylvania. Persons of great wealth were few, and about one-third were indentured servants, bound for a period of service to individuals in better circumstances. Most settled as farmers in the many rural townships, but some lingered in the "instant city" of Philadelphia as artisans and merchants. Whether rich, middling, or poor, word of the new Quaker settlement in the valley of the Delaware had sparked yet another wave of European migration to the New World.

In terms of economic development, the presence of so many sturdy yeomen and artisans, in conjunction with a small upper class, were major factors in Pennsylvania's phenomenally rapid growth. Unlike in England, or even in the Chesapeake colonies, where a fixed upper class blocked ambitious persons of humble origin, no such conditions existed in Pennsylvania. Regardless of initial status, early Pennsylvanians were confident that personal diligence, sobriety, and hard work would reward them with the socioeconomic mobility unattainable in England or in the majority of the mother country's other possessions.

In the long history of the English empire, only a handful of its colonies experienced such instant economic success as Pennsylvania. Only three years after settlement, Philadelphia was firmly enmeshed in the West Indies provisioning trade, and would soon be cutting deep inroads into New York's control of the mid-Atlantic fur trade. By 1700 Philadelphia was second in size only to Boston in the English colonies. Without question, the Delaware River Valley's fertile soil and Penn's effectiveness in promoting immigration, contributed significantly to Pennsylvania's rapid prosperity. So did the immediate arrival of a veteran merchant class. The majority of these weighty Friends arrived in the colony with sound credit, sober reputations, and perhaps most important, an already established trade enterprise throughout the empire. They obviously had come to Pennsylvania to expand their commercial enterprises and augment their wealth in the process. These individuals' shared faith and thus mutual trust, gave far-flung Quaker merchants an advantage in the competitive world of imperial commerce. Their close mercantile associations throughout the English trading system gave Pennsylvania's economy a kind of head-start.

Timing also favored Penn's colony, for it was far easier to develop a later rather than an earlier colonial enterprise. Learning from their predecessors' mistakes, Quakers came with no golden delusions and thus did not suffer any of the "starving times," which afflicted their Chesapeake counterparts in the early seventeenth century. The Pennsylvanians also benefited from having sufficiently developed colonies as neighbors, who could provision them until their farms and trades became self-sustaining and productive. When Pennsylvania farmers did produce surpluses, they could sell livestock and grain to the large West Indian market, which the older mainland colonies had stimulated into a profitable commercial network by the 1650s.

Penn's vision was to make Pennsylvania the ideal setting for family farmers producing grains and livestock for the transatlantic market (and for merchants exporting that produce). The Delaware River offered Quaker farmers cheap and easy transportation for their goods to the port of Philadelphia. In contrast to rocky New England, southeastern Pennsylvania possessed a rich soil and an easily cultivated landscape of low, rolling hills. Pennsylvania also enjoyed a relatively long growing season of 180 days, which offered a greater certainty that grains would ripen before the first killing frost of autumn.

The growing season fell just enough weeks short to discourage most colonists from growing tobacco, which would have inevitably led to greater extremes of wealth and poverty, freedom and slavery. Had Pennsylvania's topography and weather been more conducive to tobacco cultivation, plantations maintained by African slaves might have dotted the colony's landscape rather than family farms producing grains and raising livestock. Had that occurred, Penn and his fellow Quakers would have found themselves in a most vexing moral dilemma, for the belief in human equality was one of the faith's fundamental tenets. Fortunately for Penn, the majority of his brethren remained faithful to the Quaker creed, and thus, as in New England, family farms worked primarily by free labor prevailed in Pennsylvania, which meant a relatively egalitarian distribution of wealth, especially compared to the Chesapeake and Southern colonies.

Contrary to popular belief, not all early Quakers were averse to slavery, including Penn. Penn grew up with an array of household servants at his beck and call, including two African slaves, Sampson and Anthony, whom his father had purchased during his Jamaica campaign. Admiral Penn treated his two bondsmen no differently than his other, white servants. Typical for his time and class, Penn thus came to think of slavery as an unfortunate but not necessarily evil institution. The majority of slaves in England were domestic servants in affluent households such as Admiral Penn's, and thus were accustomed to better living conditions than field hands on New World plantations. The rarefied environment in which the Admiral's slaves lived affected Penn's subsequent views on slavery and servitude in general. By the time of his founding of Pennsylvania, Penn had acquired a paternalistic attitude toward slavery, viewing slaves not as a master's property but as family members. Penn's conversion to Quakerism did not change his outlook; his new creed simply added a religious dimension to his perception.

Penn agreed with George Fox's declaration that, "Negroes and Indians are as much children of God as are their masters." Penn interpreted Fox's statement to mean that the souls of black folk were more important than their bodies. Every Quaker slaveholder was obligated to provide the care and tutelage essential for the salvation of another *human being*. Penn insisted that every human being, regardless of skin color or social status, was a creature of God, equal in God's sight and so entitled to equality among men. Penn thus saw nothing wrong in controlling the labor of workmen, white or black, as long as they were accorded fair and humane treatment.

Consequently, the presence of slaves or "servants" (Quakers resorted to euphemism, dropping the objectionable terms "slaves" and "slavery" because of the challenge to their faith's egalitarianism bondage they represented) was no anomaly in Quaker Pennsylvania. Although all slaves were black and the overwhelming majority of apprentices and bound men were white, by applying the word "servant" to everyone from the lowliest slave to the highest official serving the Proprietor, Quakers hoped to disguise the fact that many members of their community, including their most renowned individual, owned slaves.

Helping Penn to further rationalize his acceptance of slavery was the institution's ready acceptance among some of his most important weighty Friends and investors. From the beginning of his venture, Penn made it clear that his objective was twofold: to not only provide a safe haven for his Quaker brethren but to be personally compensated as well for all his efforts. Since many of his wealthy patrons were willing to break with their faith on the issue of human bondage, it would be both senseless and potentially damaging for Penn to protest slavery in such circumstances. The last thing Penn needed was to lose the political and economic support of weighty Friends who were proslavery. Moreover, English officialdom, seeing the profitability to be gained especially from the slave trade, vetoed all early attempts by the Pennsylvania Assembly to reduce the volume of the slave trade by taxing importation heavily or by outright prohibition of the trafficking. The English government's promotion of slavery thus made it that much easier for Penn to justify human bondage in Pennsylvania. For Penn to prohibit slavery would be to "defy" the will of his most important benefactor, the Crown.

Penn paid more than lip-service to the acceptance of slave labor. Despite declaring that no one had the right "to inherit the sweat of the other's brow to reap the benefit of his labor but by consent," he determined early in the founding of Pennsylvania that he would staff his Pennsbury estate exclusively with black bondsmen under a white overseer. "It was better they was blacks," he said of his labor force, "for then a man has them while they live." Penn owned as many as fourteen slaves by the late 1680s. However, as Quaker anti-slavery sentiment increased, protests forced Penn to return to the use of white indentured servants on his estate by the time of his return to Pennsylvania in 1699. Although abandoning the use of slave labor on his property, Penn nonetheless continued to own slaves. By the time of his return to England in 1701 after his second sojourn at Pennsylvania, Penn still owned two bondsmen, Yaffe and Chevalier, whom he did not manumit in his final will of 1712. The Penn family "retained" both men until Yaffe's and Chevalier's respective deaths sometime in the late 1740s.

Pennsylvania's healthier and more temperate climate, which Penn had touted in his promotional pamphlets, proved to be a great boon in Pennsylvania's economic development and population growth. It was warmer than New England's and certainly more salutary than the hot, humid, malarial Chesapeake. The invigorating conditions, abundant economic opportunities, and relatively even gender divisions combined to encourage early marriages and numerous children. In 1698 a visitor reported that he seldom met "any young Married Woman but hath a child in her belly, or one upon her lap." Although immigration slowed during the 1690s, natural increase sustained a population that nearly doubled from about 11,000 in 1690 to 18,000 Pennsylvanians by 1700. Pennsylvanians simply had an overall healthier quality of life and thus lower infant mortality rates and greater life expectancies, especially compared to their brethren in the Chesapeake and England.

Upon his arrival, Penn made the establishment of his capital city one of his first priorities, immediately laying out the rectangular grid design between the Delaware and Schuylkill rivers. The town was on everyone's mind since it would encompass the most valuable land. Before leaving England, Penn had conceived the type of city he wanted to create in his colony, believing his vision would make "Philadelphia" unlike any urban center in the world. In envisioning his city, Penn appears to have been inspired by the new Piedmontese capital of Turin in Northern Italy laid out by the dukes of Savoy. Penn visited Turin during his continental tour in the early 1660s and remembered being impressed by its wide streets leading from the river Po, and the city's rectangular blocks. Penn chose his city's name, taking the two Greek words, *philos* and *adelphos*, meaning love and brother, combining them to create Philadelphia, the "City of Brotherly Love," a most appropriate name for the capital of a colony that was to be a Quaker "holy experiment" in toleration, acceptance, and the brotherhood of all people.

Penn did not want Philadelphia to be an unplanned shamble, and neither did he want it to suffer from unwholesome crowding and congestion like London and Paris. Penn remembered London, ridden by plague incubated within its own premises. He had witnessed the Great Fire and watched Londoners rebuild the city on the same haphazard, inconvenient lines. He saw too many houses built in too little space and labyrinthine streets reappear. Penn had something quite different in mind—a completely systematically designed city with straight streets running "uniform down to the water from the country bounds," and "houses built upon a line," and every house placed in the "middle of its plat, as to the breadth way of it, that so there may be ground on each side for gardens or orchards, or fields, that it may be a green country town, which will never be burned, and always be wholesome." Philadelphia was to be a neatly arranged city, distinct from older colonial towns such as Boston, with its rambling and narrow streets, crowded buildings, and frequent fires. Penn, true to his aristocratic/agrarian heritage, envisioned a "pastoral city," with tree-lined boulevards, country manor houses with ample green space for gardens and orchards, and most important, spacious city and riverside parks. Also important to Penn was the fact that two navigable rivers, the Delaware and the Schuylkill, serviced his city.

Although meticulously planned, Penn's model city unfortunately made no provision for the poor, the artisan class that provided essential city services. The addition of "backward streets," as Penn called them, with homes and shops for these people cluttered his green vistas. Commercial necessity soon usurped his riverside parks with wharves and warehouses, ironically the physical manifestations of his colony's material success. Except for its broad avenues and rectangular blocks, by the time of Penn's death, "The City of Brotherly Love" sadly resembled any crowded and filthy English seaport. Indeed, as the English visitor John Usher told William Blathwayt, secretary to the Board of Trade, although the city contained an "abundance of fine rich buildings in truth it's a monster the head bigger than the body and filled with too many inhabitants." A newly arrived merchant from Jamaica, Jonathan Dickinson, agreed with Usher, noting that Philadelphia was "so thronged with people that there is hardly a house Empty and rents grow high."

Much to Penn's eventual chagrin, the City of Brotherly Love was never an exclusively Quaker city. Besides Quakers there were Anglicans, Baptists, Presbyterians, and Swedish Lutherans in the city. Nearby Germantown had Lutheran, Moravian, and Mennonite churches. Pennsylvania early on was ethnically diverse as well. "We are a mixt people," the Quaker merchant Isaac Norris observed soon after Penn returned to England. Indeed, in addition to the English and Welsh, and the Swedes and Dutch who preceded them, there were Scots, Irish, Germans, other Europeans, African slaves, and of course Native Americans. The colony's ethnic and racial diversity meant that from the outset Pennsylvania rapidly became a model for the melting pot of later centuries.

After visiting Philadelphia's future site, Penn continued his trip up the Delaware to inspect the location of his new home, Pennsbury Manor, purchased for him from the Algonquian-speaking Lenni Lenape, or Delawares, as the English called them, by William Markham. Penn was pleased with Markham's choice; the place suited Penn's temperament perfectly, for it was far enough from

Philadelphia (twenty-four miles) to provide Penn with a retreat from the hurly-burly world of proprietary affairs, where he could live his accustomed life of a country gentleman. The actual land on which Penn's house would be constructed was in a vast, open meadow of several thousand acres.

Penn's purchase of Pennsbury represented the first of what became many transactions between the Quaker and Native American sachems. He purchased his tract in the kind of currency or "wampum" the Lenni Lenape valued: 20 white blankets, 20 kettles, 20 muskets, 20 coats, 40 shirts, 40 pairs of stockings, untold quantities of hoes, knives, glasses, shoes, pipes, scissors, combs, and tobacco. Although to the modern observer such items appear to be useless trinkets in exchange for vast quantities of land, it must be remembered that such products were of great value to the Lenni Lenape, who had been trading with white Europeans—the Dutch and Swedish settlers in the area—for decades. Moreover, by the time of Penn's arrival, the Lenni Lenape possessed more land than their reduced numbers could use, and thus welcomed the opportunity to sell some for coveted trade goods.

There is little doubt that Penn's sincere yet shrewd policy of cultivating Indian goodwill contributed significantly to Pennsylvania's rapid growth and financial success. Penn's approach allowed his colony to enjoy prolonged peace with the local tribes, avoiding the native uprisings that had devastated Virginia, New England, and New Netherland (as well as Spanish New Mexico). Pennsylvanians also benefited from the fact that by the time of their arrival in the Delaware and Susquehanna valleys indigenous peoples were relatively weak and few in number, decimated by multiple epidemics, alcoholism, because of their interaction with Dutch and Swedish traders, and because of destructive raids by both the Iroquois Five Nations (Cayuga, Mohawk, Oneida, Onondaga, and Seneca tribes) and Chesapeake colonists.

Numbering about 5,000, the Lenni Lenape were the principal Indians remaining in eastern Pennsylvania by the time of Penn's arrival. They dwelled in many small, autonomous bands along both banks of the Delaware River, moving their villages as the seasons changed, and pursuing a mixed economy of fishing, hunting, gathering, and horticulture. Harassed by the Five Nations and recently deserted by their Susquehannock allies, the Lenni Lenape needed a colonial patron to provide trade goods.

In his first meeting with them, Penn laid the foundation for peaceful relations with the Lenni Lenape, telling the tribe that

"The King of the Country where I live, hath given me a great Province but I desire to enjoy it with your Love and Consent, that we may always live together as neighbor and friends . . . [and] not devour and destroy one another, but live soberly and kindly together in the world." In this single statement Penn dissociated himself from the entire history of European colonization in the New World. In contrast to the violent intimidation, deception, and fraud often perpetrated on Native Americans by previous colonial leaders, Penn acknowledged the Lenni Lenape as the land's legitimate owners, and he publicly treated their culture with respect.

From learning their language so he would not need an interpreter when negotiating, to understanding their matrilineal society and appreciating their folkways, Penn took the Lenni Lenape for what they were—no less human ("natural sons of Providence") and no less endowed with the Inner Light than white men. Penn never underestimated or devalued the Lenni Lenape's innate intelligence and perspicacity. "They do speak little, but fervently and with elegancy. I have never seen more natural sagacity, considering them without help (I was going to say, the spoil) of tradition [formal education], and he will deserve the name of wise that outwits them in any treaty about a thing they understand." As Penn poignantly stated in a letter to the Free Society of Traders, "Don't abuse them, but let them have justice and you win them."

Penn was keenly aware of the disintegrative effects two generations of contact with the Finns, Swedes, and Dutch had had on the Lenni Lenape. Unlike most of his contemporaries, who asserted that interaction with "civilized" white Europeans had "benefited" the "savage," Penn contended the opposite: that it was the treacherous Europeans who were "corrupting" Native Americans. "The worst is that they are worse for the Christians, who have propagated their vices and yielded them tradition for ill and not for good things." Penn believed that if the Lenni Lenape had not established relations with the Europeans they would have been better off, for their inherently "blessed equable temperament" and simple life would not have been adulterated. As Penn noted, "They care for little because they want but little, and the reason is, a little contents them. In this they are sufficiently revenged [better off than] on us: if they are ignorant of our pleasures, they are also free from our pains. . . . We sweat and toil to live; their pleasure feeds them—I mean their hunting, fishing, and fowling."

Penn also observed the effects of the European "luxury" that had "filled them with anxieties" and "had raised their passions"—alcohol.

Penn greeting and shaking hands with Lenape chief to begin his
negotiations for his Pennsylvania land, including the future
site of Philadelphia.

Penn was certain "the drinking of strong spirits" was insidiously destroying their idyllic, simple life. "Sober, they are an extraordinary, sensitive people of high integrity; drunk they are helpless dupes," exchanging for rum "the richest of their skins and furs." Penn believed Native Americans' addiction to alcohol was not just another manifestation (or confirmation) of their alleged inherent, barbarous nature. To Penn it reflected something deeper: a need for relief from the intolerable tensions created by the conflict of cultural values in which they were caught.

By the late seventeenth century, Penn's peaceful policy so impressed the Native American tribes that Indian refugees began migrating to Pennsylvania, fleeing from abuse and internecine warfare in other colonies. Penn's government welcomed Shawnees from South Carolina, the Nanticoke and Conoy of Maryland, the Tutelo from Virginia, and some Mahicans from New York. As a Conoy explained to the Quakers, "The People of Maryland do not treat the Indians as you & others do, for they make slaves of them & sell their Children for Money." Welcoming the refugees was shrewd as well as benevolent. The exiles were "relocated" along the Susquehanna River, replacing the Susquehannock, thereby giving Pennsylvanians a security screen to the west of their settlements in the Delaware Valley. The outlander's villages provided a buffer, especially against the French and their Indian allies, who became particularly menacing beginning in the late 1690s. By that decade England was at war with France, and typically the conflict spilled across the Atlantic to North America. The English government called on its colonies to do their part, expecting them to provide men and arms in defense of the empire. Fortunately, the Quakers' perspicacity in locating the fugitive tribes along their western pale relieved them of having to compromise on their avowed pacifism as their native clients bore the brunt of any frontier warfare. Behind a western rampart of Indian allies, Pennsylvanians enjoyed peace and prosperity until the 1720s, when their desire for land encroached upon their Indian friends, bringing to an end what was perhaps the longest, most amicable relationship between Europeans and Native Americans.

The Quaker accomplishment is sometimes disparaged with the claim that there was little competition for land in eastern Pennsylvania between the natives and the newcomers. However, a comparison between Pennsylvania and South Carolina, both established during the Restoration, shows the power of pacifism. A quarter century after initial settlement, Pennsylvania had a population of about 20,000 whites. During the same twenty-five years, South Carolina had grown to only 4,000 whites, while becoming a cauldron of violence. Carolinians spread arms through the region to facilitate slave dealing, shipped 10,000 members of local tribes off to New England and the West Indies as slaves, and laid waste to the Spanish mission frontier in Florida. As long as the Quaker philosophy of pacifism and friendly relations with local Indians prevailed, interracial relations in the Delaware River valley contrasted sharply with those in other parts of North America.

Although one of the most farsighted, sincere, and benevolent of all Europeans in his relationships with North American Indians, Penn's primary motive was trade. Penn was well aware of the great source of profit and wealth through trade of English manufactured goods for the Indians skins and furs, and he counted on those transactions for income to defray his venture's expenses. He wanted to establish friendly trade relations not only with the Lenni Lenape, but with other tribes as well. Penn, however, was a Johnny-come-lately in the trade. New York merchants, especially those of Albany, monopolized the lucrative fur trade with the Iroquois Five Nations, who might otherwise have come down the Susquehanna to do business with Penn. If Penn hoped to "tap" into the remunerative fur trade, he had to find a way of wresting such enterprise away from other colonial competitors.

Prior to Penn receiving his charter, the future Pennsylvania and Delaware colonies were under the auspices of New York and its Iroquois Five Nations. In 1676, New York's ambitious new governor, Edmund Andros, made a number of loosely connected treaties, known as the Covenant Chain, which helped to stabilize relations with the Iroquois by allowing them to dominate the other native peoples in the northeast. Andros also allied with the Five Nations in order to bully coastal Algonquian peoples who resisted English colonial expansion. In short, the Five Nations (especially the Mohawk) and the English collaborated to increase their respective power, at the expense of weaker tribes.

The establishing of Pennsylvania did not necessarily break Andros's Covenant Chain. What did threaten the Chain, however, were Penn's trade ambitions, which portended not only to upset the delicate balance Andros had established, but also to cause intercolonial rivalry as well between New York and Pennsylvania— scenarios not welcomed by the Crown. Penn attempted to set up separate trade agreements with the Iroquois in the form of a Covenant of Friendship. Motivating Penn in his independent course was his desire to develop as extensive a trade network with as many different Native American tribes as possible. Penn wanted his colony to become the new "hub" of Native American trade, supplanting New York and New England in the process. If successful in this endeavor, Penn would significantly augment Pennsylvania's wealth and attraction as a land of limitless opportunity. Once in possession of the Susquehanna Valley, Penn could sell its fertile lands to new immigrants for ready cash and a steady quitrent income. Since neither his boundary with New York nor that with Maryland was fixed, he took full advantage of the situation, pushing especially his northern boundary as far in that direction as he could in order to break New York's (Albany's) monopoly of the lucrative Iroquois trade. The trading center Penn proposed to set up at Conestoga on the Susquehanna would be easier for most Iroquois to trade with than Albany. If Penn succeeded in his enterprise, his outpost signified instant ruin for New York. Pennsylvania was a worse threat than New France.

At this juncture (September 1683), the Susquehannocks occupied the area, and since they were Algonquian, Penn was confident his purchase would be quickly consummated, for he had already proven his "good intentions" toward the Algonquians in his dealings with the Lenni Lenape. Penn, however, was soon disappointed. The Susquehannocks could not release the land without the consent of both the Five Nations and the New York government, which neither gave. In his failure to purchase the Susquehanna Valley, Penn had underestimated his opponents, especially the Iroquois, whom he had been supremely confident he could easily befriend with his Quaker integrity, luring them and their valuable trade away from his far less scrupulous, if not predatory, English brethren in New York. However, in this instance, all of Penn's honesty and sincerity, no matter how genuine, failed to convince the Iroquois to abandon their Albany partners.

Penn underestimated Iroquois loyalty to New Yorkers, for whom the Covenant Chain had been most beneficial. Much to Penn's chagrin, the Iroquois viewed him as an interloper. Perhaps more important, Penn's attempt to encroach upon New York territory and upset the Covenant Chain created years of hostility between Pennsylvania and New York. Penn's activities undoubtedly raised concerns in England, with many at Whitehall wondering if Charles had acted wisely in giving the troublesome Quakers their own colony. It seemed that Penn and his Quaker brethren were simply incapable of behaving themselves. No matter where they went,

rsy followed them; even the native peoples of North
a could not escape their "meddling ways."

though stymied in his initial attempt to penetrate the
quehanna Valley, in 1700, when Penn returned to his colony, he
anaged to gain access to the region by a series of fortunate
circumstances. Penn's greatest obstacle had been the Iroquois, but
by 1700, they were no longer an impediment. Recently crushed by
New France and its Indian allies, they fled the area, leaving only
the original Susquehannocks, who were more than willing to
exchange their right to the valley for Penn's protection and some
badly needed goods. The treaty signed between Penn and the
Susquehannocks in April 1701 conveyed to the Quakers the valley
east of the river, thus opening up large tracts of land for sale to
colonials. Perhaps most important, the Susquehannocks agreed to
do business only with individuals or companies licensed by Penn,
and that they would trade exclusively with Pennsylvanians. The
Susquehannocks also agreed to prevent all "strange" Indians from
settling along the river until Pennsylvania's government sanctioned
the relocation. The treaty took the Indians of the Susquehanna
Valley into Penn's Chain of Friendship, dealing a grave blow to
New Yorkers' once impregnable trading partnership with the
Iroquois Five Nations. Most harmed by Penn's new pact were the
Iroquois, whose ownership of the Susquehanna territory now
ended as the once vassal Algonquian-speaking Susquehannocks
became the area's new masters. In his relationships with Native
Americans, Penn most definitely favored his own client tribes. His
faith demanded fair treatment for all. His lordship demanded distinctions. He saw no contradiction.

In the seventy-five years of English colonization of North
America, no Englishman did more to preestablish the structure
and functioning of government than William Penn. No other com-
pact compared in comprehensiveness to Penn's 1682 Frame of
Government. Yet, for all the preliminary work done in England,
Pennsylvania's first years were not marked by political order and
stability, but rather by constant tension and hostility between sec-
tions, groups, and individuals. In the first rush of enthusiasm, adventurers wrote passionately of "the Joy of the wilderness &. . . that
gladness that did break forth of the solitary & desolate Land," certain Pennsylvania was "an honorable place with Zions walls" where
God's hand was "setting up a remnant in these parts as an ensign to
the Nations." Penn too was overly optimistic and effusive, describ-
ing to potential emigrants that all current colonists were bound

together in common purpose by "heavenly Authority." During his first sojourn, he wrote to Quaker friends in England of the wonderful way in which the Spirit guided the affairs of government. According to Penn, decisions were reached harmoniously, for the Lord's presence was "ecstended [sic] dayly to us in our assemblies, so that whatever Men may say our wilderness flourishes as a Garden, and our desert Springs like a Greene field. . . ."

In reality, nothing could have been further from the truth. Even before Penn arrived, friction existed between the non-English Quaker inhabitants of the Lower Counties (eventually to become the independent colony of Delaware) and the three Quaker counties established around Philadelphia. Also causing rancor was the privileged status given to the Free Society of Traders in economic affairs. Especially aggrieved were the non-Quaker merchants, who resented Penn for granting the Traders a monopoly on the colony's mercantile activities. Within a year's time, pro- and antiproprietary factions emerged, and within the factions, individuals jockeyed for positions of dominance. "For the love of God, me and the poor country, be not so governmentish, so noisy, and open in your dissatisfactions," Penn wrote only three years after his colony had been launched. A year later he wrote in disgust that he was tempted to give Pennsylvania back to the king and let "a mercenary government" rule the Quakers if it could.

When Penn summoned his first assembly at New Castle in December 1682, he expected it to simply give his Frame of Government a rubber stamp. Much to his consternation, the assembly refused, demanding the right to read and discuss the forty "Laws Agreed Upon in England," as well as the fifty new laws submitted after his arrival. The Frame of Government clearly stipulated that only the Council had the right to initiate and debate legislation, not the Assembly, which Penn clearly envisioned as a regularized referendum, with power to vote "yes" or "no," not "maybe." If the huge, inexperienced lower house had such a prerogative, Penn feared his proposals would drown in a cacophony of opinions, and consequently, neither laws, procedures, nor proper colonial management, would be established. Penn had not anticipated such a hostile reception to his Frame of Government but there was little he could do to prevent the Assembly from abrogating much of his system. Herein lay the paradox between liberty and authority. In England, Penn had long championed Parliament's right to free debate. Was not that principle to be guaranteed in Pennsylvania? The Assembly believed so, and thus Penn had no choice but to allow that once impotent

ave a voice in running his colony. Penn knew that if he
to "negotiate" with the Assembly, such obstinacy could lead
a revolt, plunging his colony into turmoil. If that occurred,
English officials, especially those dubious from the start about
nting Penn and the Quakers a colony, had the perfect excuse to
scind Penn's charter. If Penn hoped to keep his colony and avoid
being labeled a hypocrite, he had to acquiesce to the Assembly's
demands for an increase in its power in determining Pennsylvania's
political development.

The Assembly's attempt to wrest power from Penn and his close
associates on the Council, reflected the larger tensions in
Pennsylvania between old settler and new, English and non-English,
Quaker and non-Quaker, and Penn's friends and independent
adventurers. Although often at odds with each other, they nonetheless put aside their differences in the Assembly and united in opposition to Penn and the Council's monopolization of political power.

Most disheartening to Penn was the disunity and discord among
Quakers. In many ways Penn was responsible for the tension among
his brethren, for many were upset with him for having given so
much economic and political power to the Free Society of Traders.
They had come to Pennsylvania believing it was a place where *all
Quakers* would have opportunities to improve their lives, not just a
select few. They felt duped and betrayed by Penn, for they saw his
policies, particularly the favoritism shown to the Free Society, as
discriminatory and nepotistic, no different than what Quakers had
experienced in England. The Quakers who were left out of Penn's
inner circle thus chafed at his extensive powers, creating even
among his own people an antiproprietary faction.

With such a whirlwind of opposition all around him, Penn
decided he had no choice but to capitulate to the Assembly's
demands for a new Frame of Government, which Penn agreed to in
March 1683. Most important Penn compromised on the issue of the
Assembly's right to initiate legislation. Penn conceded that the
Assembly would have the right to "confer" with the Council in legislative matters. Although more "democratic" assemblymen rightly
proclaimed "tokenism" and were leveling "undeserving Reflections
and Aspersions upon the Governor [Penn]," for the moment the
majority accepted Penn's and the Council's concession. In effect,
Penn agreed to allow Assembly members into informal consultation
with the governor and Council to suggest "such Proposals as might
tend to the Benefit of the Province." The Assembly further extracted
from Penn the mandate that he obtain the advice and consent of the

Council for every official act. Penn readily agreed to this last proposal for he knew it would be a nonissue for him because the Council was comprised of his most loyal friends, whom he could count on for supporting whatever policies he desired to implement. Beyond these modest concessions, nothing else was done to alter the existing distribution of power. For all the roiling about, in the end, Penn remained, at least for a while longer, "True and Absolute Proprietor" of Pennsylvania.

By the end of 1684, after two years of constant tension and agitation between Penn and the Assembly, political factions began to form. Although still shifting and amorphous, three increasingly identifiable groups emerged and dominating each was a coalition of merchants and large landholders. Any combination of two of these groups could overpower the third, and could consequently affect Penn's ability to maintain control of his colony. By the time Penn was about to depart Pennsylvania, his authority not only had somewhat diminished but now he was forced into playing political games— maneuvering, manipulating, cajoling, placating—one faction or the other in order to maintain any semblance of proprietary control.

The first faction comprised Penn's inner circle of staunch supporters and officeholders, men such as William Markham, Nicholas More, Welshman Thomas Lloyd, and "foreigners" such as the German Pietist, Francis Daniel Pastorius, and Lasse Cock, the acknowledged leader of the Swedish settlement in the Lower Counties, who was also an expert on Indian languages. Their power was great, for Penn had appointed them to every important office in proprietary and provincial affairs. Only a few were non-Quakers and the Council was their bastion. Occasionally some sat in the Assembly as well.

Interestingly, the second group was also almost exclusively comprised of Quakers as well, but unlike the first group they resented Penn's prerogatives and were especially upset by his blatant favoritism toward the first group. They chafed under what they considered Penn's restrictive proprietary vision and opposed his political concepts. Joining them were recently arrived merchants from New York, the West Indies, and England. Although they were Quakers and fairly wealthy, they too came to resent Penn's discriminatory and circumscriptive policies. Using the lower house as their forum, these "old" and "new" Quakers questioned the exclusive power structure Penn and his supporters had established. So long as Penn remained in his colony, his presence muted most of their demands. However, when he returned to England, they seized the

ty created by his absence to extract as much power from
ncil—and by extension, Penn—as they could accomplish.
inhabitants of the Lower Counties composed the third fac-
. The majority were either Anglican or Lutheran and non-
glish. From the moment Penn arrived, it became evident that
ongenital differences would make any sort of union between upper
and lower counties difficult if not impossible. Many issues divided
the Upper and Lower Counties. The Upper Counties, for example,
saw no need for defensive fortifications or a militia, both of which
would violate the Quaker tenet of pacifism. Moreover, Penn's brilliant Indian diplomacy obviated such needs. The Lower Counties,
however, were vulnerable to marauding pirates and later to French
raiders. They thus demanded protection in the form of coastal
forts and a home guard, which the Upper Counties' Quakers were
reluctant to give.

The most serious point of contention was economic, as the
Lower Counties' merchants feared that as Philadelphia grew, their
downriver ports of New Castle and Lewes would decline if not altogether vanish, as the "City of Brotherly Love" became regional
entrepot. Finally, the Lower Counties or "the Territories" as they
were euphemistically called at the time, feared for their eclipse politically. Because they were geographically confined, hemmed in on
their western border by Maryland and to the east by Delaware Bay,
it was obvious that all new emigrants would head north to the
Upper Counties. This migration not only would increase the Upper
Counties' population but create new counties as well, thus augmenting the Upper Counties' political power. The result would be a
loss of power for the Lower Counties in the legislature. In both
Council and Assembly, the Lower Counties' representatives tried to
preserve their autonomy from both Quaker factions to the north.

Penn's best hope for safeguarding his authority and interests in
Pennsylvania was to use his appointive powers to their fullest extent.
By his charter and Frame of 1683 he possessed sole right to commission a vast array of officers, both public and proprietary. These men
would not only be Penn loyalists, but perhaps more important, barring malfeasance, they could serve for life, thus giving continuity to
proprietary policy. Most important, Penn hoped such individuals would defend and promote his vision while insulating it from jeal-
ous encroachers. It was to the Provincial Court (early Pennsylvania's
"supreme court," which assumed appellate jurisdiction previously
exercised by the Council), county courts, and commissions to admin-
ister proprietary land affairs, that Penn appointed his most ardent and

trustworthy supporters. It was through his appointees that Penn hoped to retain his authority over his colony.

Finally, rather than appointing a lieutenant governor to rule in his stead, Penn attempted to satisfy all factions by vesting the Council with such executive power. For president of that body he appointed Thomas Lloyd, a fellow Oxford alum, and son of the eminent and affluent Welsh Quaker, Charles Lloyd. The younger Lloyd came to Pennsylvania in 1683 and immediately caught Penn's attention as the kind of dedicated and competent Quaker who could manage Penn's holy experiment when he returned to England. Penn's confidence in Lloyd's abilities was reflected in the Welshman's meteoric rise to power. In rapid succession he was appointed Master of the Rolls, Council president, and member of the Board of Propriety. In August 1684, as Penn was about to leave for England, he augmented Lloyd's power by commissioning him Keeper of the Great Seal.

Keeping Pennsylvania on a paying basis and thus himself and his family solvent, also caused Penn grief, for he was dependent on his tenants paying their quitrents. Demanding payment was a distasteful task, yet it had to be faced and understood. Thus, before leaving for England, Penn wrote a "friendly reminder" bulletin to all his renters in New Castle, Chester, Philadelphia, and Bucks counties. He hoped his "salutation," if kept congenial in tone, would disarm potential hostility toward him. Penn knew from his experiences in Ireland and England that tenants, no matter how munificent the landlord, simply did not like paying rent. Nonetheless, Penn needed the rental income and thus hoped that if he couched his intent with kindly greetings and reminders of his magnanimity, his "bearer," James Atkinson, would "gather in my quitrents among you, and you must not take it hard that I press you in this matter, for you know that I receive neither custom nor taxes but maintain my table and government at my own cost and charges, which is what no governor doth besides myself." Unfortunately, no matter what attitude Penn displayed toward his renters, he had difficulty collecting quitrents from the very beginning. He had plunged his whole life and fortune into Pennsylvania, as well as that of his family. Yet, over the years those who had benefited most from Penn's efforts found it convenient to forget all he had done to provide a new start in Pennsylvania for hundreds of fellow Englishmen.

Satisfied that all would go well under the auspices of his hand-picked and loyal officers, Penn set sail for England on August 18, 1684. He had accomplished much during his 22-month stay in his

felt good about Pennsylvania's rapid population growth
pleased by the colonists' success in establishing farms,
kept the colony from having to endure any "starving times."
zen Quaker meeting-houses, completed or under construction
oughout the colony, confirmed the Friends' success in transplant-
ng their faith. Fifty thousand acres in the Susquehanna Valley had
been set aside to be parceled out to poor families; in Philadelphia
county 10,000 acres each were set aside for a school and a hospital.
Perhaps giving Penn the greatest joy was his highly successful negotiations with the Lenni Lenape. In the history of English colonization of North America, no Englishmen proved more skilled or more
honest and sincere than William Penn in establishing peaceful and
productive relations with Native Americans. When he reached
England, he reported happily to the Quaker elder Stephen Crisp,
who had opposed Penn's enterprise, that, "not one soldier, or arms
borne, or militia seen, since I was first in Pennsylvania."

Yet, despite his successes, Penn left his colony with a heavy heart.
To the south, Lord Baltimore disputed his claim to the indispensable
Lower Counties, going so far as to encourage open rebellion among
the inhabitants. To the east, in New Jersey, the Crown's agents and
other anti-Quaker groups sent reports to England declaring that
chaos reigned in Pennsylvania. Most distressing to Penn was the discord among Friends and the resentment harbored by many toward
him. Also worrisome was the Assembly's restless straining for more
power. Individuals everywhere, Quaker and non-Quaker alike, put
their individual interests above those of the community, with only a
handful demonstrating unswerving loyalty to the proprietor. Penn's
parting prayer for Philadelphia perhaps best reflected his forebodings created by two years of wearying dissension. "What love, what
care, what service, and what travail, has there been to bring thee
forth and preserve thee from such as would abuse, and defile thee,"
the troubled Penn wrote from his ship. "O that thou mayest be kept
from evil of that [which] would overwhelm thee. . . . My soul prays
to God for thee that thou mayest stand in the day of trial . . . and
thy people save by his power."

Several factors prompted Penn to leave in 1684. Most pressing
was the need to put an official end to his ongoing feud with Lord
Baltimore over possession of the Lower Counties. From the moment
he arrived Penn had tried to reach an accord with his fellow proprietor but Baltimore refused to negotiate, insisting that the Lower
Counties were part of the original grant bequeathed to his father, the
second Lord Baltimore, Cecilius Calvert, by Charles I in 1632. There

were other differences between the two proprietors—such as the paying of rents, Indian hunting rights, and encouraging or discouraging settlers to live here or there—all of which showed that the border dispute was rapidly becoming a personal conflict between the two men.

In December 1683, Baltimore wrote to William Blathwayt, asking to be heard in person before the Lords of Council regarding his right to the Lower Counties. He hoped to be in England by the end of May 1684. He further told Blathwayt that "if my unkind neighbor William Penn or his agents are able to make out that there were Dutch seated at Delaware before my patent for Maryland was granted I will then make it plainly appear that such Dutch were usurpers." Penn had no choice but to return to England if he hoped to put an end to his troubles with Baltimore.

Also motivating Penn to return to England was the Privy Council's recent revocation of the Massachusetts Bay Company's charter. The Council also began investigating the other New England colonies. Always aware that many in the imperial bureaucracy had opposed his own grant and that the troubles with Baltimore and with New Yorkers over the Iroquois trade could be the excuses used to rescind his charter, Penn worried he might be next on the Council's list. He thus decided that his return to England was much more imperative. Penn had personal reasons for going home as well. He wanted to gather his whole family together around him in America, his sister Margaret and her husband and children, for they were all that were left from the House of Penn. Of course Guli and his own children must come, especially Guli, for he needed her presence and dignity at Pennsbury. Penn expected only a short stay; it stretched to fifteen years. Indeed, of the thirty-four years that remained to him, only two were spent in Pennsylvania.

Blessed with hardworking colonists, a prime environment, perfect timing, and peace with the Indians, despite political tensions and border disputes that frustrated and disillusioned Penn and divided his colonists, Pennsylvania prospered. Indeed, it was Pennsylvania's rapid economic development that mitigated many of the issues that could have easily ripped Penn's "holy experiment" apart at the seams. However, as long as colonists viewed Pennsylvania as a land of opportunity, in which they were able to improve themselves, political problems, at least for the moment, were nonissues in their daily lives. As Penn returned home he could take solace in the fact that his colony was economically secure; indeed, it was to date the most instantly successful colonial enterprise in the history of the English colonization of North America.

CHAPTER

9

"Another Face than I Left Them"

Penn arrived in England on October 6, 1684. He went immediately to his home for a "most precious reunion" with his wife and children. Although wanting to stay "forever," Penn knew he would not be able to enjoy his family "with a full heart" until "I have finished my business with Lord Baltimore and all his pretensions against me [the boundary dispute]. It vexes me as no other matter and I am not fit for anything nor good for anyone until I am rid of it." Penn worried that if he remained long at Worminghurst, Baltimore would seize such an opportunity to see the Privy Council and the Stuarts first, and alone. Penn feared Baltimore would convince both king and Council that Penn was the usurper and trespasser, while Baltimore was only protecting what was rightfully his from this Quaker "interloper." Penn believed his only chance of keeping the Lower Counties was for him and Baltimore to appear *together*, simultaneously before the Privy Council and the royal brothers, as Penn had convinced himself he was at a disadvantage in the dispute because of Baltimore's Catholicism. Penn was certain the nobleman would exploit this to its fullest with the Catholic James. Although on intimate terms with James, Penn worried that James's and Baltimore's "religious affinities and affection for another" would cost Penn his "Territories," for in Penn's mind, the Duke's "Catholicism affected" his every decision.

The Stuarts received Penn "very graciously, as did the Ministers very civilly." Although relieved by such a warm reception, Penn nonetheless detected that Charles, his ministers, and the Court's general atmosphere had "another face than I left them: sour and stern and resolved to hold their reins of power with a stiffer hand than heretofore, especially over those that were observed to be State

146

or Church dissenters." Apparently, little had changed while Penn was in North America; indeed he had returned to an England that was more Tory than ever.

Even before Penn left his colony he heard that Parliament was still dissolved and that Charles was "bearing down on every kind of Dissenter," and was especially vindictive "of those of the Whig strain. I suppose you'll hear [when Penn arrived in England] Lord Russell is beheaded and others as well. Essex cut his throat in the Tower." Even more distressing to Penn was the news received from his sister Margaret Lowther, that Algernon Sidney's execution "was only a few weeks away." Charles's purge and suppression of all opposition actually had begun before Penn had left England, but Penn was certain that in the twenty-two months he was away, the king would have "come to His senses," and restored Parliament. Instead, Penn came home to a virtual reign of terror, with Whig leaders proscribed daily by Charles and his ultra-Tory supporters. Causing Charles to go on such a rampage was the Whigs' attempt to prevent his brother from inheriting the throne through the Exclusion Act. Charles would never fight for his faith (throughout his reign he remained a "sympathetic" Catholic), but he was willing to risk all to defend his brother's rightful inheritance. Most important, Charles was able to rule without Parliament. The nation's economic prosperity assured him a handsome income from customs and excise taxes. French gold, in the amount of 500,000 pounds a year, also helped sustain Charles's autocracy.

Although disheartened by Charles's oppression, Penn nonetheless had little to fear personally from the king's purges. Indeed, Penn remained a Stuart favorite, as both Charles and his brother refused to see Baltimore or hear his charges against Penn without the Quaker in attendance. Penn was euphoric when he heard of the Stuarts' decree, for someone on his staff had left behind in Pennsylvania documents essential to his claim, the most important of which was the Duke of York's granting to Penn of the disputed area. Penn sent an urgent message to James Harrison to send the "York Papers" on the next ship leaving Pennsylvania. Until those records arrived, Penn believed his position untenable. As he told Harrison, "I am now here with my finger in my mouth. He [the servant who forgot the papers] would not have done me worse injury nor Baltimore a greater service if he had had the bribe of ten thousand [pounds]." Penn did not mention his problem to the Stuarts, and fortunately Charles's continued assault on the Whigs as well as his failing health made the resolution of a colonial border dispute

3,000 miles away, low on his list of priorities. Penn was relieved when notified that his appearance before the Privy Council and the king had been postponed indefinitely.

Unfortunately, Charles did not confine his wrath to just Whigs; over 1,400 Quakers were swept back into prison and many more suffered impoverishment from continuous fines. While Penn waited to present his case to the Privy Council, he once again took up the cause of liberty of conscience and of securing the release of Quakers imprisoned for practicing their faith. Interestingly, Penn did not appeal to the king for a general amnesty. Instead he engaged James to intercede with the king to secure the pardons. Penn's entreaties to James, rather than to the king, reflected his hope that once on the throne, the duke, himself a victim of religious bigotry, would be more empathetic to Dissenters such as the Quakers and would declare toleration for all English Christians, regardless of denomination.

Four months after Penn's arrival back in England, Charles II died of a stroke at the age of 56, on February 6, 1685. No doubt speeding up his demise was the treatment he received at the hands of his physicians, who "opportunely blooded and cupped him, and plied his head with red-hot frying pans." Although there had been moments of passion and violence, Charles's reign, like his personality, had been restful. On only one subject was Charles rabidly adamant: the sustaining of the Stuart dynasty. Yet, he had his doubts about a brother who, he predicted, "would never be able to hold it out for four years to an end." Charles's prophecy came true almost to the day.

Although many Englishmen feared for England's future with James's accession to the throne, William Penn was more sanguine, believing James would at last bring religious peace to England by granting religious toleration to all Christian denominations. Most important, Penn now had private access to a king with whom he could speak with even greater candor and directness than in the past, and he did so even before the coronation. As Penn wrote to Thomas Lloyd in Pennsylvania, James told his Quaker confidant that, "He declared he concealed himself to obey his brother, and that now he would be above-board; which we like the better on many accounts. I was with him and told him so. But, withal, hoped we should come in for a share. He smiled, and said he desired not that peaceable people [Dissenters such as the Quakers] should be disturbed for their religion." This was the assurance Penn wanted to hear from James, for he believed Dissenters could look to the new king with great hope for an ease of their sufferings.

Most important for Penn, James's accession to the throne marked the high point of Penn's political career, both as courtier and champion of religious toleration for all English Christians. Indeed, within two years after the start of James's reign, Penn not only assisted in the formulation of the long-awaited Declaration of Indulgence but also had become the king's right-hand man, a general spokesman for James's policies, and most impressive, as influential and powerful as the men through whom he once sought the king's favor. It was now Penn to whom countless individuals appealed or whom many cultivated the "pleasure of" in hopes of earning an audience with the king or a position within the government. Gratitude, sympathy, and expectations bound Penn to James. Penn the proprietor must also have been gratified and flattered by his new position, and probably a little blinded by hope as well.

Many of James's ministers held Penn in contempt, disapproving of him as an outsider because of his faith. Despite Tory attempts to vilify Penn in the king's eyes, the Quaker and the Catholic remained close throughout James's brief reign. Most important, Penn's intimacy with the king allowed him to use his position to promote religious toleration. What emerged in three short years was an alliance between king and Dissenter, ultimately creating a degree of liberty of conscience that transcended either one's expectations and beyond anything England had experienced.

Penn allied with James II for more reasons than just the attainment of religious toleration for Quakers and other Dissenters. Equally important to Penn was the security of his proprietary, which depended on royal grace. Such preference came to fruition in November 1685, when the Lords of Trade ruled in Penn's favor in his boundary dispute with Lord Baltimore. The Lords maintained that since the Lower Counties (eventually to become the colony of Delaware) were originally part of New York, when James agreed to cede that part of his land to Penn in 1682, it became part of Penn's proprietary. Moreover, the Lords upheld Penn's claim that no part of the Lower Counties could ever have been part of Maryland, for when Lord Baltimore received his charter, Europeans—Dutch, Swedes, and Finns—already occupied the area, and thus it was not uninhabited land, which Baltimore could claim as his.

Penn knew that James was increasingly sensitive about personal power and prerogative, especially over the colonies. Thus, in order to ensure the king's support, Penn cleverly worded his petitions by stressing that the dispute between him and Baltimore was over title to the land and was not an issue of power. Baltimore foolishly argued

William Penn at the height of his influence at the court of James II.

the opposite, asserting his "dominion" over the Lower Counties. Baltimore's verbiage irritated the touchy king. By acknowledging the king's "supremacy" (thus flattering James's ego) over the Lower Counties, Penn was assured of James's support; thus, Penn remained the legal proprietor of "the Territories." Although the area now was indisputably Penn's, his jurisdiction was limited to claiming rents only. The right to govern the Lower Counties remained on paper, a royal prerogative. Penn did not care about having such suzerainty; it was the income from quitrents he wanted from its settlers. Moreover, in effect, Penn did have political authority over the region, for its inhabitants sent representatives to the Pennsylvania Assembly, which Penn still tenuously controlled.

Penn knew how to play the courtesan game well, as his "treating" of Court power brokers with New World gifts reflected. Even before arriving back in England, Penn dispatched one of his closest aides, William Markham, with presents for both James and members of his inner circle. Markham presented James with an otter skin while Lords Halifax, North, Radnor, and Rochester received American timber—"fine pine planks"—delivered personally by William Markham to their homes. Penn hoped his "generosity" would be appreciated and "noticed" by James's councilors. It was. As Markham told Penn, the aristocrats had all become his "fast friends," whom he could count on for support in his dispute with Lord Baltimore. Although the east–west border between Pennsylvania and Maryland remained unresolved, Baltimore did not trouble Penn about it for the rest of James's reign. All further tension between the two proprietors became moot in 1689, when Maryland became a Crown colony.

Despite his triumph over Baltimore, James's display of interest in the colonies continued to worry Penn. Distressing Penn most was the possibility that James would extend his centralization schemes to Pennsylvania, incorporating that colony into a viceroyalty similar to that of the Dominion of New England. Penn knew retention of his colony would always depend on royal "favor," and loss of his province meant a great deal more than loss of power or wealth. Penn had championed for years liberty of conscience for all Dissenters. In the past, however, the best he could do was to intercede with the responsible government on behalf of the sufferers, but more often than not his activities proved futile. Now he had something more concrete to offer the religiously persecuted from all over Europe: Pennsylvania, a haven where all Christian inhabitants enjoyed liberty of conscience. To Penn, the preservation of his colony represented the most effective means of fighting persecution in England (and Europe).

Much to Penn's and other Dissenters' dismay, James initially continued his brother's policy of repressing nonconformists at home, while attempting to consolidate the North American colonies. Both posed problems for Penn. As a leading Dissenter, he was affected by James's reprisals. As the proprietor of Pennsylvania, the king's ambitions threatened to deprive him of his colony, which on paper briefly occurred in June 1686. Indeed, Penn agonized over such a prospect from the moment he arrived back in England. Causing him such anxiety were the increased reports circulated in England of his colonists' alleged unruly behavior and dissension, which could be used by the Crown as a pretext for stripping Penn of his province. As Penn urged James Harrison and other Pennsylvania Quaker leaders, "more friendly and private courses [must] be taken to set matters right in an infant province whose steps are numbered and watched; be not so noisy and open in your disaffections. If anything be amiss, let it be by more hidden and gentle ways remedied." Penn warned his colonial brethren that if they did not immediately cease their incessant "noise" (their constant bickering among themselves as well as their animosities toward him and each other), the result could be the revocation of Penn's charter and the conversion of Pennsylvania into a royal colony, a movement begun by Charles II and now a plan even more passionately embraced by his brother.

Indeed, no sooner did James become king than he ordered the incorporation of Massachusetts, Connecticut, New Hampshire, Rhode Island, New York, and New Jersey, into a consolidated supercolony called the Dominion of New England. For quite some time, James and even his brother had wanted to bring to heel the obstreperous Puritans of Massachusetts. James especially despised the sect, believing them responsible for his father's "murder." Modeled on a Spanish viceroyalty, the Dominion extended from the Delaware River to Canada. James dissolved the assemblies in all the respective colonies, administering the Dominion through a governor-general assisted by a lieutenant governor and an appointed council. The new arrangement dramatically and abruptly halted the momentum colonials had been gathering toward greater colonial autonomy defended by powerful elected assemblies dominated by wealthy elites. For governor-general, the king appointed Sir Edmund Andros, previously James's dictatorial governor of New York. Francis Nicholson became lieutenant governor, carrying out his duties in New York, while Andros and his Dominion council presided from Boston. Interestingly, allowing James to implement his consolidation agenda as well as to prorogue Parliament, and thus not have to depend on that body for income, was the substantial revenue pouring into the royal coffers from the American colonies. By the time of James's reign, the colonies had become cash cows, providing James with enough income to fund his more authoritarian regime.

Arbitrary and centralized, the Dominion regime shocked New Englanders. Reorganizing the courts and the militia, Puritan judges and officers were replaced with Anglican newcomers. On instructions from James, Andros destroyed Puritanism by defunding it, forbidding the Puritan clergy from drawing their salaries from town taxes. Moreover, the Dominion was far more expensive than the old charter governments, requiring unprecedented levels of taxation. A good portion of the increased costs of administration covered Andros's lavish salary of 1,200 pounds, an amount that exceeded the entire annual outlay to maintain the former Massachusetts government. Andros also brought along two companies of regular troops, whom he expected the colonists to provision. To raise revenue, Andros levied new taxes without an assembly and without even the support of a majority of his own council, composed largely of merchants. The Dominion regime also vigorously enforced the Navigation Acts by establishing in Boston a new vice-admiralty court, which operated without juries. The new court greatly depressed the port's business, seizing six merchant ships for violating the acts in the summer of 1686. With their incomes in contraction, New Englanders were hard pressed to pay Andros's increased fees and taxes.

Penn's fears that Pennsylvania would become part of another of James's combination schemes momentarily occurred in late May 1686, when James attempted with writs of *quo warranto*, to revoke Penn's charter for the purposes of consolidating Pennsylvania and the Lower Counties or Delaware into a new dominion. Penn knew that his dispute with Baltimore as well as his colonists' contentiousness portended trouble for his colony, for they provided the excuses both the king and the Lords of Trade and Plantations needed to rescind his charter. Most dismaying to Penn was the realization that although he and James agreed on the issue of religious toleration, their relationship was not so special (at least at this juncture) to exempt him from attacks on his charter.

In defense of his right to Pennsylvania as well as to the Lower Counties, Penn eloquently established a distinction between the terms "territory" and "dominion" or "government." By cleverly stressing that the issue was over land title not ownership, he was acknowledging the king's supremacy over *all* issues involving colonial governance while presenting himself as only the proprietor of its territory, whose *only* right or privilege was to claim its rents. Therefore, there was no need for either James or the Lords of Trade to act on the *quo warranto*, for Penn never declared, nor was it ever established in his charter, that he had "dominion" over Pennsylvania; such ultimate sovereignty always resided with the king. In short, Penn asserted that he was simply Pennsylvania's proprietor, not its *actual* governor, who remained the king. What political powers Penn assumed under his charter, he did so "at the king's pleasure," and that he never would attempt to usurp that authority. In concluding, Penn argued that if the Lords of Trade and Plantation issued a *quo warranto* against Pennsylvania, they would actually be issuing it against the king! Such a procedure would be an absurd action to take. Thanks to Penn's shrewd "redefining" of terms, the order against Pennsylvania, issued on May 30, 1686, was revoked a week later. Penn remained, for the moment, "True and Absolute Proprietor" of Pennsylvania.

Now that he was secure in his continued proprietorship, Penn felt confident he could move James toward religious toleration for all Dissenters, a cause both men believed in fervently, if for different reasons. Both were members of despised and persecuted minorities. This was the foundation for the personal bond between them as well as for their mutual interest in toleration. Yet, until circumstances forced them, neither man embraced unlimited toleration: James's goal was complete toleration for his Catholic brethren, but he initially opposed extending such status to Dissenters, whom he perceived as republicans and rebels. That James was particularly cool toward Quakers did not surprise Penn. After all, Penn had once embraced Whiggery, befriending and campaigning on behalf of the Whig-republican Algernon Sidney. However, Penn, like many other Dissenters, became Whigs primarily because of their desire for liberty of conscience, which the party advocated for all Protestant Englishmen. Nonetheless, at this juncture Penn found himself in a peculiar political position. If he continued his affiliation with the Whigs, even in the most peripheral way, he would alienate James. On the other hand, if he completely aligned himself with James and his autocracy and Catholicism, he could easily become persona non grata among powerful Whigs, and if James fell from power, Penn's personal fate as well as that of his colony would be in the hands of vengeful Whigs, who would certainly punish Penn for having supported such a despotic monarch.

Suffice it to say, Penn had to walk a most fine line, requiring his utmost skills as a courtier and politician. In the end, Penn concluded that despite all of James's personal flaws, he was king, and as such, still wielded significant power, especially in matters of religion. Penn believed that the best way he could move James to implement a toleration policy for all Dissenters was for him to personally disavow Whiggism and to convince James that it was his supposed Tory allies who were his real enemies. Penn now looked to the throne for the security of his own future as well that of his Quaker brethren.

Although wanting full toleration for all *Protestant* Dissenters, especially Quakers, until James's reign, Penn had opposed relieving Catholics from persecution. Indeed, before James's accession, Penn had castigated papists, warning fellow Englishmen that they could not be trusted and that the recusancy laws needed to be changed to distinguish Dissenters, particularly Quakers, from Catholics. No doubt there were awkward moments when James and Penn first met to discuss new strategies for toleration. Despite their previous antipathy for each other's faith, Penn and James realized that their respective sects needed each other's support if liberty of conscience for all English Christians was to become a reality. Prompting James to that conclusion was his failure to convince the Anglican Church and Tories of his good intentions.

Unable to Catholicize the realm with Tory support and Parliamentary consent, James invoked the Crown's suspending powers to subvert the law and hopefully unite Catholics and Dissenters in support of the monarchy. One of James's first moves in that direction was to grant some relief to Quakers, whom Penn assured James were no threat to his regime because they were pacifists. Thanks largely to Penn's persistent influence, in the spring of 1686, James pardoned and released from prison some 1,200 Quakers. As Laurence Hyde, the Earl of Rochester and lord high treasurer told Penn, the king commanded "not to have those poor people so troubled upon the account of their being Quakers only."

To pressure James further, Penn went "public" with his plea, publishing a tract entitled *A Persuasive Moderation to Dissenting Christians, in Prudence and Conscience: Humbly Submitted to the King and His Great Council*. In his essay, Penn exhorted James "to look upon past things as a King, and not as a man, without passion, and not suffer his own resentment or his ministers' flatteries, interests or revenges to carry him further than was good for his interest." Penn then reminded James that, "Moderation is a Christian duty, and it has ever been the prudent man's practice. For those governments that have it in their conduct have succeeded best in all ages." To drive home this last point, Penn hit James in a tender spot, using Holland and its "superlative clemency and industry" as his example of the great benefits to be derived from toleration.

Penn knew James felt threatened by the Netherlands, the residence of his devoted Protestant daughter Mary and her husband, the equally passionate anti-Catholic William of Orange. Not only were William and Mary militantly anti-Catholic, they were also next in line to the English throne. Penn hoped that by mentioning the

Netherlands, James, who was already anxious about his daughter's and son-in-law's growing popularity in England, would be more motivated to not only release Penn's brethren but to declare soon, religious toleration as well for all nonconformists. By doing so, James could "win over" to his side vital Dissenter approval and support for his government while weakening William and Mary's appeal among his subjects. For the moment, Penn could not have been more pleased with his king as well as with his own efforts, telling James Harrison that, "My *Persuasive* works much among all sorts and are much spoke of. The King shows himself merciful to all."

Although elated by the king's magnanimity, Penn, as well as James, knew that until a Catholic heir was a certainty, toleration without William and Mary's backing would be short-lived. Thus, in order to secure that support, in May 1686, James sent Penn to The Hague to find out how his daughter and her husband viewed his plan for clemency. James publicly claimed Penn was going to Holland to visit Quakers and to proselytize. However, the inner circles of both courts knew Penn was indeed James's official emissary, sent to Holland to present his king's program of toleration and hopefully extract approval for it from William and Mary. Despite attempts by William and Mary's Anglican advisers to vilify Penn in the monarchs' eyes, the Quaker persevered, determined to present his king's plea before them.

Although William was more receptive than his wife on the issue of toleration, especially for Catholics, the Prince nonetheless told Penn that it was essential to have Parliament's blessing on any toleration decree. Also, since Dissenters were clearly a minority, it would be political suicide for any English king at this moment to attempt to contravene the will of the monarchy's primary base of support, the Anglican Tories, who currently vigorously opposed toleration. Mary proved to be a more devoted Anglican than Penn reckoned, believing wholeheartedly that as the future protector of the established Church, it was her duty to protect her people's souls, which in her mind meant keeping England 100 percent Anglican. Mary thus opposed toleration of any stripe, certain it would open the door to religious and social instability.

Before returning to England, Penn, on James's instructions but much to his chagrin, was to try to persuade Mary's Anglican confessor, Bishop Gilbert Burnet, not only to endorse James's policies but to come back to England as well, where he would be rewarded for his loyalty. Apparently James hoped that if Burnet could be persuaded to embrace his agenda, then via Burnet, Mary would also be swayed. Penn knew from the outset that this latest of James's strategies to win support for his policies was doomed to failure, for Burnet despised not only Penn, but James as well. Indeed, Burnet was not about to defend the policies of a king who, just weeks before Penn's arrival, had a contract out for his assassination! Burnet told Mary of Penn's "conspiracy"; she then told her husband to ready the Dutch fleet, for Mary was convinced her father intended to invade the Netherlands with French support.

No sooner did Penn return to England than he found himself deeply involved in the formulation of James's first Declaration of Indulgence, promulgated in April 1687. It was a royal edict granting toleration not only to Catholics and Protestant non-Anglicans, but even to non-Christians, such as Jews, as well. All such individuals were now free from prosecution for breaches of the penal laws against religious dissent. The Declaration of Indulgence represented not only the zenith of Penn's power as a courtier, but more important, the triumph of almost three decades of a relentless crusade to secure for all Englishmen what he considered to be a fundamental civil liberty: freedom of conscience. To that end, Penn had courted arrests; lobbied members of Parliament; pressured Stuart advisers and placemen both in England and Ireland; and written countless tracts. Two dynamics thus far defined Penn's adult life: the quest for freedom of worship for his Quaker brethren in England and establishing a New World refuge for all the persecuted in England and Europe. Since the North American sanctuary was also to be a "holy experiment" in righteous living, Penn believed that what he was helping to guarantee in England would benefit Pennsylvania as well. In Penn's mind the colonies were inextricable parts of the same symbiotic imperial whole. In other words, what transpired in England would inevitably reach across the Atlantic and affect the colonies. As Penn told James Harrison soon after the Declaration, "If it goes well in England it cannot go ill in Pennsilvania. The time consumed in waiting has been well spent indeed."

As Penn understood from the beginning of his crusade for religious freedom, persecution was essentially political and if he wanted toleration he had to talk in political terms. Penn thus based his arguments, whether verbal or written, on his analysis of power and crafted them to support whoever seemed most likely to grant liberty of conscience. Although during the Restoration years Penn had maintained close ties with the Stuarts, he had always realized that Parliament, not the king, determined England's religious face. To that end Penn felt compelled to once again pick up his pen in defense of toleration as established by the Declaration of Indulgence and to promote the repeal of the penal laws and Test Act. Penn not only wrote several tracts and addresses thanking James, but traveled up and down England as well, preaching against further discrimination and persecution of Dissenters. Although as indefatigable an author and spokesman as ever, Penn's latest treatises and actions reflected the temperament and thinking of a more conservative, practical, and above all, politically savvy individual.

Although still believing liberty of conscience to be a fundamental civil right, Penn's new tracts were much less theoretical, not at all bellicose in tone, and most revealing, devoid of his earlier Whig-inspired notion of liberty of conscience as being part of a "contractual" relationship between the people and their government. In his 1660s and 1670s essays, Penn had proclaimed liberty of conscience to be part of an individual's inherent rights to life, liberty, and property, which citizens never forfeited even after they "contracted" for government. These "fundamental" liberties were safeguarded by a further right to legislate through elected representatives, and to participate in the execution of law, through trial by jury. Such thinking reflected Penn's belief at that time that Dissenters needed to look to Parliament, not the monarchy for their deliverance from persecution for nonconformity.

However, with James's accession to the throne in 1685 and his subsequent Declaration of Indulgence, Penn realized that his earlier contract theory in defense of liberty of conscience was antithetical to James's concept of monarchy. Nor would James welcome an attempt to bring it to his service, for he had made it clear that he believed firmly in two things: freedom for Roman Catholics, if not the establishment of Catholicism as the state religion, and his own divine rights.

Although uneasy with James's first obsession, Penn became reconciled to his king's second belief, seeing it as a potential plus for religious toleration. Perhaps most revealing, at this juncture in Penn's life he had come "full political circle"; that is, he had grown from a juvenile, petulant, apolitical religious zealot, to a politicized Whig republican, to finally what was his inherent, true conviction, a monarchist at heart, like his father. Thus, in his new tracts, Penn made only passing references to toleration as a fundamental civil right, focusing instead on equating toleration with national interest, both personal and collective. Penn now maintained that it would be in the "best interest" of all Englishmen to embrace James's Declaration of Indulgence, even for Catholics and non-Christians, for the "practical" (positive) benefits—economic, political, and social—to be derived far exceeded the negative. Although new in tone and unequivocal in loyalty and support of James, when outlining the specific or tangible advantages to be gained from toleration, Penn simply reiterated many of the themes of his earlier treatises, such as those he first introduced in *The Great Case for Liberty of Conscience* (1670).

Penn's support of James, especially his endorsement of toleration for Catholics, engendered severe criticism, not just from hard-line Anglicans but from other Protestant Dissenters as well, including Quakers. They accused Penn of being a hypocrite and opportunist. If not for personal aggrandizement, why would an individual endorse toleration for a group against whom he once railed, warning they could not be trusted. Penn refuted such attacks on his supposed change of mind toward Catholics, asserting in *A Persuasive to Moderation*, that toleration should be based on morality rather than on specific religious doctrine. Penn further explained that his earlier antipapist essays reflected his as well as other Englishmen's fears of a Catholic conspiracy. However, with a Catholic on the throne, there was no need to worry about another Popish Plot. Furthermore, if Dissenters, including Quakers, refused to extend toleration to Catholics, they would be guilty not only of bigotry, a most unrighteous sentiment, but "of a most terrible hypocrisy" as well, for all Englishmen's faiths were to be tolerated not just "select" creeds.

Penn's support of James and his policies proved to be particularly advantageous to Quakers. James rewarded Penn's loyalty with more offices and money, and shortly after the Declaration of Indulgence, James appointed Penn one of the commissioners of enquiry to look into the abuses of the penal laws by both informers and prosecutors prior to the Declaration. In this capacity Penn brought charges of perjury against informers and prosecutors who had falsely accused Dissenters with violating the penal laws. No doubt motivating Penn to perform his duty with exceptional diligence was the fact that Quakers were the sectarians most often charged and punished for their alleged violations of the penal laws. One cannot help but wonder if Penn accepted this position out of a desire to seek retribution from those individuals who for decades had so deceitfully and cruelly harassed such a peaceable people.

In September 1688, James also gave Penn the post of superintendent of hearth and excise taxes, a position, which in effect, made Penn responsible for supervising the collection of duties on two of the most lucrative commodities, tea and coffee. From the proceeds collected on such items, the king traditionally got one-fifth; Penn made sure James got one-third. Indeed, Penn later boasted that no one within the government had better proposals than he for augmenting James's income, for he wanted to see the king "well established," with a steady flow of revenue. Penn's desire to have James become as independent of Parliament as possible, in every capacity, did not bode well for Penn's future.

Although certainly no papist, it seemed the more Penn did for James, the more the king felt confident in Dissenter support for his plan to Catholicize England by fiat. Thus, to James, suspending the law was not enough; the government had to be Catholicized, the Church of England purged and disciplined, and the Tories who controlled the boroughs and shires replaced with Dissenters and Catholics. Papists received military commissions; the lord lieutenant of Ireland and the lord admiral of the fleet were Catholics, and if that was not enough flaunting of his Catholicism, James ordered a public welcome for the papal nuncio in 1687 and made his Jesuit confessor part of the Privy Council, which became a Roman Catholic cabal. In September 1688 James was at the height of his powers. Three months earlier his Catholic wife had borne him a son; the king rejoiced, but Protestant England was suddenly deprived of the single most powerful argument for obedience to the king: the expectation that the succession would pass to William and Mary. In England and in Holland, many reached the conclusion that revolution had to be risked, and on June 30, 1688, Whig and Tory magnates sent an urgent appeal to William of Orange to save their land from Catholic domination.

For Penn, a shift was occurring in high places, as one by one some of his most important allies found themselves out of power. Such was the fate of two of Penn's closest confidants, the Earl of Rochester and the Earl of Sunderland, both of whom had been edged out by James's Catholic cabal. Indeed, James's Jesuit confessor, a Father Petre, had emerged as "the first minister of state." Such status given to a Catholic priest further alienated and intensified the hatred of the nation's traditional ruling classes, to which men like Sunderland and Rochester belonged. Penn found himself in the middle of this increasing political tension, and despite a warning from his friend William Sewel that "by one and the greatest faction you are held in hatred," Penn believed he could do nothing but continue to support the king and hope to be looked upon favorably by the incoming ministers, some of whom were Dissenters.

In late September 1688 word arrived that William of Orange was preparing to sail for England as soon as conditions allowed. He was coming to restore English liberties and to preserve his wife's rightful inheritance, the English throne. At this juncture, Penn's thoughts and emotions must have been awash in confusion and insecurity; indeed he probably was close to a nervous breakdown. If William and his Whig and Tory allies succeeded in forcing James to relinquish his crown, what would be the fate of all those individuals such as Penn, who had served the deposed but despised king so faithfully? Penn had much to lose—at least his influence at Court and his reputation among his Quaker brethren, at worst his colony and maybe even his life. All depended on what mood vengeful Tories and Whigs would be in when they regained power after James's "abdication," which came sooner than Penn anticipated.

By December 1688, James found himself forsaken and alone. The queen and her infant son slipped away to France on December 10, 1688; early next morning James followed them, dropping the Great Seal of England into the Thames as he headed for the channel. Unfortunately, he was recognized and returned to London, where it had to be carefully arranged, with William's complicity, for James to be allowed to escape to France without being apprehended again.

In the vacuum between James's departure and before William and Mary's accession, uncertainty and fear gripped the nation. Vengeful Tory and Whig authorities went on a rampage, arresting anyone even suspected of having been affiliated with James's regime, and those who were considered to be part of his inner circle, were to be tried, imprisoned, or executed as "traitors." Within days of James's flight, the roundup began, and Penn was one of the first seized. Fortunately, many on the council of peers, which ruled England during this interregnum, and before whom Penn appeared, were his personal friends, so they released him on 5,000 pounds' bail, paid by two more of his supporters, Lords Wharton and Brandon. Although many Whigs regarded Penn and other Dissenters who supported James's policies as turncoats or traitors who should be punished, a good many within the party did not share this view. They contended that individuals like Penn, whom many knew had labored long and hard for universal toleration, simply believed that the best way to attain it was through the monarchy. This was Penn's defense before the council of peers, and since for the moment moderate Whigs were in control, Penn was exonerated. It appeared that many of Penn's Whig friends remembered that he was once "one of them," and thus were willing to look beyond his three-year intimate association with James Stuart and all his absolutist machinations and Catholic intrigue.

Ironically, the Tories were not so kindly disposed toward Penn, even though they had been the party of legitimacy and monarchy. However, these same Tories always had hated Dissenters like Penn, especially after he became one of James's closest advisers. Their jealousy and venom at the time knew no limits. Now with Penn's aegis gone, they could go after him with a vengeance. William Popple, Secretary of the Board of Trade and Plantations, informed Penn to what extent hard-line Tories fabricated stories about him, hoping to vilify him in the public and official view. "That you have been bred at St. Omer's in the Jesuit's College; that you have taken orders at Rome, and there obtained a dispensation to marry; and that you have since then frequently officiated as a priest in the celebration of the mass at Whitehall, St. James' and other places." "Tis fit I contradict them," Penn replied; yet, he believed his "constant zeal for an impartial liberty of conscience" impelled him to continue despite the personal risks involved. Penn was confident that when the last twenty years of his life were examined, his fellow Englishmen would realize both his loyalty and personal integrity. Such was not to be the case. Over the course of the next several months, Penn found himself arrested time and again and in greater danger than ever before in his life, all because of his devotion to the sanctity of liberty of conscience and of providing such a freedom for all his countrymen.

The Glorious Revolution of 1688 was anything but triumphant for William Penn. Indeed, destroyed was his dream of gaining full toleration for his fellow Dissenters. Also shattered was his direct influence at Court; Penn had reached the apex of his personal power during James's reign, and he never regained such preeminence. What favors or protection he needed in the future had to once again be acquired through intermediaries. When James was king, Penn did not have to play the supplicant game; he was one of the most powerful and influential men within the government, upon whose advice and counsel James depended for a variety of issues. Loss of such status not only devastated Penn personally but placed in constant jeopardy the security of his proprietorship.

For the rest of his life, Penn had to maintain a constant, wearying vigilance, trying to discern what new faction had the royal ear and whether that "interest" still believed him a traitor, and if so, would their demand for retribution result in the loss of his colony. Penn's life over the course of the next five years was anything but secure, calm, or sanguine. The king, in whom Penn had placed so much confidence and to whom he extended unequivocal loyalty, proved to be one of the most shortsighted, arrogant, and cowardly monarchs in English history, resulting in Penn's tribulations. Had James II's reign been as "uneventful" as his brother's, he not only would have died peacefully in his bed, but life for the majority of Englishmen, and certainly for William Penn, would have been much less anxious.

Not only did Penn constantly worry about losing his charter (which was taken from him in 1692 but returned in 1694) but also about what his brethren were doing 3,000 miles away from his purview. As will be seen, from the moment he left Pennsylvania, Penn's problems with his colonists proved at times to be more disturbing and emotionally debilitating than wondering whether he would be imprisoned for being a "Jacobite." Indeed, Penn became so exasperated by his colonists' behavior that there were moments when he welcomed the possibility of losing his charter. Yet, regardless of how bad conditions were in England or in Pennsylvania, or for him personally, Penn never wavered in his commitment to attain for all his countrymen their right to worship as they pleased. Penn believed that his never-ending struggle for liberty of conscience would become his most enduring legacy both in England and in the eventual United States. He was right.

10

"I Am a Man of Sorrows"

It is tempting to speculate on how Penn's life would have been different had he remained in America. In retrospect, it would have been the much wiser and safer decision, both for himself and for his colony's future. By staying in Pennsylvania, he would have been far removed, and thus insulated and unscathed, both personally and politically, from the fallout of one of the most disastrously brief monarchial reigns in English history. Indeed, Pennsylvania would have become for its founder the refuge from Old World persecution and distress he had envisioned providing for countless others. By returning to England and immersing himself in Restoration politics, albeit for the greater cause of religious toleration, it became a certainty Penn would suffer the consequences of associating with one of the most despised of English kings. Had he brought his family over, settled down in his "City of Brotherly Love," or on his estate at Pennsbury, he could have monitored his colony's progress firsthand, potentially heading off problems before they became insurmountable.

Although ultimately exonerated (thanks largely to his uncanny ability to maintain friends in high places, even under the new regime of William and Mary) a dark cloud of suspicion and recrimination hung over Penn for close to four years. Indeed, he was labeled a Jacobite (a continued supporter of James II and his return to the throne as England's *legitimate* king) and accused of conspiring with others of the same ilk with the goal of putting James back in power. As it was, he was arrested several times, his English and Irish estates were in jeopardy, and most devastating, he was stripped of his Pennsylvania proprietorship for two years. Penn spent five agonizing years proving his loyalty while attempting to erase the stigma of having been on intimate terms with James II.

In the process of such an ordeal, Penn lost touch with his province, and by the time he finally returned in 1699, it was too late; he faced a well-organized, hardened, and hostile antiproprietary combination of both Quakers and non-Quakers determined to wrest from him what little actual executive powers he had left after a fifteen-year absence. In effect, while in England, Penn had neglected his colony, causing its inhabitants to feel abandoned, and many to take advantage politically and economically at Penn's expense. Long before his return, indeed by the end of the 1680s, a disillusioned Penn realized that his "holy experiment" had degenerated into a place rife with recrimination, chronic friction, and struggle for position. It appeared that his Quaker brethren were either not as religiously motivated to be the model subjects he envisioned for his experiment or flat out disagreed with him about the nature of a Quaker society. They violated his land policy, ignored his demands for quitrent payments, and consistently challenged, if not outright refused to obey, his governing stipulations. Many colonists even disobeyed the laws passed by their own representatives as readily as they flouted Penn's.

Penn's conception of land ownership and the way in which he envisioned his colony developing demographically, best illustrate the tensions between idealistic plans and practical realities. Penn wanted a colony in which every individual had an opportunity to own land—enough to make the majority productive, profitable yeoman farmers. At the same time, he believed it essential to control the amount of land allocated to each adventurer, and where it was to be situated. He wanted to see Philadelphia surrounded by tidy, self-sustaining and contained agricultural villages. Expansion was to be closely regulated, for Penn did not want his colonists pushing into the interior, disturbing the native tribes or too far out of his governor's purview. Above all, Penn wanted to preserve the Quaker spirit of community, which he believed could only remain intact if land distribution was tightly monitored.

Penn knew that the allure of land ownership was the impetus for the majority of his brethren to have come to Pennsylvania. He wanted to ensure that all had equal access to enough land to fulfill their expectations, yet avoid at all costs what became the bane of all North American colonial enterprises: land speculation. As he declared in another of his promotional pamphlets, *A Further Account of Pennsylvania*, new settlers, "must not suffer to be drove back by them [land speculators] from comeing or [be driven] into other Provinces. . . . Let this not become like desolate Virginia and

Maryland." If the "holy experiment" was based on the needs of the community rather than the individual, then land speculation had to be prevented. If such self-aggrandizement occurred, it would lead to profiteering and acquisitiveness as it had in other colonies, thus shattering the communal bonds of the "holy experiment."

Much to Penn's chagrin, Quakers behaved no differently from other North American colonists in their desire for land anywhere it was available, ignoring all of Penn's mandates against wanton expansion. While in England, Penn heard all too frequently that dispersed farms and irregular holdings, not his planned pastoral communities, dotted Pennsylvania's landscape. More disturbing was land speculation. With settlers pouring in every few months, those with capital, such as weighty merchants, realized the opportunity for profit-making represented by land speculation. Despite appeals to their Quaker conscience, even threats, Penn could not stop the unstoppable, as land-starved and ambitious Quakers found themselves surrounded by the "temptation" of endless expanses of virgin land. As Penn was fast learning, his Quaker brethren could not resist the vast opportunities for individual accrual provided by his colony. Continued adherence to Old World creeds would gain only a modest existence in a land of plenty, while the development of more profane standards was better suited for conquering the wilderness. A subtle but pervasive and consistent transformation had begun to affect Pennsylvania Quakers, changes Penn could not have foreseen, let alone do anything about while he was immersed ever deeper in English politics.

Even more resented than Penn's land-settlement policy was the issue of quitrents. Recognizing that many settlers had spent their last money emigrating to Pennsylvania, Penn had promised a moratorium on the collection of quitrents "till after 1684." Before leaving for England, Penn instructed his commissioners to collect the rents for that year, requiring payment in coin no later than March 1685. No sooner was Penn back in England than those colonists who owed him rent reneged on their contracts signed in England before they left, promising to pay Penn when the time came to do so. Lacking hard money because they were still struggling to carve a life out of the wilderness, the vast majority of landowners viewed Penn's demands for payment as simply a means to increase his already sizable fortune. Little did colonists know how dependent Penn was on that income for his own survival. As he told his Council, "I have spent 3,000 pounds since I see London besides the bills I paid, that became due since I arrived." By the time of Penn's return to England, his out-of-pocket expenses for his colony were 6,000 pounds. Penn would not have been so anxious had his Irish holdings brought forth their usual income, but since "The Roman Catholics are mostly in power in Ireland, lands fallen there half." Penn thus looked to Pennsylvania for income, estimating collecting quitrents worth at least 500 pounds. Thus, causing Penn great distress was his colonists' "unmindful" attitude of his "exercises and expenses as to be so very slow in aiding me in my public services. What it has cost me I am ashamed to tell. I entreat thee to stir them up in it."

Unfortunately, no amount of exhorting or admonishing could get his colonists to pay Penn what they owed. Quitrents went uncollected month after month, year after year. An exasperated and angry Penn told James Harrison, that henceforth he would "sell the shirt off my back before I will trouble them any more. I shall keep the power and privileges I have left, to the pitch, and recover the rest as their misbehaviors shall forfeit them back into my hands. For I see I am to let them know, that, 'tis yet in my power to make them need me, as much as I do their supply [expected quitrent income]." Much to Penn's frustration, not even his obvious displays of rage could get his colonists to pay their "obligations." Down to the day of his death, Penn's income from his Pennsylvania quitrents never even remotely approximated what he had anticipated when he received his charter in 1682. Indeed, their attempted collection became an ongoing source of tension between Penn and his colonists; another point of divisiveness Penn might have been able to mitigate had he stayed in Pennsylvania.

Compounding Penn's colonial economic woes was his increasing indebtedness to the ubiquitous Philip Ford, whom, it seemed, had yet another piece of "paper" for Penn to sign every time he turned around. No sooner had Penn returned to England, still owing Ford close to 3,000 pounds, than Ford presented him with new account statements, showing that Penn's debt to him had increased to 4,293 pounds. Although surprised by the amount, Penn, as usual, was preoccupied with other, more "pressing" matters, and mindlessly endorsed the account without inspecting it. Only later did Penn discover that Ford billed him for about 1,000 pounds in compound interest on his debt and commissions on each transaction Ford made on Penn's behalf. There was no way Penn could pay with money what he allegedly owed Ford, and Ford had no way short of a lawsuit or public confrontation—which would have been highly distasteful in the Quaker community—of obtaining any satisfaction.

The only thing Penn could do to break the impasse, thus avoiding humiliating public exposure of his penury, was to renew his obligations to Ford, using as collateral more Pennsylvania land. Ford accepted Penn's offer, however on increasingly stringent terms. In June 1685, Penn signed a document giving Ford another 300,000 acres of Pennsylvania land, including his estate at Pennsbury if Penn did not pay him 5,000 pounds by March 1687. Ford then executed a double indemnity bond of 10,000 pounds to guarantee "performance of the covenants"; in other words, if Penn reneged on any part of their new arrangement, he would then owe Ford an additional 10,000 pounds on top of the original debt. Over the course of the next few years, Penn made periodic payments to his steward but never enough to stop the debt from escalating steadily.

A hopelessly idealistic land policy, resentment over quitrents, and the increasing belief among colonists that Penn's only concern was to extract as much personal wealth from Pennsylvania as possible, all combined to create a crisis of confidence in Penn's ability to provide effective leadership and governance from afar. By 1686, a powerful antiproprietary faction emerged, determined to wrest as much control of Pennsylvania from Penn as they could manage. The coalition that surfaced was especially potent because it not only included recent merchant emigrants but former members from Penn's inner circle as well, men who had felt abandoned by Penn when he returned to England. Allying with newly arrived gentry and merchants, these individuals formed a new Quaker elite— proud, aggressive, weighty, and most important, bent on gaining political control of the colony.

Although resolved to displace Penn, members of the new establishment were no "democrats," willing to give the "lesser sorts" a greater say in the political process in order to strengthen their position against Penn. Nor were they inclined to allow non-Quakers, even financially successful ones, a say in governance. The new Quaker grandees were just as elitist and exclusionary in their concept of government as the old privileged few; the only difference was that the new were decidedly antiproprietary. Their view was simple: Pennsylvania's future economic and political development was not to be determined by an absentee proprietor. Over the course of a decade the aggressive new Quaker establishment succeeded in reducing Penn's actual powers over his colony to the barest minimum; indeed by the time of his return in 1699, Penn's status as the "True and Absolute Proprietor" of his colony was in title only; long gone from reality was any substantive authority.

One of the main factors contributing to the increasing power struggle between Penn and the new Quaker faction was both sides' adoption of more conservative political and social views. This was especially true of Pennsylvania's Quaker leaders, who found themselves in positions of power rather than being persecuted as fanatical sectarians and excluded from all political participation. They now controlled their own society as the religious majority and thus were intent on conserving their political prominence and economic success. These social firebrands of the Old World turned conservative in the New, determined to not only keep what they had accomplished in Pennsylvania but to have the right to attain even more if they so desired. They were not about to allow a distant and aloof absentee landlord to prevent them from acquiring all that had been denied to them for decades because of their faith on the other side of the Atlantic. Moreover, in the late seventeenth-century colonial Englishmen's mind, there was a symbiotic relationship between individual, as well as communal, economic success and self-government.

As antiproprietary sentiment increased and the numbers of his faithful defenders dwindled, Penn's conviction grew that his colonists were incapable of self-government. Only a more coercive system would restore peace and stability. As Penn told Thomas Lloyd, "I hope some of those that once feared I had too much Power, will now see I have not enough, and that excess of Power does not the Mischief that Licentiousness does to a State." In another letter, Penn declared to James Harrison that, "It almost tempts me to deliver up [give Pennsylvania] to the King and let a mercenary governor have the taming of them. I hear my name is not really mentioned in public Acts of State, nor the King's [the slighting of both Penn's and James's sovereignty over the colony], which is of a dangerous consequence to the persons and things they have transacted, since they have no power but what is derived by me, as mine is from the King."

Penn's changed attitude was reflected in his stern directives to the Council and Assembly to pass—"rubber stamp"—proposals he felt essential. Penn believed even the judicial branch of government was under his control. Such a notion seems incongruent with a man who spent years championing the cause of an independent jury, free from coercion from the bench. Nonetheless, Penn instructed his officers to punish juries deciding against him in cases involving quitrents owed to him. It appears Penn increasingly came to view his own proprietary powers as more absolute than those he believed the king possessed in England.

It is tempting to conclude that an increasingly self-righteous and authoritarian Penn provoked his colonists into their factionalism and peevishness. No doubt Penn's constant paternalistic and moralistic admonishments irritated fellow saints, who resented such scolding from someone 3,000 miles away and thus out of touch with the realities of their lives in the wilderness. His heavy-handed letters were a poor substitute for his presence, which to sensitive colonists indicated that their welfare was not one of Penn's priorities. However, it was the colonists more than Penn who lost sight of their religious purpose, if they ever shared with Penn such a vision at all. Thus, compounding the power struggle between Penn and the colonial elite was the Quaker's perceived inherent, antiauthoritarian disposition, causing all who came into contact with them to label them as litigious, uncooperative, and thus ungovernable.

Despite their disclaimers, Quakers exhibited less respect for government authority and for its necessary place in human affairs than all other Englishmen, regardless of religious affiliation. No doubt prompting Quakers to adopt such an attitude was the fact that they were the most persecuted of all Dissenters in Restoration England, suffering at the hands of government more consistently and more intensively than any other religious group. As far as they were concerned, the reality of Restoration government blatantly and cruelly negated the notion that governing authority was the word of God himself and thus was to be obeyed when exercised justly and only passively and respectfully disobeyed on other occasions. To the Quakers, government was the enemy, creating and enforcing ungodly laws, twisting laws and acting arbitrarily, and depriving them of the goods and services that governments supposedly had been created to safeguard. Quakers had difficulty believing that governments that ruined them or left them to rot in jail were agents of divine authority.

That Quakers would oppose a government, created in conjunction with one of their own, is perplexing, especially when Penn pledged himself to justice in government and his laws were voted on by elected representatives, all of whom were Quakers. Two factors mitigated these considerations. First, and probably most frustrating to Penn, was the inability of his Pennsylvania brethren to separate his government from England's and to accept his authority as distinct from that of the Crown. Penn compounded this particular issue by sending his colonists mixed messages regarding their allegiance to him and England. As Penn became increasingly authoritarian, he went so far as to contend that his powers as feudal lord of both the land and the government of Pennsylvania were greater than those of the English king. Such audacious declarations demanding obeisance, caused many Pennsylvania Quakers to view Penn no differently than they viewed the distrusted (if not detested) English authorities, including the king. To many North American Friends, Penn became a disappointing, and thus an alienating, manifestation of governmental power; simply another suspect authority.

At the same time that Penn demanded such obedience, he reinforced Friends' naturally negative attitude toward English sovereignty by frequently counseling colonists to ignore and disobey the English government. He encouraged such defiance particularly whenever he thought Crown or Parliamentary acts threatened his proprietary security or when such measures, if implemented, denied him potential revenue. Of course, he made sure before sanctioning noncompliance that his people could do so with impunity. He also prompted his people to alter their legal codes to placate English authorities. However, as soon as London or colonial officials typically lost interest in colonial affairs after a few months' display of diligence, Penn allowed his colonists to resume business as usual.

Maintaining that the act of immigration represented the ultimate rejection of English authority, the final breaking away from an unredeemed society, Penn had hoped that once Quakers were safely tucked away in their own colony, free from the fear of harassment and persecution, they would no longer feel the need to be combative and litigious, a behavior Penn believed Quakers assumed in order to better protect or insulate themselves in an openly hostile environment. However, much to Penn's chagrin, transplanting did not effect any change in his brethren's attitude toward authority, even though government officials were of their own choice and religious persuasion. New World Quakers carried with them to Pennsylvania a residual antiauthoritarianism, and were just as inclined to "scurvy quarrels that break out to the disgrace of the Province"; and as irritatingly consonant with their Old World counterparts in questioning every manifestation of civil authority.

The second reason for Penn's troubles with his colonists was that neither he as a famous "Public Friend" nor the weighty counterparts he appointed to the Council could awe or intimidate the rest of the Quaker colonists into submission. Penn either naively or presumptuously believed that his exalted position within the Quaker community, as well as his title of "True and Absolute Proprietor" of his own colony, warranted his fellows' obedience. Quakers believed all individuals were equal in God's eyes and thus no one, not even the king, and certainly not one of their own, was to be respected any differently than the lowliest of society.

Compounding the lack of agreement on a common good, Quakers also extended their egalitarianism to government and laws. In the Quaker belief, all individuals possessed knowledge of the law of God through their inner light. A regenerate person thus decided for himself which human actions and statutes were in accord with divine principle, and if they were not, he could act on his own authority (with God mediating through each individual conscience), and reject them. Even those measures that were the genesis of a just Friend such as Penn were subject to such scrutiny. Thus, ironically, one of the major causes of the tension between Penn and his colonists was their shared faith; in particular a strict and literal adherence among Pennsylvania Quakers to one of their denomination's most fundamental tenets.

Leading the antiproprietary movement was Thomas Lloyd, the educated and influential Welshman in whom Penn had invested the most important offices of the colony before returning to England. Lloyd turned against Penn because of Lloyd's association via marriage, with powerful New York Quaker merchants, who dominated municipal and provincial government in that colony. Lloyd's relationship with these individuals added to his disillusionment with Penn and to his conclusion that Pennsylvania must have greater autonomy. Unlike many of his counterparts on the Council, Lloyd possessed no personal, deep-seated hostility toward Penn. Rather, he assumed the leadership of the antiproprietary faction because he believed proprietary policy simply failed to meet the colony's needs and was impossible to enforce in a community where coercion was disavowed.

Trapped in England, Penn did what he could to bring his wayward colonists in line. For two years after his return he pursued a policy of conciliation and appeals to conscience in an attempt to end the disunity and insubordination. As he told James Harrison in 1685, "Assure my servants that if they be of aid to me and Diligent, I will be kind to them in land and other things at my returne." Promises and inducements from afar had little effect, and when he realized that his pleas for cooperation and harmony were falling on deaf ears, Penn thundered to Thomas Lloyd to "Lett them know how much they are in my power and I not in theirs." Penn then threatened both Council and Assembly members that if they did not end their recalcitrance he would refuse confirmation of all laws passed since his departure, thus voiding them. If that failed to bring them in line, then he would reclaim all land sold to First Purchasers but not yet patented. "And that will be Supply enough to me and myn," Penn concluded grimly.

Penn knew verbal threats alone would not force compliance; something more tangible had to be implemented. Penn decided to attempt a reorganization of the executive arm of government, creating a commission of five deputies, with the power to enact, annul, or vary laws "as if I myself were there present." Penn naturally retained for himself ultimate sovereignty, his "peculiar royalties and advantages." Penn's instructions to the new commissioners were straightforward: end the factionalism and enforce proprietary policy. If the councilors failed to accomplish his mandates, he threatened to dissolve the frame of government without further ado. Penn made it clear to the new executives that his patience had worn thin and that he would tolerate no further encroachments "upon the powers and privileges remaining yet in me."

Unfortunately, Penn's choice of commissioners doomed his plan to failure. Responsible for Penn's new agenda were five strong-willed and incompatible individuals, whose combination compounded rather than cured the colony's problems. Nicholas More, James Claypoole, Thomas Lloyd, John Eckley, and Robert Turner were either despised by the colonists (More and Claypoole) or distrusted by each other (More and Turner doubted Lloyd's "motives"), and most damaging to Penn, only Robert Turner had any particular "affection" for his "employer."

Penn's choice of such a contentious group of individuals reflected his inherent inability to judge people. To put it succinctly, none of these men *liked* Penn personally except Robert Turner, and even he at times resented, as a fellow Quaker, Penn's noblesse oblige attitude. Most alienating to the others was Penn's increasingly self-righteous and authoritarian behavior. Despite the reality of their relationship, Penn nonetheless exhorted his commissioners to "draw not several ways, have no cabals apart, nor reserves for another, [but] treat with a mutual simplicity, and entire confidence in one another." Penn's pleas for harmony revealed how little he understood—or was willing to admit—the extent of the strife in his "holy experiment."

Compounding Penn's troubles with his commissioners as well as with other antiproprietary Quakers, was the emergence of a coalition of lesser men—both Quaker and non-Quaker, of small merchants and artisan shopkeepers from Philadelphia and small farmers from the outlying counties—who opposed the colony's domination by the Philadelphia Quaker merchants and their country allies. This challenge from below posed a more immediate and greater threat to the Quaker elite's hegemony than did their battle of wills with a distant Penn. The Assembly became the second rank's forum for their grievances, thus creating a power struggle between the increasingly entrenched and conservative Quaker-elite dominated Council and the more democratically inclined "men on the make" Assembly.

One year after implementing his new executive scheme, Penn realized it was a mistake. By 1688 Penn could count on the loyalty of only two councilors, the ever-faithful Robert Turner and William Markham. It was Turner who reported to Penn that there were "two Governors and two Councils: One within and another without." Griffith Jones, another Penn loyalist, informed Penn that Thomas Lloyd and his followers not only blatantly denied Penn's authority, but also appeared to be "raysing a force to Rebell." In one last-ditch effort at reconciliation, Penn offered the Deputy Governorship to Thomas Lloyd, telling the Welshman he could "do all as fully as I myself can do." In other words, Lloyd would have full power to run the colony on a daily basis as he saw fit, as long as his agenda did not conflict with or jeopardize Penn's proprietary interests and "vision." Such a caveat caused Lloyd to reject Penn's offer, for he was unwilling to execute Penn's long-disdained policies. Lloyd's rebuff forced an exasperated Penn into initiating his most extreme, unpopular, and eventually disastrous measure to date to bring his colonists in line: replacing the five Commissioners of State in the summer of 1688 with a former Cromwellian official and transplanted Massachusetts Puritan, Captain John Blackwell, making him Deputy Governor.

Penn's choice of a Puritan to manage his colony did not sit well with the majority of his brethren. Still fresh in the Quaker historical memory was the brutal treatment meted out by Puritans, especially in New World colonies such as Massachusetts, where Puritan magistrates routinely ordered Friends to be beaten, mutilated, or even executed. Such an affiliation did not bother Penn, who was more impressed by Blackwell's proven abilities in affairs of government, finance, and administration. As he told Thomas Lloyd, "Since no Friend would undertake the Governor's place, I took one that was not, and a stranger, that he might be impartial and more reverenced. He is in England and Ireland [where he served as Cromwell's Treasurer at War and Receiver General in the 1650s] of great repute for ability and integrity and virtue." Penn instructed Blackwell to "inspect the animosities, to use some expedient; And if no way else, authoritatively to end them, at least suppress them. Rule the meek meekly, and those that will not be ruled, rule with authority." Blackwell also was to collect quitrents and other proprietary revenues without further delay, and most important, to silence the Assembly's demand for greater powers. In Penn's mind, here was an individual, stern but devout, who hopefully would be able to establish obedience, harmony, and stability in his colony.

Blackwell's personality and authoritarian concepts of government only compounded an already-difficult situation. He was old, irascible, and a martinet, who chastised the Council, especially the Lloydians, for their multitude of "offences, Crimes, and misdemeanors" against Penn personally and for their "high usurpation of arbitrary and illegal powers" of proprietary privileges. He was there to rule in Penn's name, which, Blackwell interpreted as having carte blanche to clean house, to drive out of power the insubordinate troublemakers, such as Thomas Lloyd, whom Blackwell wanted impeached. Blackwell believed he had been sent to Pennsylvania to reclaim Penn's status as "True and Absolute Proprietor." To a former Cromwellian soldier, such an objective implied he was there to rule with an iron hand until all was set right, which meant the end of factionalism and disobedience.

Although the Lloydians had indeed usurped power as Blackwell claimed, the Puritan's uncompromising approach only strengthened his opponents' determination to bring Blackwell down before he eclipsed their power, destroying them altogether. The Council's Quaker elite received welcome support in their struggle with Blackwell from a surprising quarter—the "commoner"-dominated Assembly—who, for the moment, buried old differences with the Lloydians to join in the fight against Penn's hated Puritan deputy. Assembly Quakers perceived Blackwell to be a greater threat to their well-being than Lloyd and his followers ever presented.

In their pursuit to drive Blackwell from power, the antiproprietors ironically found Penn to be their greatest ally. Although deeply disturbed by Lloyd and his followers' attempts to usurp his authority, as a Quaker he could not allow his brethren to be "trod under" by Blackwell. For reasons unknown, other than perhaps a latent realization that he was being too overbearing with his brethren in choosing Blackwell and vesting him with broad-sweeping powers, Penn promised the Commissioners of State that if Blackwell proved too heavy-handed, he would be "layd aside." Penn's proviso stripped Blackwell of any real power, putting him at the mercy of the very men Penn charged him with disciplining. At this juncture,

Penn was desperate to return to his colony but could not. He was a "marked man" in England, constantly dodging authorities trying to arrest him for being a Jacobite and Catholic. Under the circumstances, a return to Pennsylvania was impossible; the future held only the gravest uncertainties.

Penn believed the best he could do about the crisis in Pennsylvania was to temporize. Fortunately for Penn, Blackwell had had enough of the Quakers (and the weather and mosquitoes, of which he also complained), and wanted to be released from his charge as Deputy Governor; Penn readily obliged. Penn then offered Blackwell the post of Receiver General, with full power to collect quitrents and manage proprietary revenues, which the Puritan declined, deciding to retire instead to the Puritan haven of Massachusetts.

By removing Blackwell, Penn returned to power the very alliance of merchants and landowners who were relentless in their pursuit to undermine his authority at every opportunity. In many ways, Penn had sold Blackwell out. He had ordered the Puritan to "rule with authority those that will not be ruled." However, when push came to shove, Penn cratered to his colonists' cries of tyranny and prejudice and dismissed Blackwell. Penn had handed Blackwell what turned out to be an irreparable situation and expected him to fix it, but in the end, Penn, who apparently had been paying only lip-service to Blackwell's actual authority all along, retreated. Penn's gamble with Blackwell proved disastrous, convincing even more Quakers that Penn was an unsympathetic and estranged proprietor.

In January 1690 the Council reclaimed its executive authority and chose Thomas Lloyd as its president. Lloyd, by virtue of his position as Keeper of the Seal, received the Council's approval to sit ex officio as a member of any county court. The power of the antiproprietarians had never been so encompassing. The Council acted in both executive and legislative capacities and controlled the courts as well. Thomas Lloyd exercised far-reaching powers in every sphere of government. All pro-Penn officeholders were removed and replaced with "Lloydians." As Robert Turner reported to Penn, authority was being given to those who "oppose any power to thyself, concluding [that] while the government [is] in themselves the power [is] gone from thee."

For the next several years Penn could do nothing but watch his proprietary authority continue to dissolve, for he had to deal with a much more personally urgent problem: clearing his name of alleged treason. Until vindicated of such a charge, not only was he forced to divert his attention away from his colony but he became a fugitive as well, hiding from those who wanted him arrested for high treason. Penn became a wanted man; indeed, according to some, "a very dangerous fellow," for his support of James II's autocracy, as well as for his alleged plotting with others to help James reclaim the throne. Penn thus spent the years 1689 to 1693 not only "on the run" for several months at a time, but trying as well to dissociate himself from Jacobitism while proving his loyalty to the new monarchy.

Unfortunately, in the process of trying to defend himself, his Pennsylvania charter was taken from him in 1692 as punishment. Interestingly, many of his Quaker friends as well as those he still had at Whitehall, such as the Earl of Rochester, counseled Penn to go to his colony until he could clear his name of Jacobitism and treason. Penn, however, refused to be treated like an exile, believing it better to stay in England even if he had to go "underground" for months at time, and face the charges against him head on. Penn believed that if he fled to Pennsylvania, such a move would confirm his guilt in the eyes of his enemies.

Although Penn still had friends on the inside at Whitehall, he knew that it would take more than mere connections to clear his name. He had to prove his loyalty to William and Mary. Until Penn could prove otherwise, the new king considered him one of his greatest enemies. Penn ultimately provided William III with many "services," which indeed contributed to his eventual vindication. Ironically, war with France, declared soon after William ascended the throne, provided the occasion for Penn to prove his loyalty. As Admiral Penn faithfully served Oliver Cromwell's Protectorate during wartime, all the while remaining secretly loyal to the Stuarts, his son would do likewise for another ruler of questionable legitimacy.

William and his councilors knew of Penn's close relationship with James, and realized it would be hard for Penn to automatically give the new monarchs his devotion and affection without feeling guilty for having sworn such allegiance to James, particularly since the deposed king was still alive. To many soon-to-become Jacobites, including Penn, the "Glorious Revolution," depicted creatively by the country's landed oligarchy as a spontaneous uprising by a united English people, was fundamentally a coup spearheaded by a foreign army and navy. Like so many of his countrymen at the time of William and Mary's accession, Penn was loath to commit himself to a new regime that sat so tenuously in London. Moreover, since Penn believed in the divine right of monarchs as a basic tenet of allegiance, then it was psychologically impossible for him to accept William and Mary as unadulterated rulers, despite Parliament's sanctification. Indeed, it was clear to Penn that the sovereignty of Parliament had triumphed. As one tactless member of that body reminded William, "We have made you king."

That Penn remained sentimentally loyal to the House of Stuart, as had his father, there is no doubt; that he was actively involved in conspiracies to bring James back to power is questionable: the evidence surrounding such activities implicating Penn as a willing or knowledgeable participant is circumstantial at best. Penn was without question a "sentimental" Jacobite remaining emotionally attached for the rest of his life to the sovereign he had served faithfully as a friend and confidant. In return for such fealty, James had rewarded Penn with liberty of conscience for all Englishmen. When William ascended the throne, there was no guarantee Quakers would continue to have such a freedom.

If Penn was innocent of collaborating with more fanatical Jacobites to overthrow William and Mary, then what prompted such accusations against him? The fact that James landed in Ireland in March 1689 and found ready sanctuary on Penn's estates at Kinsale did not bode well for Penn, for James intended to use Ireland as a base for retaking the English throne. Penn also allegedly aided the French war effort by shipping wheat to France from his Irish estates, thus violating the wartime embargo on French trade.

James's Irish invasion was part of what became a larger conflict between England and France known as the War of the League of Augsburg (1689–1697) or King William's War in the North American colonies. If Penn was involved in any way with James's Irish invasion, the king's defeat at the Battle of the Boyne and then his hasty return to France dashed Penn's hopes for a restoration of the Stuart monarchy. Nonetheless, as soon as the news of William's victory reached England, the roundup of suspected Jacobites began, and Penn naturally topped the list. As soon as Penn learned of the warrant for his arrest he wrote to Charles Talbot, the Earl of Shrewsbury, and the Whig secretary of state for the Northern Department. Penn knew Shrewsbury would appeal to the king on his behalf, for Whigs such as Shrewsbury wanted to cultivate Dissenter support, bringing back to the party key nonconformist groups such as the Quakers. What better way to draw Quakers back to the Whig fold, to lure them away from Catholic James and his Declaration of Indulgence, than to help in the vindication of one of the sect's most influential leaders. Thus, Shrewsbury was willing to help Penn prove his innocence to the Crown by presenting to William the Quaker's letter, swearing his noninvolvement in James's Irish invasion. Thanks to Shrewsbury's intercession, Penn remained free on bail, and when brought to trial he was acquitted for lack of evidence.

Over the course of the next two years Penn was arrested several more times on charges of treason. However, only once did he spend more than a month in jail (September to October 1689), and when finally brought to trial, he was acquitted each time for lack of evidence. After his final arrest and subsequent release in the spring of 1691, Penn disappeared for sixteen months. From June 1691 to November 1692 only his wife, a few Quaker intimates, the earl of Oxford, Robert Harley, and the earl of Rochester, Laurence Hyde, knew his whereabouts. Penn decided to go into seclusion until he could find a way to permanently clear his name.

In Penn's mind, there was no alternative to a temporary hiding; he had been caught up in a tidal wave set in motion by revolution. Realizing that the majority of his Quaker brethren would not understand his reasons for going "underground," Penn sent a letter to London Friends, dated May 30, 1691, to explain his actions. "My privacy is not because men have sworn truly, but falsely, against me; for wicked men have laid in wait for me, and false witnesses have laid to my charge things that I knew not." Penn then assured his comrades that he was not abandoning them but merely absenting himself for a while from their "love so my own afflictions will do thee no harm. Feel me near you, my dear and beloved brethren, and leave me not."

No sooner did Penn disappear than the Jacobite rumor mill went into high gear, accusing Penn of having gone to France to consort with James to plan another assault on the British Isles. According to the boatman who was to carry Penn and other Jacobite conspirators (most notably Richard Graham, Lord Preston, and the bishop of Ely), across the Channel, the Quaker indeed was headed for France. However, "the secret sailing" was "publist all over town that there was not a boy but knew it." Penn wisely decided not to go, but Preston and the others proceeded. Unfortunately for Penn, Lord Preston was caught in transit possessing letters written by Penn to James, in which Penn allegedly offered his services to the king in order to help the deposed monarch reclaim his throne.

It is very possible that Penn was headed for France to see James; indeed he might even have been seeking James's approval for asylum. Whether Penn intended to help James with plans for another invasion remains uncertain. Through his intermediary, Henry Sidney, Viscount Romney, Penn denied any knowledge of plans for another invasion by James and his French supporters. "I say, and that truly, I know of no invasions or insurrections, men, money, or arms, for them, or nay juncto to consult for advice or correspondency in order to it. Nor have I met with those named as the members of the conspiracy, or prepared any measures with them."

Most important, Penn assured Romney that the letters in Preston's possession were of "a purely, innocent personal nature in which I only inquired of his Majesty's well being and told him of events of practical and common usage and knowledge; in none of my correspondence did I or the king know of any plot, nor mention even the slightest word of such a possible occurrence in the future." Penn then freely admitted that he was going to France "to see the man and King for whom I still have great affection, and who feels much the same toward me."

Sidney believed Penn, especially after personally examining the letters. Sidney then reported to William and Mary that he believed Penn to be a "true and faithful servant to your Majesties, and that if he knew anything that was prejudicial to you or your government, he would readily discover it. He knew of no plot, nor did he believe there was any in Europe, and he was of opinion that King James knew the bottom of this plot as little as other people. He said he knew you have a great many enemies, who he was sure were more convertible against you and more dangerous than the Jacobites." Most important, Sidney believed all those who had accused Penn of conspiracy were "imposters and liars. If he had any intention of plotting against your Majesties, he would have gone abroad for that purpose long since."

Sidney, along with the earls of Ranelagh (Richard Jones) and Rochester, convinced the king that Penn should no longer be considered a threat to the government; not only had he proven his loyalty, but all previous accusations of treason were the handiwork "of evil, designing men." In November 1693, Secretary of State Sir John Trenchard delivered the news Penn had been waiting over four years to hear: that he was a free man, and as long he lived "quietly and prudently," he would remain "unmolested."

Relieved that he was no longer considered an outlaw, Penn now had to find a way to get his colony back. King William, however, proved more anxious than any of his predecessors to recover royal control of the empire, for he was interested only in the Netherlands's defense and France's defeat. To that end, all other considerations and resources were to be subordinated, especially England's North American colonies. In the new king's view, the colonies had been allowed excessive independence, which proved detrimental to the empire's interests. It was time for the colonies to fall into line, to pay and obey, and to support their sovereign's foreign policy objectives. England's empire was to be transformed into a weapon with which to destroy Louis XIV.

William was a fanatic, a soldier who cared nothing for politics and who had little interest in his fellow men except as diplomatic and political instruments or as infantry for his armies. Short, asthmatic, and stooped, with bad teeth and a beaked nose, the prince gave himself and those around him unsparingly to his single obsession—France's destruction. Any colonies refusing to comply with royal prerogatives and initiatives risked losing their charters, thus becoming Crown possessions. Such was about to happen to Pennsylvania.

As Penn had repeatedly warned his colonists, if they did not end their rancor and factionalism "the king will come down upon thee with a most unforgiving and oppressive hand. I am a man of sorrows and you augment my griefs, not because you don't love me, but because you don't love one another. Cannot you bear a little for the good of the whole at least till it please God to bring me among you?" Unfortunately, few if any Pennsylvania Friends heeded his pleas. Especially determined to disregard any of Penn's requests, no matter how urgent, plaintive, or judicious, was the ever-obstreperous Thomas Lloyd, whose control of the Council and thus of the colony was complete. No sooner did war break out with France, than Lloyd made it clear both to his neighbors—Maryland, New York, and Virginia—and to the king that Pennsylvania would not contribute to the colonial defense. When New York's royal governor Benjamin Fletcher ordered Pennsylvania to contribute to the colonies' overall protection, the Pennsylvania Assembly pleaded poverty. Lloyd's defiance did not sit well with Whitehall and the "warrior king."

The Quakers' "animositys [sic] and divisions" led the Privy Council to conclude that Penn no longer could control his colony, and thus the Crown should take it over immediately. William III was more than willing to revoke Penn's charter after hearing from his advisers of the Quakers' alleged "consorting with enemy." According to colonial informants, the Quakers not only refused to support their neighbors, but were traitors as well. They continued trading with the French along their frontier and allowed French vessels "to avail of their ports." As Maryland's new royal governor Lionel Copley further told the Lords of Trade and Plantations, the Quakers, "because of their pernicious principles [pacifism], have allowed the enemy a place to retreat to and communicate from." The alleged treason proved to be the final straw; in October 1692 Pennsylvania officially became a royal colony. The Crown appointed Captain Benjamin Fletcher governor of Pennsylvania. When Penn heard the news of Fletcher's commission, he was reported to have shouted, "Thomas Lloyd brought this to pass. Oh Sorrowful Conclusion of eight or nine years of Government."

In retrospect, Penn should not have taken the loss of his proprietary so personally or so despondently. Whitehall's desire to bring the American colonies under tighter royal control predated the 1690s. The granting of Penn's charter in 1681 was an anomaly, for it contradicted colonial policy, which since the 1670s intended to tie the overseas possessions more firmly and profitably to England. However, when it came to Pennsylvania, the Stuarts looked the other way, allowing Penn to govern his colony as he saw fit. Laws seldom reached the Privy Council for approval as his charter mandated; the Navigation Acts were violated with impunity; and most recently, Whitehall's instructions for the colony to participate in a military preparedness program by contributing money and men to the intercolonial defense system was politely but definitively rebuffed. The Quaker government knew that the English government's ability to enforce its overseas agenda was limited. Imperial decrees, like those of an absentee proprietor, were rarely heeded when the means of coercion were barely visible. However, the global war with France changed this situation markedly, at least on paper for a year.

No sooner did Fletcher arrive in Philadelphia in April 1693 than he encountered the same disdain and resistance his predecessor Blackwell had experienced some three years before. In the Quaker's view, Fletcher was no different than Blackwell, even though the king had appointed the former, not Penn. Moreover, Fletcher was an Anglican (almost as bad as being a Puritan in Quaker eyes) and a military man like Blackwell, reasons enough for immediate resentment among Quakers. Even though Fletcher carried the full weight of royal authority, with broad-sweeping powers to rule Pennsylvania in the manner he believed necessary, the Quakers were not intimidated and were determined to rid themselves of him as they had Blackwell.

Despite urgings from Penn to "tread softly and with caution," Fletcher went full steam ahead with his agenda of forcing royal prerogatives upon the Quakers. The Quakers, masters by now at oppositional politics, resisted his every attempt to govern them. They used the same tactics so effective in bringing Blackwell down: refuse to acknowledge the governor's authority until threatened with treason; have irregular and poorly attended Council meetings; push for greater powers for the Assembly; curtail the number of appointed officials; and word legislative measures so ambiguously that their meaning would be open to endless questioning and debate. As such wiles worked against Blackwell, they proved equally serviceable against Fletcher, who, in less than a year's time, requested to be "removed" as Pennsylvania's governor. The way was now open for Penn to reclaim his colony.

Aided by his Court connections as well as by the favor of King William, Penn obtained the restoration of his charter in 1694. Penn had earned the king's pleasure a year earlier by doing two things immediately after William exonerated him from charges of treason. First, despite being a Quaker, Penn helped the war effort by supplying victuals to the army and naval stores to the navy from his Irish estates. Second, following the recapture of Kinsale after the Battle of the Boyne, Penn allowed the port's renovation, converting it into a base for ships to sail out to meet French privateers, who had been harrassing English supply ships with impunity. By the end of 1694, Kinsale not only had become an important supply depot for the English navy but a fully operational naval construction yard as well. When asked by his brethren about such "un-Quakerly" behavior, Penn's rationale was that war and poverty were "looking men in the face," and thus he felt morally obligated to help "fight starvation."

The restoration of Penn's charter was not entirely inconsistent with the new imperial agenda, for English officials recognized that the Quakers could not be forced into compliance, regardless of whom they invested with the authority. Consequently, they concluded that Quaker cooperation might better be obtained through a bargain with Penn. Penn's rights of government would be restored on condition that he henceforth ensured his colonists' full participation with future requests for men and money for colonial defense and that he return to Pennsylvania and personally take charge of *his* colony. Penn initially agreed to both stipulations, and almost immediately his word was put to the test, when his agent, William Salway was informed by Fletcher that further defense of the middle colonies required Pennsylvania supplying eighty men or their equivalent in money. An anxious Penn wrote to his colonists warning them to obey the English government's demands, which they did, sending

Fletcher 250 pounds, the Quakers' computed cost for outfitting eighty militiamen for a year. Apparently, the abrogation of Penn's charter scared provincial leaders into the realization that their fate was interwoven with the shifting sands of English politics and that they badly needed William Penn's influence at Whitehall.

As far as the Crown's second mandate was concerned, Penn assured royal advisers that he *intended*, "with all convenient speed to repair thither and take care of the government and provide for the safety and surety thereof." However, at this juncture Penn had no intention whatsoever of returning "with all convenient speed" to his colony. When pressed by royal councilors, he constantly demurred, declaring there was no need for him to go at this time because he had a trusted deputy governor in the person of William Markham, whom he appointed after Fletcher's departure. Moreover, Penn claimed his presence was unnecessary; his colonists did not need him physically there because they had behaved themselves so admirably in the aftermath of the Glorious Revolution! Penn's assertion was fantastic, if not delusional; his colonists virtually ran amok politically and socially because of his absence. Nonetheless, the demand was dropped and Penn remained in England for another five years before returning to Pennsylvania.

No doubt one of the reasons why Penn wanted to remain in England at this time was because of his beloved Guli's prolonged illness. For six months Guli left her bed only occasionally, suffering from a high fever and a constant cough, probably caused initially by influenza then made worse by the onset of pneumonia. As Penn wrote to several Friends, "My wife is yet weakly; but I am not without hopes of her recovery, who is of the best of wives and women." Despite all his prayers and daily vigilance, Penn's wife and faithful companion of twenty-one years was dying. On February 23, 1694, about three hours before she died, she asked all her family to leave her room except her husband. Guli and William Penn spent their last hours alone together, "in which we took our last leave, saying all that was fit upon that solemn occasion." She sank rapidly as family members returned to the room to watch her take her last breaths in her husband's arms, her head on his chest. "She was an excelling person, both as child, wife, mother, mistress, friend and neighbor," was Penn's eulogy for her.

Guli Springett Penn was laid to rest in the Jordans burial ground, alongside four of the five children she had lost. In all she bore 11, but as of her passing, only three remained alive, 19-year-old Springett, who had become his father's constant companion of late;

16-year-old Letitia; and 14-year-old William, Jr. After burying his wife, Penn gathered up the rest of his family and returned to his Worminghurst estate in Sussex. The great, rambling manor house seemed quite empty now, but Penn eventually filled it with the warmth and affection of a second wife and another set of children. Until then, Penn pondered not only his life without his beloved Guli but the fate of his colony as well, to which he wanted to return but believed he could not, certain he still had much to do in England, both personally and publicly for himself as well as for his Quaker brethren.

For Penn the years after his return to England were filled with disappointment, frustration, anger, and despair; most of which was caused by his colonists' factionalism, contentiousness, and disobedience. All Penn wanted was for his people to financially meet their obligations to him (pay their quitrents), and obey the simple mandates of a most magnanimous Frame of Government. However, what Penn failed to realize was that his prolonged absence only exacerbated his colonists' impression that he was a distant and insensitive proprietor, whose personal concern for their problems and interests was perfunctory at best but truly nonexistent. Many believed all Penn cared about was how he could benefit financially from their efforts.

Perhaps most disheartening to Penn was his realization that his colony's unceasing turmoil brought about by his brethrens' disputatious behavior, was confirmation that they were incapable of fulfilling his expectations of Pennsylvania as a "holy experiment" in righteous, Christian living, in which Quakers were the vanguard. Indeed, Penn founded Pennsylvania as a Quaker preserve, a corner of the earth where Friends might pursue their millennium unhindered. The utopian hopes raised by Penn led to spreading disillusionment, for they elevated hopes to a level that could never be fulfilled.

Instead, Quakers, in their constant battling with one another and in their disregard for Penn's authority, proved they were no different than all the others who had come to the New World; indeed, they became just as land-hungry; just as aggressive in their pursuit of personal wealth; and just as covetous of political power and autonomy as the rest of their North American counterparts. The crucial point is that almost all of the elements distinguishing Quaker existence in Pennsylvania from that of life in England promoted rather than restrained the atomistic reality of Quaker life in the North American wilderness. The bountiful amount of cheap, available land tended to break down the sense of Quaker corporateness, which in England was a hallmark of Quaker society. The fact that Quakers were no longer a politically proscribed minority forbidden all form of political participation, led to often cutthroat and nasty competition for position and place as individuals sought to attain what had been beyond their remotest hopes in England. Finally, and ironically, because Pennsylvania Quakers were free from persecution, which in England had bonded them in mutual defense, they now no longer needed such unity and self-protection. Persecution had provided coalescence in the English Quaker community; it provided an important annealing force in their daily lives. In Pennsylvania, the absence of oppression intensified division in the Quaker community.

These same problems affected other American colonies but not as intensely as they did in Pennsylvania. The Quaker as a social type was in many ways an exaggerated manifestation of his Puritan counterpart. The vastness of the North American wilderness, which meant the availability of cheap, if not free, land impacted all settlers, regardless of their residence. Penn's system of land management only exacerbated the situation in Pennsylvania. Pennsylvania Quakers, however, differed from New England Puritans in their failure in the crucial first decade to develop a means of getting rid of their more troublesome peers. Although John Wintrop witnessed the splintering of the Massachusetts Bay Colony into "a hundred earnest little Utopias," he and the other Puritan leaders maintained a degree of stability absent in Pennsylvania, by either ostracizing dissidents or allowing them to leave the fold. By contrast, neither the Pennsylvania Quakers nor Penn would have ever sanctioned the casting out of even one, let alone several, of their fellows, no matter how disruptive they became. That simply was not the Quaker way. Indeed, such individuals were not even allowed to leave of their own volition. Regardless of the tension and rancor caused by such rebels, Quakers believed *all* the faithful must be kept tightly within their loving community, for only within the confines of Quaker fellowship could such a "problem" be resolved.

William Penn's primary goal in life was to defend and spread the message of spiritual Christianity and to make its power operative in societies beset by sin. Despite his strenuous efforts, God's kingdom did not come to Pennsylvania, and his will was not done "on earth as it is in heaven." By the time he got back his charter, he realized that he would pass from the kingdom of "this world" to the kingdom of God only when he passed through the portals of death.

11

"God Is God, and Good"

As Penn recovered from the emotional pain of Guli's loss, he turned to those closest to him, especially his eldest son Springett. Father and son became constant companions, for Penn believed it was time to begin grooming Springett not only as the Penn family's immediate heir but as the future proprietor of Pennsylvania as well. Increasingly weary of maintaining that responsibility and status, Penn was confident that if he familiarized his son now with the colony's affairs, in a few more years Springett would be ready to take over the proprietorship. Springett, however, was not as physically robust or as emotionally resilient as his father; in fact, he was much frailer than Penn in both categories. Nonetheless, Penn, like his own father, had grand plans for his son's future. He saw him at Court, wielding great influence within the Quaker movement, and of course, as the future "True and Absolute Proprietor" of Pennsylvania.

Penn also found great solace among Friends, as he once again immersed himself in a variety of activities to promote the Quaker faith. Penn's presence had been sorely missed, and when he returned his brethren welcomed him with great fanfare. In the autumn of 1694, accompanied by Springett, Penn made a pilgrimage through western England, speaking not only to throngs of Friends but to the curious as well, who turned out to see one of England's most famous sectarian leaders and public figures. In many ways, Penn's sojourn was a journey of vindication, for he wanted his countrymen to know that he had neither betrayed his faith nor his country.

It was at Bristol, the largest gathering of his trip, that Penn first set eyes on his second wife, the never-married, 23-year-old Hannah Callowhill, only child of weighty linen merchant, Thomas Callowhill. At the time of their first encounter, Penn was 49, balding, and possessed of the girth that became part of his stereotypical physical image. Hannah was shy, and not easily convinced by either her parents, other Friends, or by the torrent of love letters Penn sent her soon after their first few meetings, that Penn was the love of her life. Indeed, many accused Penn of wanting to marry her for her money. No doubt Hannah represented a very "suitable" prospect in that capacity, especially given Penn's comparative penury at the time because of the decline in income from his Irish estates and his inability to collect Pennsylvania quitrents. Penn also needed some- one to take care of him and his children, which Guli had done so well for twenty years. Moreover, Penn longed for female compan- ionship. Throughout his life, his most meaningful, intimate, and lasting relationships had been only with women, with whom he could apparently relate without feeling insecure or threatened.

Despite Hannah's initial reticence, Penn relentlessly pursued her, refusing to let either their age or personality differences prevent their marriage. His epistles literally gushed with loving tenderness, reflecting a genuinely smitten Penn. "My hand is the messenger of my heart, that most entirely loves thee, . . . And if thou Couldst believe, in how little a house I could live with thee, at least thou wouldst think I placed my happiness more in thee than any outward conveniences." One of the issues that caused a strain in their rela- tionship was her family's desire to have them live in Bristol rather than at Penn's country estate in Worminghurst. Penn capitulated, agreeing to move to Bristol, even though he liked "a citty less than a little house." Penn then rather disingenuously declared that he embraced "lowness as well as plainness" in life.

It took Penn two years to convince Hannah that he was as right for her as she was for him; that he would be "known, received, and esteemed by thee [Hannah]." Penn simply wore Hannah down, refusing to accept any answer but "yes" to his relentless pleadings. Hannah not only ultimately succumbed, but much to Penn's joy and relief, revealed a reciprocal affection and love, declaring that there was "nothing in this world so desirable or pleasant to me . . . than to love and honor thee and be united unto thee." On March 5, 1696, 51-year-old William Penn married 25-year-old Hannah Callowhill, who over the course of their twenty-one years together, proved to be a fruitful and successful mother. Of Guli's eleven children, only two survived to maturity; Hannah bore Penn seven, of whom five reached adulthood.

No sooner did Hannah enter the Penn household than she sup- ported her husband through one of his most difficult losses, the death of his beloved son Springett, in whom Penn had placed so many of his future plans. After several months of trying to fight off the ravages of pneumonia, on April 10, 1696, Springett Penn died. Penn was as devastated by Springett's death as he had been by Guli's passing. Among the seventeenth-century English aristocracy, nothing was more crushing than to lose the eldest, most promising son; in Penn's case, the heir and namesake of one of England's most legendary families. Although declaring in his eulogy to Springett that "God is God, and good," Penn must have felt, at least, momentarily forsaken by a God to whom he had been most faithful.

In his grief-stricken state Penn questioned divine will for the first time in his life, wondering how a loving, forgiving God could inflict such emotional pain on such an obedient servant, one who had devoted his entire life to His glory and the bringing about of His kingdom on earth. What sin had he committed that engendered such retribution, taking from him in just two years' time both his beloved wife and his son? After several days of such introspection, Penn concluded that God simply wanted Springett with Him, finding reassurance in his son's deathbed acceptance of his condition that "All is mercy, dear father; everything is mercy, and know there is a God, a great and mighty God, who is the rewarder of the righteous." Springett's affirmation restored Penn's faith. With his soul replenished, Penn could peacefully lay his son to rest next to his mother in the Jordans burial ground in Sussex.

Penn perhaps found his greatest consolation, not from friends and relatives, but from an act of Parliament supported by the king and for which Penn had pressed for two decades: the passage of the 1696 Affirmation Act, allowing individuals to affirm rather than swear to an oath, an action the Quaker faith forbade. Although pleased by the 1689 Toleration Act, which allowed freedom of worship to all English Protestants, including Quakers, the law still required the swearing of oaths for a host of other civil activities. Then until the passage of the Affirmation Act, Quakers remained circumscribed citizens; they could not vote, hold office, testify in court, or carry on a variety of legal and business transactions. Penn believed it was time for the removal of all legal impediments denying dissenters their fundamental English liberties. King William and his Whig allies agreed, pushing through Parliament in 1696 the Affirmation Act, allowing *all* dissenters to affirm rather than swear an oath.

Much to King William's delight, and perhaps as planned, the Affirmation Act effectively extinguished any further Quaker support for the Jacobite cause. Even a once-devoted Penn now found it difficult to remain loyal to the House of Stuart. Penn at last accepted that although he could still "love" his former king and friend, political reality made it impossible for him to continue to hope for James's return, or for any form of a Stuart restoration. The Affirmation Act enabled Penn and his brethren to transfer their allegiance to William in good conscience, and marked a crucial transformation in the process by which Penn and his fellow Quakers reconciled to the regime established by the Glorious Revolution.

Penn also found relief from his personal anguish in writing, producing two of his more seminal treatises at this time. At this juncture in his life as a Quaker, Penn believed it was time to inscribe for posterity the origin and character of the Quaker movement, which for Penn represented the quintessence of England's seventeenth-century spiritual awakening. Penn hoped to provide his readers not only with an exegesis of the Quaker faith, which he believed to be the apogee of Christianity, but also a recounting of *The Rise and Progress of the People Called Quakers*, which was published in 1694. Penn also wrote the tract to "honor the memory of that worthy servant of God, George Fox," whom Penn believed was "the greatest and most blessed apostle of our day."

To Penn, Quakerism's essence was "primitive Christianity revived"—that is, the final evolution toward the restoration of the purity of the early, elemental Christian church. Beginning with Adam and Eve in Paradise, Penn traced God's successive Biblical dispensations, proclaiming that as Adam's Fall ended mankind's purity, so dissolved the pristine nature of primitive Christianity when the Church succumbed to a "long night of apostasy." By the Renaissance the Church had become an institution of wealth, worldly dominion, and most egregious, it had married itself to the state, thus losing its spiritual purpose in the process. There was a brief ray of hope, however, with the coming of the Reformation.

While initially believing the Reformation portended great promise for resurrecting the simplicity and purity of the early church, Penn now contended that "The Reformation took some steps forward, in doctrine, worship, and practice, but these quickly failed as wickedness soon flowed over the reformers just as it had flowed over those they reformed from, so that by their fruits, you could not tell one from the other." Once the Reformation became formalized and institutionalized as in the establishment of the Church of England, its ministers "not only whipped some out of the temple, [Catholics] but others were whipped into it [forced conformity by all other

English Protestants]. They appeared to be more dogmatic than faithful, more political than pious, and that gave birth to other people"—the more radical sects such as the Anabaptists, the English Puritans, and other mystical Seekers. However, in Penn's view each of these groups was somehow flawed and imperfect; each fell short of the Truth because "what they had been seeking outwardly, with much pain and cost, could only be found inwardly": the Holy Spirit, the divine Light, "within all and is God's gift to all—it is the grace that leads to life and salvation."

For Penn, the radical Christian, religion was experience, not an intellectual process. Thus, his faith was to express itself in his daily living. Indeed, for all Quakers, their religion irradiated every act of their lives, however mundane or trivial. Quakerism was as much a way of life as a set of religious beliefs, and it definitely was not a system of thought or a set of dogmas. Penn and other Quaker leaders preferred to use the word "testimonies"—the practical, outward manifestations of the Inner Light in everyday lives—when outlining the Quaker creed. These testimonies reflected more rules of secular behavior rather than any sort of orthodox religious tenets.

Penn enumerated twelve of these testimonies—I. Fellowship With and Loving One Another; II. Loving Enemies; III. Speaking Truthfully; IV. Not Fighting But Suffering; V. Refusal to Pay Tithes; VI. Being Deferential to No One; VII. Use of Plain Language; VIII. Taciturnity; IX. Toasting; X. Their Way of Marriage; XI. Births; and XII. Burials. Although some of the Friends' testimonies or practices caused others to "give [Quakers] a rough and disagreeable appearance," Penn assured his readers that adherence to these principles did not threaten the nation's established political and religious order. Indeed, as far as loyalty to king and country was concerned, Quakers, despite "having felt the weight and severity of civil penalties," had "given the government the least trouble of any."

According to Penn, Quaker beliefs were simply "the fruits of an inward sense" God had instilled in them. Life before preaching, deeds before words, example before precept, these became the essential dynamics of the Quaker faith. Penn closed his exegesis by calling on his countrymen to embrace Quakers "as an example to you and to the nations around you. They are like a shining city built on a hill, so that by their light you may come to the Light of Jesus Christ, the Light of the World. That can be your Light and Life, too, if you would only turn from your many evil ways, receive it, and obey it." The essence of the Quaker story and faith has changed little since Penn's publication of *The Rise and Progress of the People Called Quakers*.

Penn's other signal treatise produced during his "time of sorrows" was his early blueprint for the creation of a European body dedicated to the pursuit of harmony among nations. In many ways, Penn's *Essay Towards the Present and Future Peace of Europe*, echoed similar proposals put forth by such notables as Dante, Erasmus, Henry IV of France, and Hugo Grotius, all of whom, along with Penn, presented templates for world peace. Perhaps most interesting, Penn's outline to prevent future wars and promote peaceful coexistence among the European powers came closest to the various mandates promulgated two and a half centuries later, first by Woodrow Wilson in his Fourteen Points, calling for the establishment of a League of Nations; and seventeen years later by Franklin Delano Roosevelt in his Dumbarton Oaks agenda for the chartering of a United Nations, currently in existence. Of the over forty tracts Penn produced in his lifetime, none has been reprinted more often, especially in the twentieth century, than his *Essay Towards the Present and Future Peace of Europe*.

Penn's *Essay* reflected more Penn's thoughts about political statecraft than a faith-inspired pacifism. Penn stressed, above all, the economic advantages of peace, telling his readers, whom he hoped would be the European princes currently engaged in war, that when there is peace, "our possessions are preserved: we are in no danger of invasions, our trade is free and safe, and we rise and lie down without anxiety. The rich bring out their hoards and employ the poor manufactors [artisans]. Buildings and divers projects for profit and pleasure go on. It excites industry, which brings wealth, as that gives the means of charity and hospitality." War, on the other hand, "seizes all these comforts at once. The rich draw in their stock, the poor turn soldiers or thieves, or starve; no industry, no building, no manufactury [sic], little hospitality or charity; but what the peace gave the war devours."

Equally impressive were Penn's proposed realistic solutions to the practical difficulties that might be expected to arise in such an international assembly. For example, his ingenious answer to the vexing question of precedence was to make "the room round, and have divers doors to come in and out at to prevent exceptions." Penn also stipulated that all voting be done by the secret ballot, which he believed to be "a shrewd stratagem and an experimented remedy against corruption," especially bribery. Even those "so easily cozened by money" would be able "to lie heartily to them that gave it rather than wrong their country, when they know their lie cannot be detected." All complaints were to be submitted in writing and made accessible to all members, and as far as the enactment of policy or response to a crisis was concerned, all such action required "three-quarters of the whole"; out of the ninety voting members Penn recommended that sixty-seven votes be necessary to pass any initiative. Finally, and most farsighted and unprecedented, was Penn's advocacy of disarmament as the ultimate security for international peace. Penn hoped all potential conflicts could be resolved by dialog and peaceful negotiations at his round table; his treatise remains an extraordinary attempt to find a way out of the dead end of war.

Meanwhile, no sooner had Penn reacquired his colony than he got word of what he and other Quakers believed unthinkable in their community: religious schism. The individual responsible for such a conflagration was one of Penn's former continental traveling companions, George Keith, who came to North America in 1685 as Surveyor General of East New Jersey. Penn and other Quaker leaders regarded Keith as one of their most talented and learned itinerant preachers, but a "man on the edge" as well. Indeed, Keith's mood swings were intense in the extreme, ranging from days of complete withdrawal into "deep melancholia" to sudden passionate outbursts. His behavior suggested an unstable if not deeply disturbed personality. Penn had experienced Keith's erratic "habits" during their sojourns on the European continent, but at the time he had dismissed them as simply Keith's proselytizing zeal. That Penn and other Quaker leaders allowed Keith to come to North America proved disastrous, especially for Penn.

Soon after his arrival Keith began upsetting what had been a mostly tranquil spiritual environment for Pennsylvania Quakers by calling for the imposition of doctrinal discipline on his allegedly wayward brethren. By Keith's reckoning life in the North American wilderness was eroding Quaker beliefs as Friends increasingly became more acquisitive and materialistic, forsaking their faith in the process. Keith believed it was time to establish an orderly set of tenets, to systematize primitive Quaker beliefs for his marginally educated, ingenuous New World brothers and sisters to prevent their further "dissipation." Thus, in various Meetings he proposed such unorthodox, if not "blasphemous," ideas as requiring confessions of faith from those seeking entry into the Society; the election of elders and deacons, and the silencing of persons "raw and unseasoned" or unsure of their convincement.

Finally, and most disturbing to traditional Quakers, was Keith's call for greater adherence to the Bible as the main source for spiritual growth rather than on the "inner light." It appeared that Keith was attempting to redefine Quakerism along more literal and fundamentalist lines. In effect, Keith believed it was time to make Quakerism more like "mainstream" Protestantism by establishing a body of rules, to bring greater order and discipline to meetings, ending the spiritual spontaneity that had been the hallmark of Quaker worship since the faith's inception. Keith was convinced that if his proposals were not adopted soon, the centrifugal forces of such a free-wheeling, undisciplined creed would most surely destroy what remained of Penn's "holy experiment."

Not surprisingly, the majority of Pennsylvania Quakers opposed Keith's heavy-handed proposals. From their faith's beginning, Quakers had identified the strength and appeal of their movement with freedom from dogma, the equality of all members, no clergy, and a nonliteral interpretation of the Bible. To many Pennsylvania Quakers, George Keith seemed intent on stripping their faith of its most hallowed beliefs.

It was only a matter of time before the Keithian controversy spilled into the already combustible political arena. Thomas Lloyd and his followers quickly sensed the political threat Keith posed to them, and thus moved to silence him by charging him with heresy at their Yearly Meeting. This accusation only further polarized the Quaker community, for now not only political dissent wracked Pennsylvania, but so did religious division, as Quakers determined who was orthodox and who was heretical. By condemning Keith as an apostate, the Lloydians believed their brethren would quickly line up behind them to avoid the further splintering of their cherished fellowship. The Lloydians also believed that if Keith were a "true" Quaker, he would accept the Yearly Meeting's judgment against him and stop his sacrilege. The Quaker establishment reckoned wrong; Keith became even more resolved to spread his new Quaker "gospel" with a vengeance.

Keith quickly grasped that the main reason the Lloydians wanted him silenced was more political than religious, for he directly threatened their control of the apparatus of church and state. He thus accused them of "usurping their authority over the people, show[ing] themselves too high and imperious both in Friends Meetings and worldly courts." At this juncture in the crisis, Keith knew that his redemption depended on Penn's intervention—thus the calculated use of language such as "usurping their authority," which Keith hoped would further pique Penn's attention and support, especially if Penn viewed him as a "protector" of proprietary rights against the Lloydian "encroachers." In blatant contravention of Penn's Frame of Government, the Lloydians next attempted to silence Keith and his supporters by summoning an arbitrary and dubious English law that deprived an individual freedom of speech, press, and conscience, liberties Penn had long championed and which had been denied Quakers in England.

The bitter dispute reached its climax in early 1693, only three months after the Lloydian-dominated 1692 Yearly Meeting had formally excommunicated Keith for "his Vile abuses." On the night before Sunday worship, Keithians sneaked into the building and hastily put together a gallery from which their leader could preach the next morning. The orthodox majority had long controlled the permanent gallery at the opposite end of the room and had denied the "apostate" access to it. The next morning as Quakers entered the meetinghouse for weekly devotions, they found themselves literally in the middle of verbal warfare between two groups of impassioned brethren. Harangues and accusations flew across the room, creating a din that hurt the ears. However, the verbal exchanges paled in comparison to the shocking physical outburst that followed. Brandishing axes that seemed to appear from nowhere, each group sought to destroy the other's gallery. Posts, railings, stairs, seats—crumbled before the angry blows of the two factions.

Although distressed by the news of the Philadelphia meetinghouse's destruction, Penn saw the controversy as political and "philosophical" rather than religious in nature, believing that the faith's simplicity and purity made it immune to such division and rancor, especially over "doctrinal" issues. Penn initially chalked up Keith's ranting to the Scotsman's university education, believing Keith had "come under too much scholasticism." As he told Robert Turner soon after Keith began preaching his "new" Quakerism, "Let not the learning of this world be used to defend that which the spirit of God hath brought forth." Penn was certain that once Keith started with his "metaphysics" Quakers would turn a deaf ear because what Keith was saying went far beyond the ken of the overwhelming majority. However, once both sides politicized the schism, its impact on Penn and his colony dramatically changed.

The Lloydians' heavy-handed treatment of Keith was for Penn further confirmation that their power had become so great that they now dictated religious as well as political policy in direct violation of his Frame of Government. Penn thus took Keith's side during the controversy, blaming Lloyd and his followers for pushing it to extremes, which Penn concluded they did intentionally to further entrench their own political power at his expense. Moreover, Keith, despite causing such divisiveness in Penn's "holy experiment," supported Penn's proprietary rights. No doubt Keith hoped that his endorsement of Penn's authority as proprietor would win Penn's favor, and thus Penn's approval for his religious agenda.

Perhaps most revealing and most disheartening to Penn, the Lloydians seemed to have become so "corrupted" by power that they wantonly pursued their adversaries much the same way they had been hounded and harassed in England only a few decades before. George Keith returned to England in 1694, hoping to win vindication before the London Yearly Meeting. He appeared before that body, presented his case, and after many days of deliberation the London meeting decided that it was in the best interest of the Quaker community to support the Pennsylvania decision; Keith remained persona non grata. A few years later, a bitter, disillusioned, and still disturbed George Keith joined the Church of England.

No sooner did Keith return to England, thus ending the first serious doctrinal crisis within the Quaker faith, than Penn found himself once again at political loggerheads with his provincial brethren. This time, however, opposition came from a new quarter, the increasingly aggressive and politicized Assembly. Leading the Assembly's demand for greater power was David Lloyd, Thomas Lloyd's brother. Thomas died in 1694, momentarily relieving Penn of a powerful adversary. Moreover, Penn had hoped that Thomas's passing would cause the demise of the Lloydian oligarchy, for without their ringleader, the other members of the antiproprietary cabal would not be as "inspired" to oppose him at every turn. Penn's wishes were realized to a certain degree; the old elite's domination of the Council was indeed adversely affected. However, rising out of the Council's declension because of Thomas Lloyd's death, was the Assembly's determination to gain political control of the colony. Penn now faced an even larger, more resolute body wanting to wrest from him what little power remained in his hands.

Unlike his brother, who believed control of the Council was the most effective means of curtailing both Penn's and the Crown's authority, David Lloyd sought instead to transfer power to the Assembly, which he and his followers believed was far less susceptible to proprietary or royal domination. David Lloyd reckoned provincial autonomy could best be accomplished by shifting the center of political gravity from the Council to the Assembly. The "new" Lloydians thus pressured Lieutenant Governor William Markham for a "new modelling" of government, a new charter guaranteeing the Assembly virtual control of Pennsylvania's political affairs. At a minimum they demanded that the Assembly have the right to initiate legislation, to determine when it met and when it disbanded, to regulate its own affairs, and to meet in closed session.

The David Lloyd–led Assembly timed its demand for a new frame of government perfectly. To reacquire his charter Penn had agreed to the Crown's stipulation that Pennsylvania would contribute to the colonial defense system. David Lloyd and his followers were aware of the mandate, and used it as leverage to extract from Markham a compromise or concession: that if the Assembly passed a military preparedness appropriations bill, Markham in turn would allow "discussion" of constitutional revision. The Assembly, however, did not trust Markham to keep his word; after all he was the last of a dying breed, a true Penn loyalist. The Assembly cleverly passed two bills for Markham's approval. The first authorized funds for both the war effort and his salary; the second, entitled "An Act of Settlement," called for the promulgation of a completely new frame of government, which would vest the Assembly with broad-sweeping political power. Fully aware of the Assembly's machinations, Markham protested such high-handedness, telling Lloyd and his followers that, "You have delivered mee [sic] these two bills together as if you want to tack them soe [sic] the one to the other, as that I must pass both or neither." Markham refused to succumb to such "blackmail." When the Assembly failed to pass the money bill separately, Markham prorogued the legislature for a year.

Surprisingly, the Lloydians were not outraged by Markham's dismissal of the Assembly. They knew that not only was time on their side, but so ultimately would be Penn. They were aware that Penn's charter hung precariously in the balance—that if he did not deliver what he promised relative to colonial defense, the Crown would be more than happy to revoke his charter. Penn's fears that he could lose his colony again if the Assembly failed to cooperate were well grounded. New York Governor Benjamin Fletcher, who had no great fondness for the Quakers, and whom Friends were to assist in defense, complained to Whitehall that Pennsylvanians sent "neither one man nor one penny" for his use. Fletcher further told the Lords of Trade that it was clear Pennsylvania Quakers had "as little regard for the interest of their proprietor Mr. Penn as they have for His Majesty's service."

At this juncture in the impasse, Markham believed neither he nor Penn had any alternative but to acquiesce to the Assembly's demand for a new frame of government. He believed such a concession essential if Penn hoped to keep his charter, for it had been restored on the condition his colony would comply with imperial mandates.

Markham thus yielded in 1696 to the bargain he had rejected a year earlier: if the Assembly passed a military appropriations bill he would allow them to draft a new frame of government. The Assembly and its leaders accepted the compromise, authorizing 300 pounds for Fletcher's use while quickly passing a new model of government, called the Frame of 1696, which gave political control of Pennsylvania to the Assembly and its David Lloyd–led coterie. An antiproprietary elite now dominated both Council and Assembly, ensuring that henceforth any attempt by Penn to reclaim his authority as "True and Absolute Proprietor" would be opposed by both branches of the colonial government.

Although the new charter transferred significant power to the Assembly, in no way did it reflect the further democratization of Pennsylvania society. Quite the opposite; power remained firmly in the hands of an antiproprietary Quaker oligarchy. The new frame represented the conscious attempt by the establishment to tighten their control while preventing any challenges to their hegemony, particularly from the growing non-Quaker urban populace. For example, the new frame established a residency requirement of two years before one could become eligible to vote. Such a stipulation reflected the attempt to diminish the strength of the significant influx of non-Quakers to Pennsylvania from New York and Maryland. These immigrants tended to settle in Philadelphia rather than in the surrounding countryside. To further curtail this potential threat to Quaker dominance, the voting qualifications for urban voters was stiffened to exclude anyone without a 50-pound estate free of debts. Under Penn's 1683 charter, only the payment of scot and lot (a municipal householder's tax paid by virtually every free white male) had been required. While the urban franchise became more restricted, the opposite occurred for rural voters, who saw their regulations relaxed. Before the new frame, one had to own a minimum of 100 acres to be eligible to vote; now only 50 acres was required. Like the residency requirement, the new-property provisos were designed to increase the rural Quaker vote while simultaneously reducing the increasingly non-Quaker urban vote.

Penn loyalists naturally protested the 1696 frame, claiming it was unconstitutional because it did not have Penn's approval. Technically they were correct, but their disclaimers fell on deaf ears. The Lloydians knew their hegemony was secure as long as Penn remained in England; until he returned there was little the anti-Lloydians could do to unseat the Quaker oligarchy that now controlled both Council and the recently empowered Assembly.

As reflected in the new frame's property requirements, the greatest threat to the Lloydians' domination was the influx of Anglicans into Pennsylvania in the 1690s. In 1695, Christ Church opened its doors for worship in the heart of Philadelphia, and there was nothing Quakers could do to prevent such an occurrence. In order to secure his 1681 charter, Penn had to allow for an Anglican chaplain whenever settlers requested one. Needless to say, Christ Church's appearance caused the Lloydians to despise Penn even more, for how could he countenance a church that had persecuted Friends in England for decades.

For several years Quakers had worried about the accelerating migration of non-Friends, especially Anglicans, into their colony. With the end of Anglo-French hostilities, this trend only intensified, making it readily apparent to Pennsylvania Quakers that fewer and fewer of their English brethren were willing to leave the Old World for the new. Indeed, it was a painful reminder to Quakers that despite all their attempts to attract Englishmen to their Light, they remained a marginal sect. The Pennsylvania Quaker oligarchy determined not to become (like the Catholics in Maryland) a minority in their own colony; not to be engulfed by a church that had been the bane of their existence for decades. The Lloydians believed both their faith and their political preeminence were under siege. They thus had to go on the offensive to keep Pennsylvania a Quaker sanctuary, which they believed Penn had betrayed by allowing non-Quaker immigration. They were certain Penn's permissiveness reflected a desperate and subversive attempt to try to reclaim proprietary power by using non-Quakers to bring fellow Friends to heel.

Unfortunately, in order to preserve their dominion, the leading Friends became intolerant and tyrannical in their use of power and office; no different in policies and behavior as the Puritans of New England or the Anglicans in England who had tormented the Quakers. They publicly vilified Penn loyalists. Instead of trying to end factionalism by inclusion, they excluded all non-Quakers from political office. The Lloydians even censored the Anglicans, denying them freedom of speech by suppressing an Anglican remonstrance to the king for the "free exercise of our Religion and Arms for our Defense." According to the aggrieved Anglicans, even in the courts, Quakers accepted "the word of an African slave" before they would "honor that of another Christian Englishmen because he belongs to a different Church."

The Quaker community despaired; Quakers were supposed to be different; their colony was to have been a haven where all Christian faiths were tolerated, where freedom of speech and press were inalienable rights, and where political dissent was recognized and guaranteed as an essential component of a free society. Perhaps most important, it became clear to Penn that his consensual ideal had been completely shattered by his brethren's inability to join hands in the work of building a reconstructed society. It was yet again dishearteningly obvious to Penn that he had placed his expectations of his colonists too high. They were simply incapable of bringing about his utopian vision of Pennsylvania as an example of righteous, loving, selfless Christian fellowship.

In fairness to all the Pennsylvania factions that had emerged by the late 1690s, their presence, in many ways, was the logical result of important natural factors that Penn had failed to understand or recognize from the beginning. His long absences from the colony only exacerbated these inherent dynamics. Much of the colony's bitter factionalism and struggle for power was the result of the realities of life in the wilderness and the very nature of his "holy experiment," which Penn could not control, especially from his home in England. From the beginning, immigrant composition significantly impacted the colony's politics. The majority of settlers were only a step or two above the indentured servant class—yeomen farmers and artisans, and thus the gap between wealthier and the less endowed settlers was so marginal that upward mobility, especially in a land of limitless opportunity, was a reality rather than a pipe dream for increasing numbers of colonists. Such fluid conditions allowed for the rapid rise to political power of self-made individuals, a rough-hewn lot, who came to believe they had as much a right to participate in politics as their supposed "betters."

By comparison, only a handful of weighty Friends had left England to settle in Pennsylvania, and few of those had the requisite education or experience in public affairs to manage a colony. Penn could not even count on those individuals who were university-trained to enter the political arena; they preferred instead to pursue opportunities with far greater potential remuneration. No matter how hard Penn tried, he could not attract sufficient numbers of educated, experienced men willing to assume his colony's political leadership. In short, Penn had created on paper a political system based on the rule of a dual elite—proprietary and provincial—which the masses were to embrace. As Penn insightfully wrote, "the Great fault is, that those who are there, lose their authority, one way or other in the Spirits of the people and then they can do little with their outward powers." Quaker religious values simply were not strong enough to withstand the atomizing realities of life in the wilderness or suppress the natural desire for personal political and economic aggrandizement.

Penn had to contend not only with increasingly factious fellow Quakers, but also with an English government determined to bring the wayward colonies, especially the proprietary ones, under greater imperial control. Prompting such a reaction from the Crown in the last year of the war with France was the flood of reports from royal officials detailing how colonists, especially those residing in North America, violated the Navigation Acts with regularity and impunity, hurting the war effort. Indeed, according to Edmund Randolph and Francis Nicholson, the Crown's two main troubleshooters and informants, the colonies' illegal trade deprived the Crown of an estimated 50,000 pounds annually. To a military imperialist such as William III, such blatant disregard for royal policy and authority was unacceptable, for such activity was not only disobedient but treasonous as well.

More alarming to colonial officials was the colonists' growing political estrangement and increasing sense of autonomy; a belief that their respective assemblies were equal to Parliament in sovereignty, thus exempting them from having to obey Parliamentary decrees. This political self-consciousness proved to be far more detrimental to England in the long run than the immediate issue of trying to stop their illegal trade. As the royal governor of Maryland (then later of Virginia), Francis Nicholson, told the Board of Trade, "A great many people in these Colonies, especially under proprietors and in Connecticut and Rhode Island, think that no law in England ought to bind them without their consent; for they foolishly say that they have no representative sent from themselves to the Parliament in England, and they look upon all laws made in England, that put any restraint upon them, as great hardships."

Although Nicholson and Randolph undoubtedly inflated the numbers and exaggerated colonial noncompliance of the Navigation Acts out of personal contempt for the American colonists, there nonetheless existed more truth than falsehood to their claims. There was no denying that England's North American subjects were becoming more self-reliant, and in the process, they evaded the laws, especially those they perceived as restricting their trade, and hence their material advancement. However, since neither Randolph nor Nicholson was headed for greatness in England because both lacked family connections and court patrons, they had sought colonial appointments to use as possible subsequent stepping-stones to higher offices in England. Both men were hardcore Anglicans who opposed nonconformity, religious or otherwise, and resented the disobedient colonists among whom they were forced to live. They thus became, along with many others in similar conditions, zealous advocates and enforcers of English dominion over the colonies.

Since both men abhorred nonconformity, Pennsylvania naturally became the focus of their vigorous compulsion to bring the colonies to heel. In their trips through the colony, they saw little that pleased them. They reported that both Philadelphia and New Castle had become hotbeds of illegal trade and havens for pirates such as Henry Avrey, the most notorious buccaneer in North America at the time, from whom they bought or received goods free in exchange for providing Avery a hideout. Maryland tobacco streamed into the colony, where it evaded the king's customs, and was then illegally shipped to Scotland or Europe in barrels labeled as "bread" or "flour." Vessels from all the European countries could be seen in Philadelphia's harbor, trading freely with the Quakers.

Most disturbing to the Crown was that even when caught "red-handed" for violating the Navigation Acts—a rarity—the likelihood of an individual being convicted by a colonial judge and jury, who were often his neighbors and friends, was remote. The legislature virtually asserted its independence from the Crown by omitting from colonial laws the customary preface acknowledging the English monarch as "their sovereign Lord and King." As Robert Quary, another ubiquitous royal lackey complained, in Pennsylvania, "the King's interest was never so much abused. They do what they please, and your officers must take what the Merchants will give them." In the view of English officials, the Navigation Acts had proved impossible to enforce not because of a flawed system, but because colonial common-law juries, attorneys general, and even colonial governors (particularly those of the proprietary colonies) shirked their obligations to support Crown policies. In more ways than not, their assessment was accurate, especially with regard to Pennsylvania, where Quaker antiauthoritarianism, individualism, and oppositional politics, remained strong, with Friends determined to resist any encroachments on their political and economic freedoms.

Such flagrant disregard, if not open contempt, for English laws infuriated the government. Thus, in 1696 Parliament passed a new Navigation Act, designed to stop the smuggling and "for preventing frauds and regulating abuses in the plantation trade." However, the act's real teeth was the establishing of vice-admiralty courts—a juryless tribunal of three Crown-appointed judges—throughout the colonies, assigning them complete jurisdiction over violations of the trade acts. Until the creation of the vice-admiralty courts, the Crown had no effective means of prosecuting colonial offenders of the navigation laws. Most egregious, colonials charged with violation of the Navigation Acts would be denied the right to a trial by a jury of their peers.

No doubt such a measure outraged the colonists, especially the Quakers and Penn, who had championed the right to a trial by jury as one of the most sacred liberties in a free society. Equally disturbing to Penn was the act's mandate that henceforth the appointment of governors in proprietary colonies would require approval by Whitehall. Randolph declared such a proviso essential "to bring the Governments of Proprietys [sic] to a dependence on the Crown." Another of the measure's decrees that especially affected Penn was the prohibition of land sales to non-English subjects, which included the Scots. This particular stipulation hurt Penn financially, depriving him of potential purchasers of land and payers of quitrents. Finally, to enforce the measures and to bring the colonies under tighter royal control, the Crown established the Board of Trade and Plantations. All these actions reflected the Crown's awareness of the degree of autonomy the colonies had gained, especially the proprietaries.

News of the forthcoming vice-admiralty courts prompted a defiant David Lloyd to declare such courts illegal, and that anyone who supported such usurpation by English officials to be a greater enemy to the "liberties and privileges of the people than those that established and promoted ship monie in King Charles the first time." Lloyd's bluster emboldened other Quakers, who believed Penn's return to favor at William III's court would shield them from such royal interference. Confidence in Penn and the bravado of brethren like Lloyd encouraged Pennsylvania's leading merchants to proclaim that the King's only function was "to receive a bear skin or two yearly." As far as Pennsylvanians were concerned, English laws reached no farther than the boundaries of the mother country.

Penn initially welcomed the Crown's more hard-line approach to colonial affairs. He saw both the Navigation Act and the creation of the Board of Trade as potential aides in helping him to regain control over his colony. However, Penn quickly realized that the last thing the Crown wanted was to see proprietors' power increased; indeed the Board of Trade wanted the opposite, hoping eventually to turn all the proprietary colonies into Crown colonies. Penn was very aware of this objective, having witnessed Lord Baltimore's loss of Maryland for alleged Jacobitism, as well as his own forfeiture of Pennsylvania for similar reasons. Moreover, the new Navigation Act and all its components hurt Penn financially, by not only restricting emigration to his colony, which represented potential revenue, but his other plans to develop Pennsylvania's economy as well, such as expanding the fur trade and increasing commercial ties with the West Indies. Although Pennsylvania and the Carolinas successfully resisted the Board's efforts, under both William, and his successor Queen Anne to transform their status, Penn nonetheless lived in constant fear of losing his proprietorship. His strategy was to try to stave off the Board's aggression until he could deal with the Crown directly. He knew that trying to negotiate with a hostile, antiproprietary Board would be fruitless. Perhaps at no other time in his career as a courtier was Penn pressed to use all his political wiles and acumen in order to keep his colony. That Penn succeeded in this endeavor is confirmed by the fact Pennsylvania survived as a proprietary colony, owned by the Penn family, down to the American Revolution.

In defending his proprietorship against Randolph's evidence of Quaker complicity in all manner of illegality, Penn denied some of the charges, upholding his government's integrity while attempting to shift the blame to the customs service, which he asserted was rife with incompetence and corruption. Although there was much truth to Penn's accusations of malfeasance and ineptitude within the customs bureaucracy, he knew it would be folly to try to make the service the real culprits. Penn knew his colonists evaded the Navigation Acts as often as they could get away with it, and thus he was trying to put the best possible face on a plainly difficult situation. That his colony was being especially "picked on" because of its religious orientation there was no doubt; other mainland colonies, as well as those in the West Indies were just as flagrant if not more so in their violations of the Navigation Acts. Believing that by demonstrating a personal loyalty to England's interests he could hope to ward off this latest attempt to deprive him of his colony, Penn offered English officials his own program for more effective regulation of trade.

The illegal trade flourishing in the colonies genuinely concerned Penn, and he recognized that the lack of cooperation among individual governors compounded the colonial defense issue. He also wanted to neutralize Randolph's influence at Court. Penn thus produced two proposals: one to address the defense issue, while the other focused on the illegal trade problem. In his attempt to find alternatives to the Board's solution of simply turning the propri-etary colonies into royal colonies, Penn had to walk a fine line between appearing to be either too much in favor of greater provin-cial autonomy and advocating greater English hegemony.

Penn's *A Briefe and Plaine Scheame how the English colonies in the North parts of America may be made more useful to the Crown and one another's peace and safety with a universal occurrence*, was the result of consultation with fellow proprietors and colonial agents. True to his Quaker faith, Penn wanted a consensus among all involved, for he believed no program or plan would be popular or successful if it came about by fiat, whether dictated by the Crown, by the Board of Trade, or by the proprietors. Penn believed all the issues causing the current tension between the Crown and the colonists could be resolved amicably and "with great satisfac-tion to all" if both sides agreed to adopt his proposal. In order to accomplish this end, more of three things were essential: people, time, and discipline.

Penn believed that much of the contraband business was the result of the restrictions placed on intercolonial trade by the Crown. Thus, all such impediments were to be eliminated, replaced by a free exchange of goods among the colonies, such as there was in England between counties. It was in this context that Penn's three principles of people, time, and discipline came into effect. There had to be enough people to produce the needed products. Consequently, the present emigration ban on non-English subjects had to be lifted. Penn believed postponing payment of customs duties for seven years would promote greater investment in the colonies because individuals would not have to worry about potential profits being eaten up by such imposts. To offset the temporary loss of revenue for the Crown, Penn proposed an increase of tariffs on imported foreign goods. Lastly, workforce measures should be established so that industry could flourish. Wages should be high enough that the common folk would no longer live hand to mouth, but not too high, which Penn believed would lead to excessive living, destroying the sobriety and diligence essential to economic success.

Relative to the colonial defense issue, Penn believed that if the Crown demanded quotas, then the colonies themselves should have the right to establish the numbers through representatives meeting "in one common assembly." Penn first expressed such an idea to his friend John Locke, one of the first commissioners on the Board of Trade, who convinced his cohorts to allow Penn to personally present his "scheme more fully" before the Board. Penn proposed the creation of a continental congress in which each colony would send two representatives, establishing a body of twenty individuals who would meet at least once a year to "hear and adjust all matters of complaint or difference betweene [sic] province and province" over issues such as supplying quotas of men during wartime, debts, and illegal trade.

Although the exigencies of war prompted Penn to devise his plan, he believed his idea was even more applicable during peacetime "for adjusting the differences that might arise between the colonies in civil matters, not military." Penn envisioned the creation of a permanent union, whose object would be to foster "a better understanding" among the colonies as well as to ensure their "public tranquility and safety." Penn assured the Board that of course his gathering would be under the supervision of a "specially appointed King's commissioner, who shall have the chair and preside in the said Congress." Unfortunately, only two Board commissioners, John Locke and Richard Coote, the first Earl of Bellomont, found Penn's "scheme" intriguing. The rest of the Board rejected his proposals, no doubt because they smacked of increasing colonial autonomy. The Crown was not in the business of decentralizing. Quite the contrary; it sought to bring the colonies, including Pennsylvania, more directly under its control. Despite its rejection, Penn's "scheme" reflected that as early as 1696 Penn grasped the nature of a vexing problem and suggested a possible solution—the distribution of powers between central and local governments.

By the summer of 1699, the torrent of complaints coming from the pens of Quary, Randolph, Nicholson, and other colonial officers, proved too overwhelming for Penn to continue to parry at Court. Although many believed Penn "hath greater interest at Court now than ever he had in King James's reign," he nonetheless found his proprietorship to be in jeopardy once again. Penn knew his colonists' fifteen-year general unruliness in conjunction with their most recent refusal to obey the Navigation Act contributed significantly to this latest attempt to nullify his charter. Moreover, as Robert Turner informed Penn, many colonists had lost faith in him because they thought he had sanctioned their loss of liberties and privileges. In Turner's view, Penn had no one to blame but himself for his current crisis, for "Thou hast left us too much to ourselves and the mismanagement of others. My advice to thee is that thou take speedy repair to here [Pennsylvania] to settle the government before it is beyond redemption and thou lose your Colony."

Pennsylvanians had become habituated to self-rule, and the longer Penn remained in England the more his colonists disregarded his proprietary prerogatives. Recognizing that he had stayed away from his colony too long, and willing to accept personal responsibility for the situation in Pennsylvania, Penn nonetheless believed that his present difficulty was more the result of an anti-Quaker conspiracy instigated by Quary, Randolph, Nicholson, and Jeremiah Basse of New Jersey to see Penn stripped of his charter. Penn contemptuously referred to these individuals as the "little tools" of the antiproprietary groups operating out of Whitehall. Indeed, few men could bring Penn to the edge of profanity, but Randolph was one of them. As Penn told Robert Turner, "He [Randolph] is the Scandal of the Government, as arbitrary a villain as lives. The Fellow is crafty and industrious but as false and villainous as possible. His name and a lye goes for the same thing 1000 Miles upon the Continent of America."

Undoubtedly, officials such as Randolph had it in for Penn. However, by this time in Penn's life, the years and events had crowded in on him, dulling his earlier optimism and tempering his utopian zeal. All his efforts from afar to achieve stability in Pennsylvania and to obtain compliance with proprietary policy had failed dismally. Penn concluded that only by returning to Pennsylvania and personally implementing Crown policy could he preserve his charter. Thus on September 3, 1699, accompanied by his wife Hannah and daughter Letitia (19-year-old William, Jr., or "Billy," and his pregnant wife remained in England) Penn set sail for North America, arriving in Philadelphia three months later.

By the late 1690s, in the eyes of many Pennsylvania Quakers, Penn, the Crown, and the Parliamentary laws that restricted their economic activities and thus their ability to succeed in the New World, were all the same, and held in similar contempt. If this was the end result of his absence, Penn, an intelligent man, surely must have sensed such consequences. Again, the question must be asked, why did Penn stay away from his colony for so long? It will always be difficult to know for certain, because in Penn's mind he believed that what he accomplished in England in those fifteen years benefited all Englishmen everywhere. In many ways he was correct; his countrymen owed him a debt of gratitude for his tireless campaign for liberty of conscience, which was finally realized in England in the 1690s. However, while Penn performed such deeds in England, his colony suffered, largely as a result of his absence. Would his brethren have "degenerated" regardless of his presence? Perhaps, but certainly not as quickly as they did during his nonresidence; his prestige and charisma would have kept most in line.

The larger issue that must be raised is this: Had Penn stayed, would he have become as antiauthoritarian, as anti-imperialist as his fellow Quakers? Would the same environmental, economic, and political realities of life in the wilderness have affected Penn in the same way they were transforming his brethren? This is likely, for as Penn witnessed with his colonists (albeit from a distance), no matter how righteous the determination to resist the profane temptations of this world, when such provocations offered the potential of great wealth and power, they proved impossible to resist. Indeed, of all the English emigrants to North America, the Quakers possessed the most intense inherent disposition for such an identity change. What Penn failed to grasp was the metamorphosing phenomenon of life in the New World that was slowly but efficaciously changing his colonists into a new species of humans called "Americans." Had Penn remained in his colony he too might eventually have succumbed to the same overwhelming natural forces that were recasting his brethren into Americans. It would have been interesting, if, in the process, William Penn had become an even greater early American icon than he already is.

12

"This Licentious Wilderness"

Penn hoped his return would set things right and possibly even restore Pennsylvania to its founding principles. He was still a venerated figure in the Quaker community, and signs of his old charisma, which had been so important in recruiting settlers in the 1680s, seemed to reappear. To his dwindling number of loyalists, Penn's resurfacing rejuvenated spirits and hopes that proprietary strength and leadership would be resuscitated. To others who had never seen him, Penn was a legend, a larger-than-life image come to life. Coming to save his more humble brethren from themselves was a member of one of England's most honored families, a leader of the English Quaker movement, and a confidant of kings, Penn's personal influence was still considerable. Thanks to a gala reception, a sanguine Penn believed he could redeem his colony from all the turmoil and contentiousness that followed his departure. For a while, old grievances faded away as a renewed sense of common purpose pervaded the colony. As the rising young Quaker merchant Isaac Norris noted, "Things in Church and Government seem to goe [sic] well."

Sadly, all of Penn's hopes for a regenerated holy experiment dissipated five months after his return, as his colonists resumed their personal squabbling and rancor. All factions were united, however, in their determination to resist Penn's attempts to reclaim his status as "True and Absolute Proprietor." More distressing to Penn, and certainly more detrimental to the retention of his charter, was his colonists' equally steadfast commitment to obtain greater autonomy, especially from the Crown. Such combined resistance to legally constituted authority made Penn once again "a man of sorrows." Indeed, by the end of the first year of his return, his optimism for salvaging the "holy experiment" had evaporated. He no longer spoke

209

of plans to reunify his colony, but referred to Pennsylvania instead as "this licentious wilderness."

Penn returned to a colony that looked nothing like the infant society he had left fifteen years earlier. Fifteen thousand people now resided in his holy experiment, and his "City of Brotherly Love," Philadelphia, had become the second-largest city in English North America. Only Boston was larger. By the time of Penn's arrival, Philadelphia boasted a population of over 5,000 inhabitants. Most impressive was the city's mercantile success, confirmed by the volume and variety of goods exported, ranging from whale oil to furs to tobacco to even iron and copper. Quaker-owned vessels carried wheat, flour, and lumber to the West Indies, returning with sugar and rum and bills of exchange. The latter, functioning as an international currency, were used to purchase woolens, tools, and hardware from the mother country. Such enterprises had made Philadelphia the colonies' leading emporium, and in the process transformed humble Quakers into some of the most affluent merchants in all of North America. "If anyone were to see Philadelphia who had not been there before," wrote the city's Swedish minister in 1700, "he would be astonished beyond measure that it was founded less than twenty years ago."

Much of the population boom of the 1690s was the result of internal emigration, as a steady stream of families, mostly from New York and Maryland, moved to Pennsylvania, seeking relief from militia duty, high taxes, and religious and ethnic discrimination. Once peace returned to Europe in 1697 and the Atlantic was again safe for travel, the overwhelming majority of English passenger ships leaving for North America had Pennsylvania as their destination.

Penn was under tremendous pressure from the Privy Council to bring his colony in line with Parliamentary and royal mandates. Before sailing for North America, it had been made clear to Penn that upon his arrival he was to immediately remove William Markham as Lieutenant Governor, David Lloyd as Attorney General, and Anthony Morris as Commissioner of the Peace for their bold flaunting of Crown authority. Penn was to also ensure his colonists' compliance with the Navigation Acts, their obedience to the admiralty court, prevention of piracy, and the establishment of a militia for the province's defense. Shortly after his arrival, Penn succeeded in pushing through the General Assembly a strongly worded declaration condemning illegal trade, thus satisfying London authorities, at least on that count.

On a personal level, Penn also hoped to extract some sort of income from his colonists other than from quitrents whose collection had become a farce. Penn believed his brethren owed him some form of reliable compensation for the years of personal anguish and penury their unanticipated selfishness and acquisitiveness had caused him to suffer. By the time of his "second appearance," Penn had sunk 25,000 pounds into his "holy experiment" but had realized a return of only around 1,000 pounds. This was hardly the remuneration Penn envisioned when he received his charter. At the Assembly's first meeting upon his return, Penn pushed the gathering to pass a revenue bill for his "welfare" a "proprietary tax," which much to Penn's humiliation, was voted down "verry handsomely [unanimously]." Apparently, Pennsylvania Friends remained convinced that Penn was a wealthy opportunist, still trying to extract from them whatever he could to line his own pockets. As a rather insulting sop, the Assembly voted to pass a tax on liquor, whose receipts would be allocated to Penn as "income." Penn accepted the offer, hoping the amount he received would be significantly more than his quitrent receipts, which by this time were less than 10 pounds a year.

To augment such a pittance, the ever-resourceful Penn thought of another source of potential revenue: the retention of seized pirate booty. When captured in the colonies, buccaneers were to be returned to England for trial along with all their contraband, which was given to the king. Penn, however, believed that when *his* colonists assisted in the apprehension of such individuals (a rare, if ever, occurrence), or when their ships and cargo were brought to Pennsylvania ports, he should be awarded a portion of the value of the stolen goods to help pay the costs of "retention," as well as for policing the coasts and shipping prisoners back to England.

The Privy Council rejected Penn's request; pirate treasure was too lucrative for the mother country to allow even a small percentage to remain in colonial hands. Despite Quaker protestations to the contrary, London authorities knew that Friends were some of the pirates' best colonial customers, allowing them safe haven and eagerly buying their goods. Penn's campaign against illegal trade and piracy contributed to the erosion of his popularity. His charter in perpetual jeopardy, Penn was obliged to do all in his power to implement the Privy Council's demand that he rid the colony of pirates and illegal traders. However, his actions in that direction built resentment, so much so that in letters to prominent English officials Penn spoke of his increasing disfavor because he had removed popular officeholders who had earlier aided buccaneers seeking refuge in Philadelphia. Until the royal navy could cleanse New World waters of pirates, and until they could count on colonial support in such an effort, freebooting would continue.

Finally, Penn wanted the Assembly to address the Frame of 1696, which he never officially sanctioned. He wanted a new charter, but such plans also foundered because the Lower Counties refused to accept any constitutional arrangement that allowed for Quaker control of their affairs. At this juncture in the relationship between the Upper and Lower Counties, it was becoming clear to Penn that he would soon have to grant "The Territories" their independence, for their inhabitants had rejected both his and Quaker suzerainty since Pennsylvania's founding.

In carrying out his charge of removing certain individuals from office, Penn particularly relished firing David Lloyd, who to Penn represented the most serious threat and obstacle to resurrecting proprietary authority. Penn not only wanted Lloyd removed from office but prosecuted as well for "high crimes and misdemeanors" against both the proprietor and the king. However, to Penn's surprise, the Anglican Judge of the Admiralty Court, Robert Quary, intervened, cautioning Penn not to prosecute Lloyd. Even though Quary despised Lloyd because of his anti-Anglican policies, Quary believed that engaging Lloyd in court would cause a backlash of antiproprietary sentiment. Although there was no love lost between Quary and Penn, at this particular moment, the men's mutual contempt for Lloyd superseded their antagonisms.

Quary was committed to the enforcement of authority and supremacy, and to that end, he sided with whoever would best help him attain that objective. Seeing the wisdom in Quary's counsel, Penn momentarily suppressed his animus toward Lloyd and refrained from initiating legal proceedings against the Welshman. Although Penn dropped the case, his dislike for Lloyd was nonetheless public knowledge. Much to Penn's chagrin, the potential showdown between the two revealed that Lloyd's popularity and prestige was far greater than Penn's throughout the colony. Indeed, Pennsylvanians believed Lloyd to be the most vocal and dedicated defender of their rights against external authority, which to Penn's great dismay, now included himself as well as the English government.

Why was David Lloyd such a threat to both Penn and colonial officials? Several factors caused such hostility and alienation, including Lloyd's obsessive hatred of Penn and a desire for revenge for the loss of his public and proprietary offices. So embittered was

Lloyd after his removal, that his resentment of Penn and all who supported the proprietor was boundless. From the moment of his dismissal, all of the passion Lloyd had reserved for opposing royal decrees in the 1690s he now vented on Penn, devoting the rest of his life to waging a political and personal war on the proprietor and all his agents.

Lloyd was convinced that Penn's policies were premeditated attempts to curtail colonial rights. Portrayal of Penn in such light was not only unfair and inaccurate, but also dismissed the important dynamics of Pennsylvania politics, which Penn could not control, especially from afar. Although often offending colonial sensibilities, Penn was not vindictive, autocratic, or hungry for power. It was stability and unity he longed for, along with proprietary revenue. Many Quakers believed this about Penn, such as Isaac Norris, who blamed Lloyd for causing the conflict. "There is some who by Linking [the] imaginery with the true Intrest of the Country therewith Couch & Cover their own Interests & disguise & do so perplex affairs as to almost give the Honest and Undesigning to Dispair of any Reconciliation or progress to a Settlement."

Although shunned by his wealthier Quaker brethren as a rabble-rousing parvenu, Lloyd was a gifted man: a brilliant orator, a student of the law, a skilled advocate, and a master at parliamentary maneuver. There was no mistaking his power. He presented himself as the people's tribune, defending their rights against the arbitrary authority of the Crown, the proprietary, and their respective minions. In many ways Lloyd's beliefs and behavior reflected the characteristics of the archetypical New World rebel—railing against established authority, translating personal grievances into personal crusades, and often manufacturing, then propagating the notion that conspiracies were afoot designed to take away the peoples' liberties. To David Lloyd, William Penn was a willing accomplice in this nefarious plot, and thus resistance to his proprietary authority was wholly justified. Lloyd was a Whig of the American variety, and he had a counterpart in nearly every colony. Perhaps most important, the conflict between Penn and Lloyd revealed that the legacy of Quaker antiauthoritarianism and oppositional politics were important influences in the shaping of American revolutionary ideology.

Like Isaac Norris, James Logan, who became Penn's most important proprietary official in Pennsylvania, also believed Lloyd was nothing more than a self-interested, demagogue, animated by a personal vendetta against Penn. According to Logan, Lloyd, despite his "smooth language and pretenses," could not "conceal his resentment of thy taking, as he calls it, his bread from him [Penn's removing him from office], this expression he has several times dropped, overlooking his politics through the heat of his indignation."

Logan, a 24-year-old former schoolteacher, had accompanied Penn on his return to America. He so impressed Penn with his erudition that the proprietor offered him a job as his private secretary. Logan was a language prodigy and also a fine mathematician and a burgeoning scientist with a particular interest in botany. However, it was not Logan's scientific expertise that impressed Penn, but rather his mathematical skills, which Penn believed would make Logan a good secretary (and accountant), especially when it came to administering proprietary policy, of which the collection of quitrents and other revenue was utmost on Penn's mind.

No sooner did Logan arrive in Pennsylvania than Penn put him to work collecting quitrents from those who were in arrears (each landowner owed Penn a shilling or a bushel of wheat a year for each 100 acres). In addition to rents, Penn wanted his secretary to "look carefully" at the collection of fines, forfeitures, and escheats—all outdated relics of feudalism and thus impossible for Logan to recover. After enduring a year of futility, a dejected Logan reported to Penn that he had collected barely 12 pounds in quitrents and less than fifty from the sale of lands, and most of it went to satisfy Penn's local creditors. Penn, Logan later wrote, "had hopes on his Arrival of raising a considerable Sum here, which was not then easily practicable; therefore during his first year here, to the great dissatisfaction of his friends who had received him with transports of joy he was hard to the People; and thereby lost the affection of many who had almost ador'd him."

In an attempt to placate Crown authorities, Penn appointed to positions of authority loyalist non-Quakers. Such a move only further alienated his already hostile brethren. To the post of Chief Justice of the Provincial Court, Penn designated John Guest, while Robert Assheton became the new Attorney General. Both were Anglicans. Penn selected Assheton and Guest to offset Anglican complaints that only Quakers received justice in Pennsylvania. Penn's appointment of Anglicans only confirmed the belief among many Quakers that their proprietor was willing to sell them out for his own self-preservation, that their well-being was of little concern, and that all Penn continued to care about, and thus the only reason for his return, was to collect his rents. In the eyes of many Quakers, so desperate was Penn for money and retention of his charter, that he not only allowed non-Quakers to come to Pennsylvania, but now appointed to positions of power individuals notorious for their hatred and persecution of Friends.

Little did Friends know of the pressure on Penn to place Anglicans in control, which royal officials believed was the only way political stability could be restored in Pennsylvania and obedience to Crown policies ensured. In a letter to Thomas Callowhill, Penn's father-in-law, James Logan confirmed the animosity toward Penn that appeared universal among Friends. "Never was there any person more barbarously treated or baited with undeserved enemies. He [Penn] has been able to foil all attacks from public adversaries [colonial officials] but 'tis his fortune to meet with greatest severities from those that owe most to him."

Resentment toward Penn and resistance to his attempts at reestablishing proprietary authority became so intense that by the summer of 1700, a weary and disillusioned Penn abruptly changed his agenda. Penn now shifted ground, completely abandoning all attempts to force his colonists to obey imperial mandates and turned openly against Quary and Randolph, whom he believed had railroaded him into betraying his own people in order to enhance their own respective ambitions. No sooner did Penn change his mind than he began reappointing Quakers to a variety of important government positions. Penn believed he had been used by colonial officials, who hoped his attempts to reclaim proprietary power would provoke so much animosity and obstruction of his policies that the Board of Trade would conclude Penn was incapable of bring order to his colony, and thus would revoke his charter and make Pennsylvania a royal colony; a prospect that undoubtedly delighted sycophants like Randolph and Quary, who were confident that they would be rewarded with even greater sinecures for helping to bring about Penn's demise as a proprietor. Randolph, Quary, and other Crown officials saw the end of Quaker government in sight.

Realizing he had become a pawn, Penn went on the offensive, accusing Randolph, Quary, and other officials of deception. Their cries of Quaker discrimination against Anglicans were a ruse—fabrications contrived to conceal their real intent, which was to subvert proprietary government in his colony. "Church is their Cry, and to disturb us is their Merit. . . . They misrepresent all we doe, and would make us dissenters in our own Country." In Penn's view, the Anglican "interlopers" left no stone unturned in their efforts to provoke dissension and antipathy between him and his colonists, to undermine his authority and obstruct his government, and to paint him with the brush of incompetence, and of possessing, like his brethren, anti-imperial and antiauthoritarian sentiments.

Penn also rightly accused colonial officials of corruption and ineptitude in carrying out their sworn duties. Many, such as Quary, engaged in all manner of illegal trade, importing and exporting a variety of merchandise without paying the required duties by bribing customs officials to look the other way or simply by labeling contraband by another name. According to Penn, "They do as they please while all others must be Racked by all the Severities he [a colonial officer] shall think fitt for their Discouragement in Rival trade put upon them." Worse were the vice-admiralty courts, whose justices were as venal, incompetent, and crooked as other royal bureaucrats. If there must be such tribunals in America, Penn exclaimed, they must be staffed with experienced, honest individuals, "for as these manage, a great Discouragement is given to trade." The notoriety of Philadelphia's vice-admiralty court had already caused scores of ships to divert to other colonial ports, negatively impacting the City of Brotherly Love's economy. As Penn reminded his friend Robert Harley, Speaker of the House of Commons, it was trade that made the wheels of the empire turn. However, colonial officials, by their unconscionable extension of power, were greatly inhibiting such enterprise. "They have swallowed up a great part of the Government here," Penn wrote, "giving our people the greatest discontent, looking upon themselves as less free than at home, instead of greater privileges, which were promised."

Ever the advocate, Penn also attacked the vice-admiralty courts' legal right to exist in his colony, invoking the privileges of such jurisdiction granted to him by his charter from Charles II. Penn asserted that according to his charter, he had equivalent power to that of any Crown agency or Parliament, of vice-admiralty authority in his colony. Penn then argued that in his view such courts were unconstitutional, for they condemned one's property without due process, of which the most important component was an individual's right to a jury trial. The vice-admiralty courts were thus an egregious contravention of a fundamental English liberty being denied to Englishmen in North America, while those in England continued to enjoy such rights. Penn believed that his New World brethren were being discriminated against because of "where they have chosen to Inhabit. What is the right of the English subject at home should be allowed here," he adjured, "since more and not less [liberty] seems the Reason to Plant this Wilderness."

Although Penn defended his colonists and his proprietary to the best of his abilities, the forces arrayed against him were too powerful for him to defeat; he was losing the battle of influence in London and thus the struggle to keep his charter. In April 1701, the Board of Trade introduced into the House of Lords a "resumption bill," calling for the revocation of all proprietary charters based on the claim "that the severing of such power and authority from the Crown and placing the same in the hands of subjects hath by experience been found prejudicial and repugnant to the Trade of this Kingdom and to the welfare of his Majesty's other plantations in America and to his Majesty's revenue arising from the customs by reason of the many irregularities committed by the Governors of those plantations and by those in authority under them by incouraging [sic] and countenancing pirates and unlawful traders."

Although distressed by this latest declaration against his proprietary, there was little Penn could do to defend his rights from 3,000 miles away. The best he could do until he returned to England was to continue to present his case through lawyers and other intermediaries. Penn also wrote a broadsheet entitled *The Case of William Penn, Esq. As to the Proprietary Government of Pennsilvania*, which he had his son, William III, circulate. In his essay, Penn argued that to divest him of his dominion over his colony was tantamount to depriving him of his property without his consent. "Powers are as much property as soil; and this is plain to all who have Lordships and Mannours [sic] [manors] in England." Penn also reiterated the many advantages to the Crown provided by proprietary government, the most salient being that a royal official had no other interest than to serve his time and collect his salary, while a conscientious and loyal proprietor such as himself, "performs all manner of Services of great Benefit to the Nation and Your Majesty's Welfare." Finally, Penn reminded the government that he, not the king, nor any members of the Lords of Trade or Parliament, had poured "twenty thousand pounds sterling to bring it [Pennsylvania] to pass." Instead of enriching Penn, his colony "pays not the debt owed my father. I wish myself twenty years younger for if I could live longer I would hope to enjoy the fruit of my labor and receive the return of my deep and sinking experience."

Fortunately for Penn, the resumption bill did not pass Parliament, at least at this go-round. "The multiplicity of other affairs"—impending war with France over the issue of the Spanish Succession—appeared to preoccupy members of Parliament more than whether or not William Penn remained the proprietor of Pennsylvania.

Parliament, however, did find the time to take away Penn's right of government for the Lower Counties, eventually transforming them by the time of Penn's death in 1718, into the independent, royal colony of Delaware. Although angry at having lost "the Territories," Penn was relieved that at least for the moment he still retained Pennsylvania. Penn knew, however, that he was not out of the woods relative to keeping Pennsylvania. He heard that although currently distracted by other events, Parliament more than likely would approve the resumption bill at its next session. Faced with this prospect, Penn announced in August 1701 that he must return "with due haste" to England to try to stop this latest assault on his proprietorship by individuals "gaping for Perferments under the Specious pretence of Serving the king's Interest."

While Penn battled with fellow Quakers and colonial officials, his first child with his second wife Hannah, was born at his Pennsbury estate on January 28, 1700. John Penn, known as "the American," was the only one of Penn's children born in the New World. Also bringing Penn momentary joy during his depressing feud with his colonists and English placemen was the news that his first grandchild, a girl, had been born to William, Jr., and his wife. The happy couple named their daughter Gulielma Maria in honor of Penn's first wife and Billy's mother.

Since Penn found Philadelphia too crowded, crime-ridden, and noisy, his Pennsbury estate became his refuge, particularly when Pennsylvania politics got too rough for his heart and mind to handle. Pennsbury was about twenty miles up the Delaware River from Philadelphia, and it was a most definite English transplant, replicating in size, shape, and accoutrements, Penn's country home in Worminghurst. Pennsbury had poplar-lined walkways, formal gardens, and manicured lawns; all the typical and fashionable trappings inside and out of the home of an English squire. Penn commuted between his suburban home and the statehouse in Philadelphia in an ornately decorated six-oared barge, similar in style and ostentation to the ones used on the Thames by the English aristocracy on their Sunday outings. Even though he was among his more humble brethren, Penn had no intention of trying to "bond" with his more rough-hewn colonists. Penn wanted to make it clear to all that he was "the lord of the manor," and thus believed it essential to project and reinforce such an image by flaunting as often as possible his wealth and status.

Perhaps the greatest solace Penn found during his second American sojourn was that his colonists, despite constantly quarreling among themselves, had maintained exceptionally peaceful and profitable relations with their Native American neighbors. Penn thus found the tribes eager to meet with him in council in Philadelphia to cement another peace treaty. The Articles of Agreement, signed by Penn and the chiefs of the Conestogas, Shawnese, Potomacs, and Onondagas, reaffirmed their friendship and trust, as both parties agreed never to injure or defraud one another. The tribes promised to respect Pennsylvania laws and remain loyal to the Crown. Speaking for both himself and his heirs, Penn assured the tribes they would be protected from trade abuses and that they could settle anywhere within his colony they wished. At what would be his last conference with Native Americans, Penn, for the first time in his transactions, used an interpreter. At all previous meetings Penn had spoken directly to the chiefs in their native tongue. By the time of his first departure, Penn spoke not only fluent Algonquian but Iroquois as well. However, his fifteen-year absence had caused him to lose his fluency, requiring his present use of an interpreter.

Not surprisingly, Penn also found at the Council meeting leaders from several refugee tribes—Senecas, Shawnees, and Piscataway/ Conoys—all of whom had fled their original homelands because of maltreatment by European colonists and other Indians. They too were anxious to become part of Penn's protective "Covenant of Friendship." Penn of course agreed to incorporate them into his colony, not only for humanitarian but for financial reasons as well, for all the Indians made their living primarily by hunting and the trading of furs, which was a great boon to Pennsylvania's economy and thus Penn's potential for personal income. Regardless of Penn's motivation for such munificence, as the missionary John Heckewelder observed years later, "Never will the Delawares forget their elder brother Miquon [Penn], as they affectionately and respectfully called him," for during Penn's time, "Pennsylvania was a last, delightful asylum" for Native Americans.

Before returning to England in 1701, Penn suggested to James Logan that the Assembly should grant him a fur trade monopoly for his compensation in lieu of tax receipts. Logan counseled Penn not to put forth such a proposal, for "the merchants will never bear it. Contrivance and management may give thee a share with the rest, but more is not to be depended upon." It appeared that the fur trade was too lucrative an enterprise for Penn's acquisitive, self-serving brethren to relinquish, let alone share, with an absentee landlord, even though it was Penn's diplomacy and solicitous cultivation of the Indians' trust that had brought such a profitable business to his fellow Quakers.

Although denying Penn fur trade receipts, the Assembly did vote to replace the liquor tax awarded to Penn earlier with a stipend of 2,000 pounds paid annually as recompense for all personal costs incurred since the founding of Pennsylvania. It appeared that the Assembly's generosity was a show of appreciation for Penn's spirited defense of provincial rights against the Crown's "usurpers"— Quary, Randolph, and the like. For several months in late 1700, the most influential men in the Quaker community, many of whom had openly defied Penn's authority and publicly vilified him, now shamefacedly rallied behind him, realizing that he was all that stood between their security and autonomy and their coming under royal dominion. Indeed, for a while it seemed that most of the issues between Penn and his colonists could be successfully compromised. However, such hopes disintegrated when Penn announced in August 1701 that the new antiproprietary bill pending before the House of Lords necessitated his return to England.

Penn's impending departure resurrected old divisions, but none were more acrimonious than those between Quakers and Anglicans, with the former determined to wrest from Penn as much provincial autonomy as possible, while the latter worked assiduously and clandestinely with colonial officials such as Quary, to ensure Pennsylvania's transformation into a royal colony. Nothing was more important to the Anglicans than keeping the Quakers divided, for their contentiousness could be used by the Churchmen to prove that Friends were inept in matters of state and thus that there was a need for a Crown takeover. Compounding this political tug-of-war between the two groups was the bitter religious enmity that existed between Anglicans and Quakers, dating back to the Restoration, when Anglicans persecuted Quakers. Now, Quakers were being asked to peacefully coexist in Pennsylvania by both Penn and the Crown. To Friends, *their* colony was the long-promised fulfillment of sectarian visions, while to the increasing numbers of Anglicans, enjoying support from England, it was time to end Quaker control of Pennsylvania and transform the colony into a Church of England stronghold. It was thus imperative that before Penn left, he must allow the Friends complete self-government as a hedge against the reestablishment of royal government and Anglicanism, or the possibility that he might not return in time to protect them against such an onslaught.

The influx into Pennsylvania of other denominations and their toleration by an uneasy Quaker majority would eventually give the colony renown as the epitome of New World acceptance of religious diversity and the embracing of the sanctity of liberty of conscience. Ironically, for Penn, religious pluralism proved the death knell for his "holy experiment."

No sooner did Penn announce his impending departure, than the David Lloyd–led Assembly seized the opportunity represented by Penn's leaving to begin the process of creating a new frame of government. Lloyd and his followers were determined to strip Penn of the last vestiges of his proprietary power. Once again, Penn's belief that his affairs in England were more urgent, requiring his immediate attention, proved fatal to his proprietary status. Perhaps at no other time as the "True and Absolute Proprietor" of Pennsylvania was Penn's presence more crucial, especially if he hoped to retain what few prerogatives he had left. Remaining in his colony rather than returning to England was the imperative. However, as seen in numerous instances, Penn constantly looked for any excuse he could find either to leave Pennsylvania when there or postpone a return to his colony when in England. At this juncture in Penn's life, it appeared that the reality of owning a colony and being responsible for its human, political, and economic upkeep conflicted sharply with Penn's initial proprietary vision.

From the beginning, Penn saw himself as a quasi-feudal lord, expecting both economic and political fealty from his people in exchange for providing them with a means to escape persecution and an opportunity to start a new life in North America. Penn also assumed that those whom he engaged to rule in his name, his "vassals," would do exactly what he prescribed in the best interest of all, particularly if he magnanimously allowed for a substantial degree of self-government. However, what Penn never appeared to accept was that his semi-feudal expectations and personal prerogatives were anachronistic to the majority of his colonists. Nonetheless, Penn believed that of all Englishmen, his fellow Quakers would be the most appreciative of having such privileges after decades of torment. In Penn's view he had not only liberated the Friends from a cruel tyranny but had entrusted them as well with the responsibility to establish a "holy experiment" in righteous, Christian living and fellowship. If this was Penn's conception, then in his mind there was no need for his presence. Friends, filled with the desire to be examples to the world, would not require his constant supervision to comport themselves appropriately.

Moreover, Penn found it difficult to adapt to colonial realities, to circumstances bearing scant resemblance to what he expected two decades earlier when his plans for Pennsylvania lay on the drawing board in London. He was simply unwilling to adapt his original blueprint to unforeseen conditions as he watched his outdated policies and expectations erode the affections of large numbers of colonists. Yet, through it all, and largely because of his own financial problems, Penn refused to accept the fact that Pennsylvania would never become the profit-making enterprise he initially envisioned. Penn never succeeded in enforcing his will, whether it related to the collection of quitrents or gaining his colonists' respect for his status as proprietor and thus acceptance of his authority to govern them.

It also must be remembered that Penn, despite all his lip service to Quaker plainness and simplicity, was "to the manor born"—an aristocrat, who, like many of his English counterparts, was comfortable being an absentee landlord, overseeing his estates from afar while allowing others to manage daily affairs. As long as the profits flowed into his pockets, Penn saw no need for prolonged stays at his various holdings. This was precisely how Penn attended to his Irish estates, and this was also the manner in which many Englishmen, who owned plantations on Barbados, Bermuda, or Jamaica, conducted their business as well. Being an absentee landlord was de rigueur among many of England's land-owning grandees.

Penn, however, literally could not afford to indulge in such aristocratic niceties and pretense, especially given the nature of his colonists. If Penn expected to profit from his colony while simultaneously enjoining his people to respect his authority, then his presence for more than a few years at a time was essential. Pennsylvanians needed to see that Penn genuinely was concerned for their well-being, that he was capable of managing the colony on a daily basis, and that he could protect them not only from the vagaries of wilderness living but from the capricious, self-serving encroachments of colonial officials as well. But his fifteen-year absence left Penn's colonists feeling abandoned and betrayed by the individual whom they believed was their messiah and protector. Penn's subsequent return to England after staying for only twenty-three months confirmed the view of the majority of Friends that their once-revered proprietor cared little about their future welfare. Sadly, many of the colonists' perceptions of Penn were accurate.

With time running out, Penn yielded to a plan of government that differed little from the Frame of 1696, which he had vehemently opposed. However, on the eve of his departure, Penn had no alternative but to accept a new frame of government called the Charter of Privileges, promulgated in October 1701 and remaining in effect until the American Revolution. As Penn anticipated, the new document confirmed the Assembly's sovereignty; that body now solely had the power to initiate, amend, or repeal legislation. The Assembly, not William Penn, now governed Pennsylvania. Indeed, no assembly anywhere in the colonies at this time wielded as much power as Pennsylvania's. Although it appeared Penn was being forced to capitulate to the David Lloyd–led Assembly, in reality he was only acknowledging a fait accompli; Lloyd and his followers had been chipping away at Penn's powers for over a decade and had already accomplished most of their objectives during the years of his absence. In many ways, all they were doing now was legitimizing the Assembly's privileges within Penn's presence and with his consent.

Although the new charter formalized the Assembly's ascendancy as Pennsylvania's governing body, Penn retained certain proprietary prerogatives, such as his or his governor's right to appoint Council members. Those chosen, however, served in an advisory capacity only; the Council was stripped of all legislative power, thus making its appointees purely titular. In effect, the Charter of Privileges established a unicameral legislature in Pennsylvania. Interestingly, the new frame did not represent "the final triumph of democratic principles," as some historians have contended. For one, universal manhood suffrage was not established, as the franchise remained restricted to rural landholders and urban taxpayers, a narrower base than first envisioned by Penn but still broader than any other colony.

Much to Penn's satisfaction, the new charter maintained freedom of conscience for all Pennsylvanians; no one who professed belief in one Almighty God would be harassed, and anyone who believed in Christ could hold office. Finally, and in many ways recognition of an accomplished fact, the new frame contained a proviso granting Delaware, which had seceded from Pennsylvania ten years earlier, the right to form its own government. Although initially approving the new document under duress, Penn later admitted that he also agreed to the Frame of 1701 because he believed Parliament was going to strip him of his proprietary regardless of his personal plea before them upon his return. If his colony's fate had already been decided, then Penn wanted to shield his colonists from an arbitrary royal governor. He believed the new frame of government provided such protection.

Penn's dream of a brotherhood of the godly had long since fallen victim to Quaker internal divisions, personal rancor between Penn and the Lloydians as well as between Quakers and Anglicans, and imperial tension. The Charter of Privileges, by formally separating executive from legislature, simply confirmed the holy experiment's final demise. The new charter was the result of conflict and strains Penn could not effectively deal with while preoccupied with affairs in England, supposedly forcing him to remain there until they were resolved. Yet, because the new plan recognized and even balanced the diverse interests of proprietor and assembly, empire and colony, the Frame of 1701 was infinitely more workable than the once-dreamed-of utopia.

Penn's brief sojourn to Pennsylvania proved a disheartening failure. Although initially placating Crown officers by promising to enforce the Navigation Acts, once Penn realized that their intent portended disaster for himself and his colonists, he reversed his purpose, vigorously defending provincial and proprietary liberties. While his about-face won him Quaker support, at least for the moment, it only intensified the wrath of colonial officials, both in England and in Pennsylvania, who accused Penn of defying imperial mandates. With his proprietary chronically in jeopardy, Penn was compelled to return to England to defend his charter. Although proprietary government, at least in theory, would last another seventy-five years in Pennsylvania, it nonetheless had lost is most prestigious advocate in the New World.

Although forced to relinquish power to the Assembly, Penn hoped that through James Logan and a combination of Quakers and Churchmen (Anglicans) still loyal to him he could preserve enough authority to perhaps someday reclaim his full status as "True and Absolute Proprietor." Naturally, this possibility depended heavily on Penn returning to his colony and staying permanently. This was Penn's intent, and thus before his departure, he appointed to various key offices both Anglicans and Quakers, all of whom had remained loyal to him over the years, despite his petulance, arrogance, and often high-handed measures. However, it was in James Logan that he placed his principal confidence, telling the young Scotsman, "I have left thee an uncommon trust." Penn appointed Logan to the most important positions: Provincial Secretary, Clerk of the Council, Receiver General, Commissioner of Propriety, and Proprietary Secretary. Perhaps at no other time during his proprietorship did Penn have in place a more loyal and formidable coterie of both provincial and proprietary officeholders, thus making his influence greater than at any time since the earliest days of settlement. No wonder Penn left feeling sanguine about the possibility of reclaiming in the near future his former status and authority.

However, as Logan and Thomas Story reminded Penn, if he hoped for such an outcome, then it was imperative that "thou return to this place with all speed and haste; wee implore thee not to tarry long in England or matters hither may come undone and become irretrievable upon thy return." Penn assured all his placemen that he indeed planned to stay in England only long enough to secure his retention of Pennsylvania.

Penn may have left behind a powerful group of loyal, carefully placed supporters, but they would have to contend for political supremacy with the Lloydians, who controlled the county courts, the Assembly, and the Philadelphia city government. It was in these vital sectors that the Lloydians' strength loomed the largest. Among the general populace, the Lloydians had the support of Philadelphia's middle class as well as that of the majority of landowners in Chester County. It was the merchant class that was still "up for grabs," and whichever faction—Lloydians or Penn loyalists—who garnered their allegiance, would go far in determining Penn's future hold on Pennsylvania.

Penn wanted his wife and daughter to remain in America while he returned to England, "for only a short while." Hannah, however, flatly refused; she had had quite enough of the New World. Penn tried to convince his wife there was nothing for her economically in England, for under the laws of primogeniture, if anything could be salvaged from his English and Irish estates, the money automatically would go to his son Billy. However, Pennsylvania holdings were a different matter and if Penn were to die, all his New World property would go to Hannah and their son John. Penn thus believed it essential for Hannah to stay so she could not only become better acquainted with her colonial brethren, whom she might some day have to "govern," but to learn to manage an estate as well. Penn's entreaties fell on deaf hears; Hannah Penn *was* returning to England with her husband, son, and stepdaughter. On November 3, 1701, the Penns boarded the *Dolmahoy* and set sail for England.

"A Soure Temper'd People"

After thirty-five days at sea, Penn arrived in England on December 8, 1701. He returned home to a country on the verge of war once again with its old nemesis, France, which had violated the 1697 Treaty of Ryswick by invading and capturing the Barrier Fortresses in Flanders and Brabant, held by the Dutch in Spanish territory. While William Penn parried with the antiproprietors and Crown officials in his colony, England joined with Holland and the Holy Roman Empire, forming the Grand Alliance, to counter Louis XIV's aggression. Within a year's time, Europe once again was engulfed in a major conflict, the War of the Spanish Succession (1702–1713).

Penn knew another European conflagration would undoubtedly affect his proprietary status, providing the government the excuse it needed to strip him of his colony. Crown officials had not forgotten alleged Quaker "disloyalty" during the last war, and to ensure no such "treasonous activity" occurred again, it was more than time for the nullification of all proprietary charters, especially Penn's. Indeed, the revocation of Penn's charter was a priority; his colony's reputation as a hotbed of illegal trade, contentious political factionalism, and failure to participate in colonial defense programs seemed to present the most convincing case for imperial reorganization, particularly with a major war looming. With such antiproprietary sentiment against him at all levels of officialdom, no sooner did Penn arrive in England than he immediately went to London to try to defend his right to his colony.

Penn not only had to counter the charges leveled against him and his colonists by colonial and Crown officials, but by the Church of England as well, led by the Bishop of London, Henry Compton.

Compton and his minions published several tracts decrying "the deplorable State of the English Colonies where they have been in a manner abandoned to Atheism; or, which is much at one, to Quakerism, for want of a clergy settled among them." Penn knew that more than pride of empire or love of church fed grist into the propaganda mill against him. For individuals such as Robert Quary, Jeremiah Basse, Edward Randolph, and a host of others, career advancement and other personal rewards, which would surely come their way as a result of colonial unification, was their principal motivation to revile Penn and his colonists. Penn expressed such awareness to Lord Romney, to whom he looked for support against these "knaves" and "beggars" who wanted to strip him of his proprietorship so that "some people may have more Governments to exercise, & Governors to goe halves with—a corruption that has been thought to raigne [reign] too long already."

Beginning in April 1702 and over the course of the next two years, colonial officials, led by Robert Quary, and Penn, hurled charges and countercharges at each other before the Board of Trade, Parliament, and ultimately the Privy Council, where fortunately for Penn, his influence far exceeded that of Quary's or any other bureaucrat. It was before the Privy Council and the House of Commons where Penn made his most cogent defense, asking its mostly Whig members whether "the heat of a few churchmen, headed by a Flanders camp parson, under the protection of the Bishop of London" be sufficient to abrogate a charter granted two decades before to ensure Quakers the right to "enjoy their conscience more quietly?" Penn found it difficult to believe the government could be convinced by a handful of "officious and turbulent persons" to nullify proprietary charters when Pennsylvania was proof positive that "the colonies thrive [more] in proprietary hands than under the immediate government of the Crown." Penn used Virginia as an example of how in the eight decades after it became a royal colony its economic value to England was not nearly as great as Pennsylvania's, which in less than three decades under Penn's auspices, was on its way to becoming one of the empire's most profitable colonial undertakings.

As Penn pointed out, which was the better gauge of a colony's worth: its growth and trade with England or the particular form of its charter? Although Penn's lucid arguments undoubtedly impressed many at Court and in the House, sentiment among members of the Board of Trade and of the House of Lords still favored a Unification Bill, which would result in the revocation of Penn's charter. Such appeared to be imminent when William III suddenly died in the spring of 1702, causing Parliament to abruptly end its session.

Just before the king's death, Penn achieved a minor victory in the battle to keep his colony: Robert Quary lost not only his campaign to rescind private charters, especially Penn's, but his job as judge of the vice-admiralty court at Philadelphia as well. An embittered Quary wrote the Board of Trade, who had relieved him of his position, that his firing only further emboldened an already smug Penn, who along with his fellow Quakers believed "that the Lords of Trade and Plantations are Mr. Penn's Enemies, and that he values them not, having a greater Interest [favor at Court and in Parliament] than all of them, and [he] shall be able to Carry on all his designs in spite of them."

The accession of Queen Anne, James II's last daughter, and thus the last Stuart to sit on the English throne, once more brought Penn into the bright rays of royal clemency and favor. Not only did Anne's assent bode well for Penn politically but religiously as well, for the new monarch was a devoted tolerationist, committed to upholding the 1689 Act of Toleration as well as the 1696 Affirmation Act. No sooner did Anne become England's ruler than she formed a new ministry composed solely of Whigs, many of whom Penn had befriended over the years. Penn's old friend, one of the original "Chits" during the reign of Charles II, Sidney Godolphin, was appointed lord treasurer; Robert Harley again became Speaker of the House of Commons; and Penn's new acquaintance, soon to become one of the most powerful and popular men in England as well as one of Penn's key supporters and benefactors, John Churchill, Earl of Marlborough, commander-in-chief of English forces abroad. Together these men formed an exceptional trio of powerful individuals, known at the time as "the triumvirate."

Penn's relationship with these men gave him direct access to the very heart of power in England, which Penn deftly parlayed into his favor, allowing him to keep his colony. As a confident Penn informed James Logan, "The scene is much changed since the death of the king, the Church party advances upon the Whigs, and yet I find good friends, sorely against some people's will [the Lords of Trade]," who still hoped to nullify Penn's charter via yet another Resumption Bill.

The turning point in Penn's struggle with the Lords of Trade to keep his colony occurred in the fall of 1703 when the "triumvirs" arranged for Penn a personal audience with the queen at Bath. Penn spent two hours with Anne, during which time Her Majesty not only agreed to allow Penn to keep his colony for "one year" without any interference from the Lords of Trade, but also assured Penn that she would uphold Quakers' and other nonconformists' right to liberty of conscience. At the end of their meeting, Penn thanked the queen, and much to his surprise, Anne responded that, "I am so well pleased that what I have said is to your satisfaction, that you and your friends may be assured of my protection."

In many ways the queen's reply was a double entendre, implying much more than merely a personal guarantee of the Quakers' right to worship; Anne also was referring to Penn's proprietary status as well as to his colonists' security under his charter, to all of whom she was pledging her "protection." Thanks to the triumvirs' intercession on Penn's behalf, Anne was assuring Penn she favored his continued position as proprietor of Pennsylvania, and that she would do all she could to safeguard his interests.

Anne made good her promise to Penn, when with the help of her ministers, she persuaded both Parliament and the Lords of Trade to drop the resumption bill for the year 1703, emphasizing that the war against France on the Continent and in North America should be their focus, not attempts at imperial reorganization. Moreover, Anne impressed on both those bodies that any talk of unification or resumption bills at this time could alienate the colonists, whose support in the war was vital to preserving English interests in North America. A relieved Penn wrote Logan that thanks to his Court connections, "a great reformation and relief has occurred, & for which American Governments owe me their good will."

In late 1703, Penn shocked the Queen, her ministers, and the Lords of Trade when he offered to sell his right to govern Pennsylvania (but not his proprietary or "feudal" rights to all of the colony's land) to the Crown for the 30,000 pounds he had invested so far in the province and the guarantee that Quakers be allowed to practice their faith freely. There were many reasons prompting Penn to make such an offer at this time in his life and career as a proprietor, the most important of which was personal indebtedness, especially to Philip Ford, who claimed Penn owed him more than 20,000 pounds. After two decades of constant battles with his cantankerous and obstreperous colonists, Penn had simply grown weary of all the problems, most of which were beyond resolution, no matter what approach he tried. Penn finally realized that his fellow Quakers were politically uncontrollable, and that for his own future well-being, the time had finally come to disabuse himself of all notions that the political situation was still salvageable, that he could reclaim his right to govern them, that the fear of becoming a royal colony would somehow miraculously bring them to their senses, and that they would come to appreciate and welcome Penn's authority. Since none of that was about to happen, Penn concluded that it was time to relieve himself of such a burdensome and heartbreaking responsibility, and allow someone else to assume such an onus.

But there was perhaps another reason for Penn's offer that had nothing to do with being a weary proprietor. It was possible that Penn's proposal to sell Pennsylvania's government was a shrewd ploy to *ensure* he kept his proprietorship in toto. There is substantial evidence indicating that throughout the years when the Unification Bill remained under Parliamentary consideration that Penn used the tactic of suggesting the sale of Pennsylvania's government while simultaneously trying to hold on to his charter. Ever the calculating courtier, Penn knew that 30,000 pounds was an outrageously exorbitant amount to ask from a government knee-deep in a war that would last thirteen years and cost millions of pounds. Moreover, many members of Parliament as well as the Queen's ministers (and Penn's friends) opposed imperial reforms, particularly during a time of crisis.

In the view of these individuals, especially to a military-minded adviser such as the earl of Marlborough, nothing should be done to disturb the status quo in the North American colonies, whose support in the war was crucial. Ministers such as the triumvirs also believed that much had been done since 1696 to regularize the relationship between the colonies and the mother country. Give those measures more time they argued, and when the desired results have been realized, there will be no need for the abrogation of private charters. Penn knew his timing was perfect, for international events were pushing the issue of proprietary charters into the background. As he told James Logan, all matters relating to the colonies moved "with unspeakable dilatoriness" because of the priority given to "forraign [sic] affaires."

Penn's maneuvering eventually achieved the desired results. By 1704 the Lords of Trade had dropped their campaign against the proprietary colonies in general and against Pennsylvania in particular. As Penn wrote to James Logan, "I am more likely to keep my government than ever, or to have some equivalent for it; and take this from me: *that if you do but the Queen justice in her revenue, and discountenance illegal trade*, you will not be molested hence, but protected. This the *ministry* assures me here." A relieved and jubilant Penn received further confirmation that he had the Queen's favor as well as that of her ministers when his governor Andrew Hamilton died, providing him an opportunity to appoint another. Penn's choice of the Anglican John Evans as Hamilton's successor sailed through official channels without an eyebrow raised in opposition. Unfortunately for Penn, Evans proved to be a disastrous choice. Penn, never a good judge of character, chose an individual with no qualifications for the position other than his father being a friend of Penn's. Moreover, the 26-year-old Evans was a pretentious, arrogant fop, who made his contempt for the colonials he was sent to govern widely known. That Penn would send such a stripling into the political jungles of Pennsylvania at a time when his colony was consumed by political unrest and uncertainty reflected not only Penn's inherent inability to choose competent individuals and the low regard most Englishmen had for their colonial counterparts, but also Penn's difficulty in finding capable men, especially ones possessing sufficient savvy to try to govern the notoriously defiant Quakers.

Penn instructed Evans to "keep up the Powers of my Graunt . . . and in no wise suffer them to be broaken in upon by any refractory or factious Persons whatever." Evans initially concealed his disdain for the Quakers, seeking the Council's advice on how best to proceed. However, by the end of his first year in office, Evans's true colors emerged, as he prominently displayed his sense of self-importance and dislike for the Quakers as well as implementing policies guaranteed to incur the Friends' wrath, especially the Lloydians. By 1708, the outcry against Evans was so great that Quakers appeared on the verge of revolt.

The Evans tumult made Penn's discouragement with his colony nearly complete. Refusing to admit that he had once again chosen the wrong individual to represent his authority, Penn blamed David Lloyd for the recent upheaval. He condemned the Welshman as "a traitorous person, a delinquent and vile ingrate." As Penn further railed to James Logan, "What Proprietor and Governour would care one jot what becomes of such foolish, if not wicked people."

Penn dismissed Evans in 1708 without consulting the Board of Trade because by then the *duke* of Marlborough had arrogated to himself, with the Queen's blessing, the appointment of colonial governors. The duke insisted on military men, recommending to Penn that he appoint Captain Charles Gookin. Although opposed to Marlborough's choice, Penn was in no position to challenge the duke, for Penn was in debtor's prison as a result of money owed to

Philip Ford. Nonetheless, Penn warned Marlborough that the likelihood of his Pennsylvania brethren accepting another military governor was remote, for such an approach had been tried twice in the past, and both times his colonists made life so miserable for appointees that they each resigned from office.

Marlborough rejected Penn's counsel, certain that times and conditions had changed in Pennsylvania and that the Quakers surely would not dare defy the preference of the most powerful man in England. As Penn predicted, Gookin would ultimately go the way of Blackwell and Fletcher, for like his predecessors, Gookin was temperamentally unfit to adjust to the Quaker style of civil government. Gookin viewed Quaker opposition to his authority as Penn's surrogate as insubordination. Although an honorable man who intended well on Penn's behalf, Gookin, like Blackwell and Fletcher before him, soon found himself in open war with both Council and Assembly; a conflict he was destined to lose. Although sympathetic to his colonists' pleas to remove Gookin, Penn was helpless to do anything until he could find a way out of debtor's prison. Interestingly, the man who had insisted on Gookin's appointment proved to be the key to Penn's release: the Duke of Marlborough.

Ever since Penn began accruing a debt to Ford in the mid-1680s, he had used his colony as collateral. He first mortgaged, then leased, then sold Pennsylvania to Ford, but Ford never attempted to take control of the colony. Penn made sporadic payments to his steward, but the amounts fell far short of covering what was owed and consequently, the debt escalated steadily. By 1696, Ford claimed that Penn owed him close to 11,000 pounds. At this juncture Penn had little choice but to deed his entire colony as collateral in order to assure Ford of payment. A year later he rented Pennsylvania back from Ford at an annual rate of 630 pounds, which Penn paid in part over the next several years.

Penn never settled his accounts with Ford; he treated his obligation more cavalierly and recklessly than Charles II had handled the money owed to Admiral Penn. When Ford died in 1702, he bequeathed the proprietorship of Pennsylvania to his widow and children. Bridget Ford, however, wanted cash, not an unruly colony 3,000 miles away. Penn refused to pay a penny more to the Fords, leaving them no alternative but to sue Penn in court for 20,000 pounds, which was more than his entire colony was worth. To ensure that they would receive some sort of compensation, Bridget Ford sued Penn in three different courts, the Exchequer, Common Pleas, and Chancery. In October 1707, the Common Pleas awarded the Fords 2,908 pounds, which Penn refused to pay, choosing instead to endure the humiliation of a seven months' stay in debtor's prison. In January 1708, 62-year-old William Penn walked through the gates of the Fleet, London's famous debtor's prison, becoming for the final time in his life a prisoner for conscience's sake. Penn had refused to pay the Fords because he was convinced that the Fords had falsified their bookkeeping in order to fleece him of thousands of pounds over the course of almost two decades.

Seeing such an exalted figure as Penn in a debtor's prison upset the English Quaker community. Weighty brethren came forward offering to raise money to help Penn pay his debt to the Fords. Penn initially rejected the Friends' generosity, believing that the over 14,000 pounds the Fords demanded he owed them was outrageous. Penn, however, changed his mind and accepted his brethren's solicitude when the Lord Chancellor, the Duke of Marlborough, intervened in the case. No doubt Penn's friendship with the duke prompted Churchill's intercession on Penn's behalf. However, also motivating Marlborough was the Fords' "arrogance" in petitioning the Queen to issue a new charter granting the Pennsylvania government to them. There was no way an aristocrat of the duke's stature and influence would allow a parvenu family such as the Fords, to take away the property of a friend and peer.

In demanding Pennsylvania, the Fords overplayed their hand, incurring the Duke's ire who, now became determined to settle this matter for Penn. He personally invited the Fords to his office and after about an hour's time, the Fords agreed to cut Penn's debt in half, to accept 7,600 pounds as a final settlement. According to Isaac Norris, who witnessed the exchanges between the Fords and the duke, "The Lord Chancellor declared positively that the equity of redemption still remained in William Penn and his heirs; as to taking the Government, that could not be, for it would not be decent—to use his own words—to make Government ambulatory; He spoke more fully and handsomely than I can repeat and, in a word, their petition was laid aside, and the Queen will be advised not to answer it."

The duke's rebuff forced the Fords into negotiation with Penn, who, after conferring with Marlborough, agreed to pay the 7,600 pounds and was released from the Fleet in August 1708. As Penn informed James Logan, "The Fords seem to embrace accommodation, and several Friends and others not of our profession [Marlborough] interpose to mediate it. Seven thousand pounds looks to be the sum." Since Penn was bankrupt, he accepted as a "gift" 6,600 pounds from fellow weighty Quakers Henry Gouldney, Joshua Gee, Silvanus Grove, John Woods, his father-in-law, Thomas Callowhill, Thomas Oade, Jeffery Pennell, John Field, and Thomas Cuppage, and 1,000 pounds from the Duke of Marlborough. In October 1708, the Penn–Ford dispute finally came to a close when a relieved Penn wrote Logan that, "My business is agreed with the Fords, and writings in hand for ratification." Penn once again owed his freedom to a powerful courtier with whom he shrewdly had cultivated a friendship. Moreover, like Admiral Penn, who had rescued his son many times from such ordeals, John Churchill was also a warrior and hero, the victorious general of the decisive battles of Blenheim (1704) and Ramillies (1706) during Queen Anne's War.

Was Philip Ford really the unethical, opportunistic knave Penn portrayed him to be? Conversely, was Penn a self-absorbed, easily duped, reckless spendthrift? A fool when it came to money matters? To cast such simplistic aspersions on either man's character is both unjust and insufficient in explaining what occurred. Ford certainly did not participate in any questionable practices with Penn's money in his early years of employment. He was a principled man, who worked very hard for Penn and for Pennsylvania's success. Moreover, the two men got along fine on a personal level, and for several years Ford appeared to be managing Penn's Irish estates and other finances well. However, once Penn's interest shifted to his North American colony, Ford's vigilance in overseeing Penn's Irish property and other enterprises waned, and thus Penn's rental income from those holdings declined as expenses from other ventures mounted. Ford, however, made sure there was enough cash on the credit side for him to use personally to start his own dry goods business. Although there is no hard evidence that Ford falsified his bookkeeping as Penn later claimed, the fact that Ford and his family's lifestyle improved significantly during the years after 1684 causes one to wonder if Ford hadn't indeed engaged in some "creative" accounting with Penn's money.

Nonetheless, according to the records, after 1684, Ford received no compensation for the multiple labors he was called upon by his employer to perform. No doubt Ford came to resent Penn, for while he labored away on Penn's behalf without being paid, his boss continued to live the gentleman's life. It is thus plausible that Ford's feeling that Penn was taking advantage of him caused Ford to doctor his accounts with excessive charges. They were paper charges, however, for Ford never personally collected his debt. His wife collected, but only roughly half what Ford's books said he was owed.

As for Penn, he was by no means a total fool and reckless spend-thrift. He was a premier recruiter of colonists. He sold land at attractive and well-calculated rates in order to profit. However, in retrospect, he needed to have charged a higher price per acre in order to make enough money to cover the expenses involved in an overseas colonial enterprise. Yet, in many ways, Penn found himself in a conundrum relative to land sales in Pennsylvania. If he had charged more for his land he might have generated more personal income, but he would not have been able to lure so many colonists to Pennsylvania. Only about half of the First Purchasers actually came to Pennsylvania in the 1680s and worked the land, either with indentured servants, some with African slaves, or directly themselves. The rest stayed in England and assumed the status of absentee landlords. However, their collective commitment, at least on paper, ensured the colony's success. Unfortunately for a trusting Penn, few of the First Purchasers, especially those who came to Pennsylvania, ever paid him in full for the land they bought, and virtually none paid him the quitrents they owed.

They also refused to pay taxes to help defray his costs of colonial government, and when asked to vote him some sort of annual salary or stipend, a parsimonious Assembly grudgingly agreed to a pit-tance amount. Had Penn received from his colonists what they agreed to pay him for all his efforts in creating a place of refuge for them, he would have had no crisis with Ford. Sadly for Penn, his colonists were like his Irish and English tenants—they had an inher-ent prejudice against landlords, especially absentee ones. Finally, and perhaps most injurious to Penn's finances, was a character defect: his refusal to live within his means, to adjust his lifestyle and spending habits to his income, especially as it declined after the founding of Pennsylvania, requiring a less extravagant existence. Penn preached bourgeois thrift but practiced noblesse oblige.

After his return to England, Penn typically so immersed himself in a variety of public affairs that he neglected both his old and new families. The latter felt especially aggrieved and abandoned by his prolonged absences and preoccupation with external matters. Although Penn was at home with his second wife Hannah long enough to sire seven children, more often than not, he was gone from his family, either in London at Whitehall, trying to hold on to his colony, or traveling about the English countryside preaching the Quaker Light. Hannah knew the moment she agreed to marry Penn that he suffered from wanderlust. She accepted that reality, recon-ciling herself early in their marriage that she, like her New World brethren, would be beholden to an "absentee" proprietor/husband. Most disturbing to Hannah was that her children scarcely knew their father. Her two sons, John, going on three and Thomas, a year-and-a-half, initially ran away from Penn when he "visited" them. Hannah had to convince the boys that this man in their house was not a stranger, but their father.

By 1703, Penn had three children, John, Thomas, and a daughter, Hannah Margarita, whom he did not see for the first time until she was three months old. In the four-and-a-half years of his daughter's brief life, Penn saw her only five times, and once for only a day. By this time Penn also had three grandchildren: his son William, Jr., or "Billy" had two children, and his daughter Letitia, who had married William Aubrey in 1702, had delivered her first child, William IV, at Worminghurst in March 1703. By the time of Penn's release from debtor's prison in August 1708, at the age of 63, Hannah had borne seven children, the oldest of whom, "John the American," was only seven. Five of Penn's children by his second wife would reach adulthood; Hannah Margarita and his sixth child Dennis would not. Over the course of the remaining years of his life, and especially after he suffered his first stroke in 1712, neither his five remaining children that he had sired with Hannah, nor his four grandchildren, would come to know Penn personally, and certainly none of them by the time of Penn's death, comprehended or appreciated what a legendary name and status they now all possessed.

Causing Penn greater emotional pain than his estrangement from his children by his second marriage was the disappointment and heartbreak William III brought to his father. Much to Penn's chagrin, his son, although raised a Quaker, preferred, in behavior and attitude, the robust life of the Cavalier. Indeed, he was more his grandfather's son than the progeny of his righteous and deeply serious father. "Billy" Penn was a pampered, self-indulgent, bon vivant playboy son of an aristocrat, who could care less about the responsibilities and demeanor incumbent upon him as the future proprietor of Pennsylvania. Indeed, young Penn saw Pennsylvania as nothing more than a potential cash cow to enrich his lavish lifestyle. Although Penn was hardly an easy person to get along with, Billy possessed none of his father's outstanding qualities such as dignity, perseverance, loyalty, and integrity.

William, Jr., lived in and of the moment, and when sent to Pennsylvania on his father's behalf, representing proprietary interests and supposed authority, all young Penn accomplished was to further disgrace the family name by engaging in all manner of debauchery and dissipated behavior, ranging from drunkenness to brawling, to the "frequenting of the Caves for purposes of fornication" with Indian women and other colonial females of "loose morals," according to James Logan. Nonetheless, Penn had great hopes for Billy, grooming him as best he could to be the next Proprietor.

When Billy returned from his last sojourn to Pennsylvania in 1705, and based on reports from Logan about his son's disreputable conduct, barely escaping arrest for involvement in a tavern brawl, Penn came to the sad conclusion that his son was ill fit to become the next proprietor, and informed him so. An angered and alienated Billy distanced himself from the Penn household, spending most of his time abroad. He was not at his father's deathbed in 1718, and he died two years later in France from wounds incurred during a sword duel.

Once Penn accepted the reality that his son was not fit to be the future proprietor of Pennsylvania, he once again looked to the Crown as a possible "inheritor" of his colony, particularly its government. After two decades of enduring accusatory letters, invective, and recrimination, and long harangues on the rights of the people and legislative bodies, by 1710, Penn had had enough. He concluded that the unrelenting Lloydian outcry against proprietary prerogatives and upper-class privileges had infected the whole community, engendering a chronic feeling of resentment against authority of any kind.

Most disheartening to Penn was his perception that his colonists, because of the agitation caused by men like the Lloyds, had developed a deeply suspicious view of the world. People who had been drawn together by ties of religion and background now looked suspiciously, if not menacingly, at each other. The old sense of community had been lost. Penn could expect no further support or affection from his colonists, lamented Logan, for "every man is for himself. Pride has become a national Infirmity & there is a general Infatuation gott among us, as we are generally too full of ourselves, and empty of sence to manage affairs of Importance."

In one of his last missives to the Pennsylvania Assembly, Penn vented years of frustration and anger at his colonists, especially the Lloydians' usurpation of his executive authority as vested in his lieutenant governors. To Penn, nothing could be "more destructive" to good government than "to take so much of the provision of the executive part of the government out of the Governor's hands and lodge it in an uncertain collective body [the Assembly]." Penn also had personal reasons for doing what he was about to do. "The attacks upon my reputation, the many indignities put upon me in papers sent over hither into the hands of those who could not be expected to make the most discreet and charitable use of them; resolves passed in the Assemblies for turning my quitrents, never sold by me, to the support of the government, my lands entered upon without any regular method; my private estate continually exhausting for the support of that government; both here and there, and no provision made for it by that country; to all that I cannot but add the violence that has been particularly shown my secretary [James Logan]."

As reflected in his letter to the assembly, Penn had finally reached the disheartening conclusion that the Quakers' antiauthoritarianism had made them temperamentally unfit for government; that the frontier conditions of Pennsylvania had only intensified this inherent disposition of the Quaker character. Indeed, the "howling wilderness" had made his people completely intractable, borderline paranoid in their determination to resist all forms of external authority. Even officials elected from among their own ranks encountered resistance. By this time in his life, nobody understood this "colonial syndrome" better than Penn. "There is an excess of vanity," Penn wrote, "that is Apt to Creep in upon the Crowd, in which they were lost here. [They] think nothing taller than themselves, but the Trees, and as if there were no After Superior Judgment to which they should be accountable."

As an antidote to such pride (or perhaps a nascent nationalism) Penn believed that all his brethren should take turns revisiting England in order to regain a sense of humility and civility, which, in Penn's view, the "howling wilderness" had completely subverted, bringing out the most negative characteristics of the Quaker personality. Penn hoped that by returning to England, Quakers might "lose themselves again amongst the Crowds of so much more Considerable People." With their sense of "decency" and comity hopefully restored, they would return to America a righteous and humbled people, and thus "much more Discreet and Tractable and fit for Government." Unfortunately, Penn's cure for his wayward colonists was never implemented; they remained, according to James Logan "a soure temper'd people."

With such a grim view of his colonists, Penn believed he had no other choice but to try to once again sell to the Crown his right to govern Pennsylvania. Thus, in February 1711, Penn began negotiations with the Lords of Trade, offering to relinquish political control of his colony for 20,000 pounds, the same amount he had proposed eight years earlier. This time, however, he would accept payment over a seven-year period instead of taking an immediate cash settlement. Intrigued by Penn's proposal, the Lords of Trade agreed to present it to the Queen as long as Penn's surrender of Pennsylvania was "absolute and that he renounce all right and claim or pretention whatsoever." Penn agreed.

Queen Anne accepted Penn's offer, and papers were drawn up for signatures; however, in May 1712, Penn suffered a mild stroke, postponing for a few months the transfer of Pennsylvania's government to the Crown. In the meantime, Penn wrote a new will, ensuring that his colony's government would not fall into the hands of his profligate son Billy. Penn stipulated that if he should die before the agreement was officially finalized, Pennsylvania's government was to be entrusted to Robert Harley, Earl of Oxford, and his friend, Lord John Poulet. The two peers were to act as trustees until the Queen was ready to transform Pennsylvania into a royal colony.

Penn bequeathed all of Pennsylvania's land to seven trustees in England, including his wife, and to five in Pennsylvania, including James Logan. His three grandchildren—two of Billy's progeny as well as his daughter Letitia's child and Letitia directly—were to receive 10,000 acres each in America. Penn named Hannah sole executrix, and to her he left all of Pennsylvania's rents and all of his personal estate. When they came of age, all of his children by his second marriage inherited the rest of Pennsylvania's land, to be divided equally among them. Billy was to receive 1,000 pounds from Penn's estate but not an acre of Pennsylvania land. By the drawing of his will, Penn no longer had any land in Ireland and in England, only his Worminghurst estate, where his daughter Letitia lived with her family and his new manor at Ruscombe, where Penn lived with Hannah and his second family.

Meanwhile, the Crown agreed to Penn's surrender terms, but as expected, Whitehall cut the price from 20,000 pounds to 12,000 pounds. Penn nonetheless accepted the Queen's counteroffer, with the caveat that she was to advance him 1,000 pounds immediately, which Anne readily agreed to do. Soon after receiving his money Penn suffered another stroke, in October 1712. Penn was writing a letter to James Logan, informing him of what had transpired since Logan's return to Pennsylvania three months earlier. While beginning the fourth page of his missive, Penn's right hand suddenly stopped writing, wilted by paralysis, and he lost consciousness. Hannah finished Penn's letter, telling Logan she had to do so because her husband "was taken with a second fit of his lethargich illness, like as about six months ago." Hannah was confident, however, "in the comfortable prospect of his recovery. And I am ordered by the doctors to keep all business from him till he is stronger." Like her husband, Hannah too was anxious for Logan to "use thy utmost diligence to settle things [in Pennsylvania] and returns for our comfort and quiet those whose mean spirits have contributed to my dear husband's illness." Hannah Penn was convinced that Penn's strokes were the result of his incessant troubles with his colonists.

A year later, Penn had "just reached home [his new estate at Ruscombe], when he was seized by the same severe illness that he has twice labored under," Hannah informed James Logan. This third stroke completely debilitated Penn, confining him to his bed for most of the rest of his life. From this point on—January 1713—to the end of his life, Penn was dependent on the care of others. Those who came to see him found the Proprietor "pretty well in health, and cheerful of disposition, but defective in memory, nor could he deliver his words so readily heretofore," wrote Penn loyalist Thomas Story to James Logan on a visit to England and to Ruscombe. Story remained in Europe for several more years, traveling among meetings in England and the Continent, returning to Ruscombe to give Hannah Penn what help he could, since she was now in charge of Pennsylvania. On his last visit to Ruscombe in 1716, Story reported to Logan on Penn's condition. "His memory is almost lost, and the use of his understanding suspended; so that he was not so conversable as formerly, and yet as near the Truth in the love of it, as before. When I went to the house I thought myself strong enough to see him in that condition, but when I entered the room and perceived the great defect of his expressions, for want of memory, it greatly bowed my spirit, under a consideration of the uncertainty of all human qualifications, and what the finest of men are soon reduced to."

During that same summer, Hannah took Penn to Bath, hoping that the curative waters would help revitalize him somewhat. "Thy poor father holds through the Lord's mercy as well as at home. He drinks about a quart of the Bath water and has a good stomach after it," she wrote home to her sons. Whatever ameliorative affects the Bath waters had on Penn did not last long, for no sooner did he return home than he continued his gradual declension. Sometime in July 1718, the 73-year-old Penn came down with chills and a fever, probably some form of influenza, and on July 30 of that year, between two and three in the morning, William Penn died. He was laid to rest at Jordans, next to his beloved Gulielma and among so many of his children from both marriages.

Epilogue and Legacy

When William Penn established his "holy experiment," he envisioned that his colony's government would reflect not only the best of the English liberal (Whig) tradition in politics but be unswervingly committed as well to religious liberty. Government, Penn wrote when developing his 1682 Frame of Government, was "a part of religion itself, a thing sacred in its institution and end." Penn was also a traditionalist, believing that the recognized leaders of the Society of Friends naturally would be conceded political preeminence in his colony. The Quaker creed was to be the all-powerful mechanism of social and political integration and cohesion, in which all the faithful joined together in stewardship or obligation to the community. Penn believed that the same ideals and ideas that bound Quakers together in England would hold them together in the New World.

However, no sooner did Friends arrive in Pennsylvania than the overwhelming forces of life in the wilderness began to undermine adherence to the Quaker ethos. It was as if the "temptations" or promise of material success, which appeared all around them in the form of almost limitless amounts of land and other opportunities, simply overcame their devotion to the Quaker way of being. Everything Quakers either lacked or were denied in England they found in abundance in their colony and at their ready disposal for their immediate taking. Regardless of how modest the income or simple the livelihood, all took a fierce pride in their accomplishments.

Quakers saw themselves as people who had suffered years of persecution at the hands of petty English authorities, endured a long and hazardous ocean crossing, toiled through droughts, epidemics, boom-bust economic conditions, weathered religious controversy, and resisted Puritan governors, Anglican imperialists, and proprietary placemen. Through it all, they had carved out a niche in the New World, a quality of life few, if any, had dreamed possible, and certainly unattainable in England.

Quakers thus came to vigorously oppose any proprietary or royal policies they perceived as restricting their pursuit to have in the New World what had been denied them in the Old World. In order to ensure that their new reality of success continued unimpaired, Quakers deemed it essential that their political system allow and protect their newfound freedoms. As a result, Penn's vision of his colony being a "holy experiment" in righteous, Christian living, quickly fell by the wayside, as his brethren acted first as ambitious, covetous settlers and only secondarily as members of an organic Quaker community. "Particular men doeth for themselves," complained John Blunston, an early leader in the settlement process. This observation was reiterated repeatedly throughout Pennsylvania's developing years—by John Blackwell, who was appalled by the exorbitant prices Quaker merchants charged their fellows; by James Logan, who constantly complained to Penn that self-interest ruled Pennsylvania life; and of course by Penn himself, who forever lamented his colonists' excessive individualism and acquisitiveness at his expense, both financially and spiritually.

Perhaps most distressing to Penn because it most directly affected his vision of what Pennsylvania was to be, was his colonists' refusal to accept the "proper relations amongst men," which to Penn meant acquiescence to the ancient sense of deference to persons known "for their wisdom, virtue, and ability," as his Frame of 1682 articulated. Penn expected his colonists to accept his authority to govern them at all times and thus obey his mandates and the power vested by him to his surrogates. However, no sooner did Penn leave his colony in 1684 than the Quakers' inherent antiauthoritarianism emerged, and in a short time, Penn found himself having to deal with a people determined to resist his every charge, regardless of the form his authority assumed. It made no difference to his people whether his entreaties to accept his right to govern them came in letters or in person, or in the shape of a governor; if they believed Penn's decrees prevented them from pursuing the improvement of their lives, or violated the liberties they had taken upon themselves to grant each other, then massive resistance to proprietary power was the order of the day.

Even the most loyal of Penn's supporters, men like James Logan and Isaac Norris, admitted to a disillusioned Penn before his death that life in "the howling wilderness," had revealed that Quaker principles were "destructive or repugnant to Civil Government." It was clear to Norris that after almost three decades in Pennsylvania, Friends "must either be independent and entirely by ourselves; or, if mixed, partial to our own opinion." Finally, by the time of Penn's death, and much to his simultaneous joy and sadness, Pennsylvania had become known for its hospitality to liberty of conscience. However, as all manner of Christian sects poured into Pennsylvania, Quakers were forced to stand by almost helplessly, accepting into their colony religious groups who had nothing but contempt for the Quaker faith, making Friends "dissenters in their own country," as Penn frequently lamented.

In planning his Zion, Penn refused to accept his faith's contradictory tendencies, which doomed his original conception to failure. It was not until the last years of his life that he finally understood that Quaker religious principles were incompatible with the political responsibility he had entrusted to his people. He would have found great solace, however, in his brethren's fulfillment of the Quaker mission to reform the world, rather than withdraw from it. Quakers' subsequent bold work in the fields of abolitionism, humanitarianism, and civil liberties would have greatly gratified Penn, for such endeavors reflected the realization of a significant part of his vision for his "holy experiment." Perhaps most important, by the time of the American Revolution, Penn's wayward saints had succeeded in becoming the embodiment of the national conscience.

Depending on the side of the Atlantic on which one stands, William Penn has a dual image. In England he is regarded as a significant historical figure, while in the United States, he assumes the status of an icon, one of early America's most legendary and revered individuals. The only known portrait of Penn as a young man is the one of him in armor, currently hanging in Christ Church at Oxford University. There are no other known pictorial representations of him in England. By contrast, in the United States there are several paintings and statutes of Penn, especially in Pennsylvania and Delaware, but they are all facsimiles of a much older Penn; indeed most appear as caricatures of a portly, balding, plainly dressed, rather dour middle-aged man. None come close to the flatteringly sublime depiction at Oxford.

Although not given iconic status in England, Penn nonetheless influenced religious and political thought at a pivotal time in English history. Throughout Penn's life, the hand of God was being pushed back by the mind of man. Authors branded in their own days as dangerous atheists became respected thinkers. English intellectuals believed the fundamental tenets of the Scientific Revolution were as applicable to the sociopolitical realm as they were to the cosmos.

They were certain the new scientific methodology represented man's best hope to liberate himself from the consequences of Adam's fall; man's power over nature, not God's grace, would henceforth be his salvation. In politics, men talked about man-made societies and the inalienable rights of life, liberty, and property, not of governments instituted by God or the divinity of kings.

Penn never fully embraced the new secular ethos. He still believed that God was more than a first cause, a divine and marvelous clock-maker, who started the universe but then disengaged, allowing man to discover the natural laws with which He imbued the universe. Although in his treatises Penn spoke the secular language of his time lucidly and convincingly, in the final analysis, like his Puritan counterpart John Winthrop, Penn believed men, governments, and laws were answerable to God, and thus they must at all times be wise, just, and moral. Indeed, the very institution of government finds its source in the cosmic pattern. "Magistracy," wrote Penn, "is an ordinance of God." Therefore, all government officials are morally responsible to God for their conduct. Moreover, every magistrate is the guardian of public morality in the largest sense of the term. If men and the governments they create and the laws they promulgate violated God's trust, then it would be only a matter of time before God's retribution would be visited upon such a reprobate people.

Although Penn believed governments to be divinely instituted, he nonetheless drew from the purely material political philosophies of Algernon Sidney, John Locke, Thomas Hobbes, and James Harrington, what he felt was worthwhile for his colony as well as for his greater crusade for liberty of conscience for all his countrymen.

Unlike the Puritan Errand into the Wilderness, which asserted individuals had fallen from grace and thus only a handful of visible saints could rule, Penn claimed that the light within everyone entitled all to participate (in varying degrees) in the political process. Although believing individuals to be inherently good, Penn nonetheless accepted that people were susceptible to passions that overcame their reason or disposition to do good, causing them to become depraved or corrupt. Reflecting the influence of men like Locke, Hobbes, and other seventeenth-century thinkers, Penn concurred that when individuals proved no longer capable of living in a "state of nature," just and moral laws administered by wise and virtuous men had to be instituted to safeguard society from degenerate individuals. Penn believed law to be "the prime necessity" of human society, for disobedient men, having refused to conform to "the holy law within," must therefore be subject to "the just law without."

To Penn, good laws reflected the quality of the individuals responsible for their proclamation. In other words, the dignity of government was dependent on human morality. As he declared in the preface of his 1682 Frame of Government, "I know some say, Let us have good laws, and no matter for the men that execute them; But let them consider, that though good laws do well good men do better. . . ." Penn insisted on the moral responsibility of the governing class to maintain at all times a genuine humility and understanding that God's love extended to all men regardless of their station. Penn thus believed it was imperative that those entrusted by the people to govern in their name did so righteously, as God-inspired and God-fearing human beings. Unfortunately, Penn's experiment of placing government in the hands of supposedly good men was tested repeatedly and found wanting each time, at least in his view.

Although implicit in many of his political writings was the social contract theory, Penn by no means believed in republicanism, political equality or popular self-government. Indeed, when helping Penn construct the Frame of Government for Pennsylvania, Algernon Sidney and others criticized Penn for not creating, when given such carte blanche in his charter, a government based on republican ideals. In Penn's mind there was no direct correlation between government by consent and popular sovereignty or democracy; indeed the two were mutually exclusive rather than symbiotic, as they would become to later generations of Americans. In Penn's political frame of reference, the people's consent, or input, was confined to the promulgation of laws and constitutions, and the right to an indirect participation in the governing process. They were to defer at all times to their socioeconomic superiors, who by their material or educational accomplishments, experience in public affairs, or other distinctions had earned the right to govern in the people's name. To Penn, and the majority of his contemporaries, the different levels among individuals, was an implicit part of God's design for the human condition. In Penn's world, the roles of men and women; master, servant, and slave; nobility and commoner were well known, understood, and accepted.

Penn did agree, however, with republicans like Sidney, that individual authority such as that of a king should be limited by a superior and nonpersonal agency, the law, which evolved by and from the consent of the people. In the final analysis, the principal purpose of government thus became for Penn "to support power in reverence with the people, and to secure the people from the abuse of power; for liberty without obedience is confusion, and obedience without liberty is slavery."

Perhaps greater than Penn's contributions to political theory, especially his thoughts on constitutional government, was his indefatigable struggle against religious bigotry and oppression. Not even the scurvy dungeons of the time could dampen Penn's zeal to obtain for all his countrymen the right to liberty of conscience, which after years of personal, unrelenting crusading and the suffering of all manner of humiliation and punishment, Penn saw come to fruition by the end of the seventeenth century. Indeed, William Penn was in the vanguard of clarifying for his time the fundamentals of an Englishman's birthright. He never stopped insisting on the triune nature of political freedom—the right to life and the security of property, the consenting and representational power of the people in the making of laws, and the right of a fair trial by jury.

Although Penn's "holy experiment" of Pennsylvania failed to live up to his expectations in virtually every capacity, it nonetheless reflected the breadth, depth, and tolerance of mind that conceived an endeavor in social living founded on the principles of humanity's inherent goodness rather than depravity. Although failing as a "holy experiment" in righteous, Christian living and communal and political harmony, Pennsylvania nonetheless produced the first successful venture in ethnic and religious pluralism. In many ways, the "melting pot" called Pennsylvania, became the cauldron from which the American ethos grew.

Equally impressive and insightful was Penn's relationships and compacts with Native Americans, whom he believed were no less human, no less endowed with the Inner Light than white Europeans. Penn succeeded as few white Europeans did anywhere in the New World in establishing a mutually beneficial and trusting rapport with Native Americans, largely because he did not regard them as savages and heathens but as fellow human beings whose culture was to be respected and valued at all times. Penn's willingness to treat Native Americans with such dignity turned Pennsylvania into a refuge for many other tribes fleeing from the harsh, if not brutal treatment in the other colonies.

The world is also indebted to Penn's "breadth and depth of mind" for another reason: he was among the first of European intellectuals and leaders to propose an international parliament to settle disputes and preserve world (mainly European in Penn's time) peace. His *Essay Towards the Present and Future Peace of Europe* can rightfully be considered the philosophical progenitor of the

World Court, League of Nations, and United Nations. Nor is it to be forgotten that Penn was the very first to propose a legislative and executive union of the colonies more than a half a century before Benjamin Franklin offered an almost carbon-copy of Penn's design at the Albany Conference at the beginning of the French and Indian War. Although none of Penn's ideas for ending conflict came to fruition during his time, he nonetheless can be credited with sowing the seeds of international arbitration to be permanently planted in our own time.

Penn was, above all, a man of faith. Unlike his Puritan counterparts, who believed life on earth was one, long tormenting, hopeless journey to all but a handful of the Elect, Penn believed hope was always present; God's light was everywhere, available to all individuals. In a way, the Quaker doctrine of the Inner Light announced the end of the Puritan age and the beginning of the brighter, free age to come. Beginning in Penn's time, two powerful forces have come to define much of Western culture: the attainment of intellectual and political liberty and the ongoing reformation of humanity's moral and spiritual nature. Both dynamics converged in the personality of William Penn and came to define much of his life.

As Penn grew older, the distance between him and his Quaker brethren widened, and ironically, he became as imperious and uncompromising as his father. Indeed, he became the man his father wanted him to be, and in many ways, more successful than his father even dreamed possible for a son who had rejected so much of his pedigree. Penn owned a colony as large as England and was a landlord on a massive scale. However, after becoming "True and Absolute Proprietor" of Pennsylvania, Penn displayed an increasingly authoritarian personality, becoming quarrelsome and vindictive, especially as his colonists' determination to curb his executive powers intensified. His prolonged absences from his colony and isolation in England caused him to become more rigid, tactless, and given to self-pity, believing his Quaker brethren never appreciated all he had done for them. Penn often referred to himself as the "Old kind abused landlord" without self-consciousness.

Despite possessing such an overbearing and truculent personality, Penn's contributions to the spiritual and political development of Englishmen and Americans were of great historical significance. He conceived of and established a society in which all inhabitants were guaranteed freedom of religion, equality before the law, and rights secured by a written constitution, which also placed checks on the proprietor's power. Interestingly, the vision that made these things possible came from a lifetime of resistance to the authority of others, whether it came in the form of Anglican ministers and civil authorities, or in the shape of colonial bureaucrats and placemen. Penn's wealth and status led to influence and favors at the Stuart court, which in turn, allowed his musings to become reality, especially his image of a Quaker haven in the New World.

William Penn knew well that an experiment never really ends. Indeed, he never intended for his colonial endeavor to reach finality. Perhaps therein lay the essence of the American ideal: it was Penn's faith-inspired vision of creating in the wilderness of North America a place where all who came would be guaranteed fundamental human rights that no one should be denied because of their skin color, gender, or religious beliefs. Over time, as the American character and identity evolved, it became apparent that of all the European people who came to North America in the seventeenth and eighteenth centuries, it was the Quakers and their leader William Penn, who had left the most enduring imprint on the shaping of the American creed, which to this day cherishes and espouses the liberties William Penn first established in Pennsylvania.

Study and Discussion Questions

Introduction

1. What is the image, if any, many Americans still have of William Penn?

2. What are some of the "realities" about Penn's life, career, and personality that many history books and Penn biographies fail to reveal or develop?

Chapter 1

1. What kind of man and father was Admiral Penn?

2. While growing up, what kind of relationship did young William Penn have with his father?

3. How did the dynamics of Penn's relationship with his father contribute to his eventually becoming a Quaker?

4. Why was Admiral Penn arrested and sent to the Tower on his return from the West Indies expedition?

5. How did Quakerism differ from all other forms of orthodox or traditional Christianity?

6. What fundamental beliefs defined the Quaker faith?

7. From the moment of their founding the Quakers became one of the most persecuted sects in English history. Why?

Chapter 2

1. Why did Sir William want Penn to attend Oxford?

2. Why did young William Penn dislike Oxford?

3. Why was Penn expelled from Oxford?

4. Why did Admiral Penn send his son to France?

5. What two events interrupted Penn's attendance at the law school of Lincoln's Inn and how did those events impact his life?

6. Why did Admiral Penn send his son to Ireland?

7. William Penn became a "convinced" Quaker while in Ireland. By what circumstances and experiences did that occur?

Chapter 3

1. How did Sir William react to his son's becoming a Quaker?

2. What three fundamental Quaker tenets did Penn articulate in *The Sandy Foundation Shaken*, and why did his essay create such controversy?

3. Why was Penn arrested and imprisoned for publishing *The Sandy Foundation Shaken*, and what was his father's response to this ordeal?

4. Why did Penn write the first edition of *No Cross, No Crown* while confined to the Tower?

5. What were Penn's main arguments in *No Cross, No Crown*?

6. Why did Penn appear to recant his position on the Trinity in his apologia, *Innocency*?

Chapter 4

1. In securing the release of imprisoned Irish Quakers, what did Penn realize about his family name and status?

2. Under what act and with what charge was Penn arrested at the Gracechurch Street meetinghouse?

3. Why were William Penn and William Mead found in contempt of court?

4. Although charged with violating the Conventicle Act, Penn's alleged "crime" and court appearance quickly escalated into what far greater legal issue?

5. As a result of the Penn–Mead trial, what became an inalienable right for all Englishmen?

Chapter 5

1. Within months of his release from prison, Penn was incarcerated again. He was charged with violating what Parliamentary acts?

2. While confined to Newgate prison for six months, Penn wrote another seminal tract, *The Great Case of Liberty of Conscience,*

Once More Briefly Debated and Defended. What were Penn's main arguments or themes to prove that to deny one liberty of conscience was not only morally wrong but illogical and economically and politically detrimental to England as well?

3. Why did Penn relate better to women, especially those of the upper classes than with the majority of his male Quaker brethren?

4. What was Charles II's Declaration of Indulgence, and why did it last for only a year?

5. In *Spirit of the Truth Vindicated*, Penn established the Quaker concept of apostasy. What did Penn and the Quakers mean by that term?

6. What Quaker leader went to North America, and upon his return, what did he want to see come about for his brethren?

7. What was the purpose of the Meetings for Sufferings?

8. Who were the Whigs and Tories, and what were their respective political ideologies?

9. What was the "Popish Plot" and how did it affect Penn?

Chapter 6

1. Where was the Quaker's first sanctuary in North America, and how did it come about?

2. Although inheriting a sizable fortune from his father, Penn proved to be a poor money manager. Why?

3. Why did New Jersey prove to be an unsatisfactory Quaker haven?

4. What economic, political, strategic, and personal factors contributed to Penn's receipt of his charter for Pennsylvania?

5. William Penn not only received one of the largest colonial charters in English history but one that granted him great power and authority. What rights and privileges did Penn have as "True and Absolute Proprietor" of his colony?

6. Why did Penn ultimately call his colony "Pennsylvania"? What did he initially want to name his Quaker refuge?

Chapter 7

1. What were Penn's main objectives in establishing Pennsylvania?

2. What kind of society and political environment did Penn envision Pennsylvania becoming?

3. Why did the *Frame of Government* go through so many revisions and editions before finally being promulgated?

4. Was the final *Frame* a liberal or conservative document?

5. What did the final draft reveal about Penn's political thinking?

6. What kind of settlers or immigrants did Penn hope to attract to his colony, and why?

7. How did Penn attract both people and money to Pennsylvania?

8. As revealed through the final *Frame of Government* and his other actions in promoting and establishing Pennsylvania, was William Penn a "liberal"? A "conservative"? Or was he, perhaps, somewhere in between?

Chapter 8

1. What was Penn's attitude toward the use of Africans as slave labor?

2. What socioeconomic and physical factors contributed to Pennsylvania's rapid material and demographic development?

3. What was Penn's vision for his "City of Brotherly Love," Philadelphia?

4. How did Penn regard Native American culture?

5. How did Penn personally as well as his colonists collectively, benefit from Penn's enlightened treatment of Native Americans?

6. The moment he arrived in his colony, Penn faced unanticipated opposition to his authority. Why? What realities about his brethren and life in the wilderness did he fail to recognize?

7. What three factions emerged in Pennsylvania which over time would come to challenge Penn's authority as "True and Absolute Proprietor"?

8. Upon Penn's return to England in 1684, what issues and problems remained unsolved and smoldering in Pennsylvania?

Chapter 9

1. What issues bonded Penn and James II?

2. Why did many within James's government resent Penn's status and relationship with the king?

3. What was the Dominion of New England and why did its creation worry Penn?

4. Why did Penn become one of James's closest advisers?

5. Why did Penn's support of James's policies arouse opposition not only from Whigs but from Tories and Dissenters as well, including Quakers?

6. Penn paid a high price for his loyalty to James Stuart. After James fled England, what happened to Penn?

Chapter 10

1. Should William Penn have stayed in Pennsylvania? Why or why not?

2. What issues between Penn and his colonists caused the continued erosion of Penn's authority in Pennsylvania as well as a loss of confidence in his ability to govern his colony?

3. Why did Penn allegedly owe Philip Ford so much money?

4. Why did Pennsylvania Quakers resist Penn's authority as "True and Absolute Proprietor"?

5. Why did Penn's appointment of Captain John Blackwell prove disastrous?

6. Who was a Jacobite, and why was Penn accused of such an affiliation?

7. Why did Thomas Lloyd and his followers oppose Penn so vigorously?

8. Why was Penn's charter taken from him in 1692? What did he do to get it back two years later?

9. What realities of life in the North American wilderness did Penn never fully comprehend that caused his Pennsylvania brethren to allegedly lose sight of their purpose in coming to the New World?

Chapter 11

1. Why were Penn and fellow Quakers pleased by the passage of the Affirmation Act and why did King William rather enthusiastically support the measure?

2. What were the major themes of Penn's treatise, *The Rise and Progress of the People Called Quakers*?

3. What was the Keithian Schism and how did it impact Pennsylvania Quakers and Penn?

4. Why did Penn acquiesce to the Assembly's demand for a new Frame of government?

5. The influx of what particular religious group greatly alarmed the Quakers, and why?

6. According to colonial officials such as Edmund Randolph, how were Pennsylvania Quakers "misbehaving," and how did their activities affect Penn's image and role as proprietor?

7. Penn typically believed the issues causing tension between the Crown and colonists could be resolved peaceably. He thus proposed solutions to end the grievances in *A Briefe and Plaine Scheame how the English colonies in the North parts of America may be made more useful to the Crown and one another's peace and safety with universal occurrence*. What did Penn believe must be implemented in order to end the problems?

Chapter 12

1. How had Pennsylvania changed during Penn's fifteen-year absence?

2. Why was David Lloyd such a powerful figure in Pennsylvania and thus a threat to both Penn's status as proprietor and colonial officials as well?

3. By the time of his return to Pennsylvania, the majority of Quakers had come to resent if not despise Penn. Why?

4. Although initially intending to come down hard on his colonists for disobeying English laws, thus jeopardizing his charter, Penn reversed himself and came to his colonists' defense. Why?

5. Why did Penn agree to a new frame of government, the Charter of Privileges, promulgated before he returned to England in 1701?

6. Given all the trouble his colonists had caused him while he was in England, one would assume that Penn would have realized that his prolonged absence was the cause for many of these problems. Why did Penn not stay in Pennsylvania? Why did he believe he had to return to England?

Chapter 13

1. How did the ascension of Queen Anne benefit Penn, especially the retention of his charter?

2. Why did Penn offer to sell to the Crown his right to govern Pennsylvania in 1703?

3. Why did Penn's choices for governor have difficulty with governing Pennsylvania?

4. What caused Penn to become so indebted to Philip Ford, ultimately resulting in Penn serving time in a debtor's prison?

5. What kind of relationship did Penn have with his second wife and family?

6. Why did Penn's son, William III, cause his father such heartbreak and disappointment?

7. By the time of his death, what conclusion had Penn reached about his New World brethren and his "holy experiment" called Pennsylvania?

Epilogue and Legacy

1. Why did Penn's vision of Pennsylvania as a "holy experiment" prove to be a heartbreaking failure, at least in Penn's expectations?

2. What were some of Penn's most important contributions to the histories of both the United States and Great Britain?

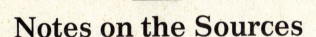

Notes on the Sources

Indispensable to the writing of this biography of William Penn were *The Papers of William Penn*, a four-volume effort under the auspices of Richard S. Dunn and Mary Maples Dunn, published by the University of Pennsylvania from 1981 to 1987. Although the majority of information contained in the volumes focuses on Penn's relationship with his Pennsylvania colonists, the series also includes a substantial microfilm collection containing invaluable manuscripts concerning Penn's life in England. Since this study encompasses Penn's life on both sides of the Atlantic, the microfilmed documents in conjunction with the published material allowed for the creation of a much more complete profile of William Penn the man, Quaker, husband, father, writer, and politician.

Beginning with Joseph Besse's 1726 publication of *A Collection of the Works of William Penn, of which is Prefaced a Journal of His Life with Many Letters and Papers Not Before Published*, there have been over thirty-five biographies of Penn focusing on different aspects of his life. Penn's nineteenth-century biographers tended to emphasize Penn as the pious Quaker and champion of liberty of conscience or as The Great Colonizer. Penn the man remained an enigma until the late 1950s, when Catherine Owens Peare produced *William Penn: A Biography*. Based on sound scholarly investigation, Peare did an admirable job of providing readers with a much more complete picture of Penn the man, his life, and his accomplishments. However, her study remains hagiographic in presentation and overall assessment. In short, the Penn that emerged was more saintly than real.

The 1960s witnessed an outpouring of works on Penn with each attempting to capture a different aspect of Penn's life and career. The first to undertake such an approach was Edwin P. Bronner, who, in *William Penn's Holy Experiment: The Founding of Pennsylvania, 1681–1701* (Philadelphia: Temple University Press, 1962), questioned whether Penn's colony was a success. The best work on Penn's relationship with James II is Vincent Buranelli's *The King and the Quaker: A Study of William Penn and James II* (Philadelphia: University of Pennsylvania Press, 1962). Buranelli contends that motivating Penn to sustain his relationship with James, regardless of the king's autocratic ways and political blundering, was Penn's religious motives; his belief that James represented the best hope for religious toleration for Quakers and other sectarians. In *William Penn and Early Quakerism* (Princeton, NJ: Princeton University Press, 1973), Melvin B. Endy, Jr., concentrates on Penn the Quaker, asserting that animating all of Penn's secular undertakings was a higher spiritual purpose.

The first to attempt to separate Penn from his Quakerism and present him as a savvy Restoration politician was Joseph Illick in *William Penn the Politician: His Relations with the English Government* (Ithaca, NY: Cornell University Press, 1965). Produced shortly after Illick's groundbreaking work was Mary Maples Dunn's equally thought-provoking study, *William Penn: Politics and Conscience* (Princeton, NJ: Princeton University Press, 1967). Dunn's book examines how Penn reconciled his political activism with his faith, willing to combine the two in order to achieve a better world not only for his fellow Quakers, but for all Englishmen as well. Perhaps the best synthesis of both Illick and Dunn is Mary K. Geiter's *William Penn,* one of the selections in Pearson's Profiles in Power series (Essex, England: Pearson Education Limited Series, 2000). Geiter focuses on Penn as one of Restoration England's most powerful insiders, whose Court connections were to be envied and which he shrewdly parlayed into great advantage for himself, his Quaker brethren, and his colony. Without question, the most complete biography of Penn, based on the most extensive use of his correspondence and family papers, is Harry Emerson Wildes's *William Penn* (New York: Macmillan, 1974).

Two works were particularly helpful in understanding Penn the prolific writer of essays and treatises, *The Witness of William Penn,* edited by Frederick B. Tolles and E. Gordon Alderfer (New York: Macmillan, 1957), and Paul Buckley's *Twenty-First Century Penn* (Richmond, IN: Earlham College Press, 2003). Buckley's work is rather unique in that he translates into modern English what he believes to have been the five most important of the over 150 treatises Penn wrote during his lifetime.

When doing a biography, it is essential to see the individual in the economic, political, and social milieu in which he or she operated.

Such was the purpose of *The World of William Penn,* a collection of essays, written by the foremost scholars of the time, edited by Richard S. Dunn and Mary Maples Dunn (Philadelphia: University of Pennsylvania Press, 1986). Especially helpful were Mary Maples Dunn, "The Personality of William Penn"; Richard S. Dunn, "Penny Wise and Pound Foolish: Penn as a Businessman"; Francis Jennings, "Brother Miquon: Good Lord!"; Ned Landsman, "William Penn's Scottish Counterparts: The Quakers of 'North Britain' and the Colonization of East New Jersey"; Edwin R. Bronner, "Quaker Discipline and Order, 1680–1720: Philadelphia Yearly Meeting and London Yearly Meeting"; Caroline Robbins, "William Penn 1689–1702: Eclipse, Frustration, and Achievement"; Stephen Saunders Webb, "The Peaceable Kingdom: Quaker Pennsylvania in the Stuart Empire"; and Nicholas Canny, "The Irish Background to Penn's Experiment."

Since Penn actually spent more time in England than in North America, it is imperative to give readers as clear, concise, and accurate an account of his English life as possible in a short biography. Especially important is an understanding of the political environment in which he operated. All of the following are indispensable when trying to understand Penn's political world. Douglas R. Lacey, *Dissent and Parliamentary Politics in England, 1661–1689* (New Brunswick, NJ: Rutgers University Press, 1969). Lacey's work focuses on the efforts by the nonconformist sects, including the Quakers, led by Penn, to achieve toleration. A scholarly yet readable general history of the period that complements Lacey's work is Ronald Hutton's *The Restoration: A Political and Religious History of England and Wales, 1658–1667* (London: Oxford University Press, 1985). For biographies of the men with whom Penn could count on for support throughout his life and career, see John Kenyon's *Robert Spencer, Earl of Sunderland, 1641–1702* (London, 1958), and Brian W. Hill's, *Robert Harley: Speaker, Secretary of State and Premier Minister* (New Haven, CT: Yale University Press, 1988). There are several good biographies of Charles II. Without question the most readable and enjoyable is Antonia Fraser's *Royal Charles: Charles II and the Restoration* (New York: Random House, 1979). For more scholarly accounts of Charles's life and reign, see John Miller, *Charles II* (London, 1991), and Ronald Hutton, *Charles II* (London, 1991). Good, concise, readable general histories of Restoration England, including the Glorious Revolution, can be found in Lacey Baldwin Smith's *This Realm of England: 1399–1688* (Lexington, MA: D.C. Heath and Company, 1976); William B. Willcox's *The Age of Aristocracy: 1688–1830*

(Lexington, MA: D.C. Heath and Company, 1976); Robert Beddard, ed., *The Revolutions of 1688* (Oxford: Clarendon Press, 1991); Dale Hoak and Mordechai Feingold, eds., *The World of William and Mary: Anglo-Dutch Perspectives of 1688–89* (Palo Alto, CA: Stanford University Press, 1996); and Jonathan I. Israel, ed., *The Anglo-Dutch Moment: Essays on the Glorious Revolution and Its World Impact* (New York: Cambridge University Press, 1991). For the event's impact on the North American colonies, see K.G. Davies, "The Revolutions in America," in Beddard, ed., *Revolutions of 1688,* pp. 244–270; Richard R. Johnson, "The Revolution of 1688-9 in the American Colonies," in Israel, ed., *The Anglo-Dutch Moment,* pp. 215–240; and Richard S. Dunn, "The Glorious Revolution in America," in Nicholas Canny and Alaine Low, eds., *The Origins of Empire: British Overseas Enterprise to the Close of the Seventeenth Century* (New York: Oxford University Press, 1998), pp. 445–466.

For understanding the personalities and dynamics of colonial Pennsylvania politics and Penn's relationship with his colonists, there is no better place to start than with Gary B. Nash's seminal work, *Quakers and Politics: Pennsylvania, 1681–1726* (New Edition; Boston: Northeastern University Press, 1993), and Craig W. Horle and Marianne S. Wokeck, eds., *Lawmaking and Legislators in Pennsylvania* (Volume I; Philadelphia: University of Pennsylvania Press, 1991). For a general understanding of colonial Pennsylvania history see James T. Lemon's *Best Poor Man's Country: A Geographical Study of Early Southeastern Pennsylvania* (Baltimore: Johns Hopkins University Press, 1972); Joseph E. Illick, *Colonial Pennsylvania: A History* (New York: Charles Scribner's Sons, 1976); Arthur L. Jensen, *The Maritime Commerce of Colonial Pennsylvania* (Madison: University of Wisconsin Press, 1963); Stephanie Grauman Wolf, *Urban Village: Population, Community and Family Structure in Germantown, Pennsylvania, 1683–1780* (Princeton, NJ: Princeton University Press, 1976); Frederick B. Tolles, *Meeting House and Counting House: The Quaker Merchants of Colonial Philadelphia, 1682–1763* (Chapel Hill: University of North Carolina Press, 1948); Sally Schwartz, *"A Mixed Multitude": The Struggle for Toleration in Colonial Pennsylvania* (New York: New York University Press, 1987); and Barry Levy, *Quakers and the American Family: British Settlement in the Delaware Valley, 1650–1765* (New York: Oxford University Press, 1988). Perhaps the best, most current, and highly readable treatment of colonial America is Alan Taylor's *American Colonies* (New York: Viking Press/The Penguin Group, 2001). Taylor challenges the traditional

Anglocentric focus of colonial history by exploring the many other cultural influences that helped shape the American character and determined the dynamics of much of the pre-Revolutionary period.

For Penn as well as his Quaker brethren's relationships with Native Americans and African Americans, Gary Nash's *Red, White, and Black: The Peoples of Early America* (Third Edition; New York: Prentice Hall, 1991), remains the best study of colonial American race relations. On Penn's attitude toward slavery as well as those of his fellow Quakers, see Jean R. Soderlund, *Quakers and Slavery: A Divided Spirit* (Princeton, NJ: Princeton University Press, 1985). For Penn's relationships with Native Americans, see C.A. Weslager, *The Delaware Indians: A History* (New Brunswick, NJ: Rutgers University Press, 1972). Also see Eric Hinderaker, *Elusive Empires: Constructing Colonialism in the Ohio Valley, 1673–1800* (New York: Cambridge University Press, 1997). For the Covenant Chain, see Matthew Dennis, *Cultivating a Landscape of Peace: Iroquois-European Encounters in Seventeenth-Century America* (Ithaca, NY: Cornell University Press, 1993); Francis Jennings, *The Ambiguous Iroquois Empire* (New York: W.W. Norton, 1984); Daniel K. Richter, *The Ordeal of the Longhouse: The Peoples of the Iroquois League in the Era of European Colonization* (Chapel Hill: University of North Carolina Press, 1992); and Daniel K. Richter and James H. Merrell, eds., *Beyond the Covenant Chain: The Iroquois and Their Neighbors in Indian North America, 1600–1800* (Syracuse, NY: Syracuse University Press, 1987).

Essential to any biography of Penn is an understanding of the imperial context in which he operated. However, works on this theme are relatively few compared to imperial studies on the American Revolution. Nonetheless, those I found most useful for this biography were the classic works of Charles M. Andrews, *The Colonial Period of American History* (in four volumes; New Haven, CT: Yale University Press, 1934–1938), and Winfred T. Root, *The Relations of Pennsylvania with the British Government, 1696–1795* (New York: D. Appleton and Company, 1912). For the English empire in the seventeenth century and the Navigation Acts, see Robert M. Bliss, *Revolution and Empire: English Politics in the Seventeenth Century* (New York: Manchester University Press, 1990); John J. McCusker, "British Mercantilist Policies and the American Colonies," in Stanley L. Engerman and Robert E. Gallman, eds., *The Cambridge Economic History of the United States*, Vol. 1, *The Colonial Era* (New York: Cambridge University Press, 1996), pp. 336–362; Nuala Zahediah, "Overseas Expansion and Trade in the Seventeenth Century," in Canny and Low, eds., *The Origins of Empire,* pp. 398–422; and John H. McCusker and Russell R. Menard, *The Economy of British America, 1607–1789* (Chapel Hill: University of North Carolina Press, 1985). Also see Ian K. Steele, *Politics of Colonial Policy: The Board of Trade in Colonial Administration, 1696–1720* (New York: Oxford University Press, 1986); Alison Gilbert Olson, *Anglo-American Politics, 1660–1775: The Relationship Between Parties in England and Colonial America* (New York: Oxford University Press, 1973), and her later study, *Making the Empire Work: London and American Interest, 1690–1790* (Cambridge, MA: Harvard University Press, 1992). A good examination of the problems surrounding the Navigation Acts and the individuals charged with enforcing them is Michael Garibaldi Hall, *Edward Randolph and the American Colonies, 1676–1703* (Chapel Hill: University of North Carolina Press, 1960).

For the impact on the colonies of the Nine Years War and the War of the Spanish Succession, see Douglas Edward Leach, *Arms for Empire: A Military History of the British Colonies in North America, 1607–1763* (New York: Macmillan, 1973); Mark Kishlansky, *A Monarchy Transformed: Britain, 1603–1714* (New York: Penguin, 1996); and Ian K. Steele, *Warpaths: Invasions of North America* (New York: Oxford University Press, 1994).

Index